PRIMULAS

Primulas

The Complete Guide

Mary A Robinson

The Crowood Press

First published in 1990 by
The Crowood Press
Gipsy Lane, Swindon
Wiltshire SN2 6DQ

British Library Cataloguing in Publication data
Robinson, Mary A
Primulas.
1. Gardens. Primulas. Cultivation & exhibition
I. Title
635.933672

ISBN 1 85223 313 3

PICTURE CREDITS

Colour photographs by Michael Robinson.
Plates of *Primula marginata* 'Holden Clough', *Primula* 'Mrs J. H. Wilson' and Gold
Lace Polyanthus 'Kaye's Strain' by Les Kaye.
Front cover and Plate of *Primula marginata* 'Pritchard's Variety' by Michael Myers.
Line illustrations by Mary A. Robinson.

Typeset by Acūté Design, Stroud, Glos
Printed in Great Britain by Billing & Sons Ltd, Worcester

Contents

Acknowledgements

Thanks to Michael Robinson for the time and effort in producing most of the colour plates. To Ruth Turner for constructively reading the manuscript, and to Les Kaye and Michael Myers for the loan of their slides.

Foreword

Michael and Mary Robinson have grown a wide range of plants for many years and their colourful exhibits have consistently won many high awards. With the ever increasing interest in many groups of primulas, Mary has created this delightful book on their cultivation in a most practical and charming manner.

Many of the more modern varieties are included and the book reflects the instinctive insight of an author wishing to pass on the knowledge gained from first-hand experience. Both the enthusiastic gardener and the cautious beginner are well catered for, as the text is easy to read, yet essentially informative, which all gardeners will greatly appreciate. There are also many primulas included which have not been written of in depth before, yet the author remains mindful that all are still in cultivation and therefore available. The section on many of the show and alpine auriculas grown today is written in a manner that greatly enhances their current revival.

The Primula family is vast and has always attracted the enthusiast as well as the average gardener. The dedicated enthusiast will always seek out a new discovery to test his or her skill, while the average gardener gains equal pleasure from a display which is easy to cultivate. However, readers will find this book refreshing in its contents and may even be tempted to extend their own knowledge by becoming more adventurous.

Mary has the constant support of her husband Michael, whose colourful photography completes this very worthwhile book which I feel will be welcomed by all plant lovers.

Brenda Hyatt

Author, *Auriculas:*
Their care and cultivation

Introduction

Having been invited to write a book on primulas, the first problem was what to include and what to leave out. The primula genus is huge, and on consideration it becomes increasingly clear that no book of this size could encompass the whole subject. The task should be to provide the prospective grower with the information necessary to grow and enjoy this beautifully varied genus, and to illustrate it with plates of plants that are reasonably available.

It is essential to remove the mystery surrounding this enormous family, and to present the information in a manner that can be understood by the general gardener as well as the botanist. Inevitably any specialist subject uses jargon, but this will be kept to a minimum, and a full list of the technical terms used is included in the glossary.

The popularity of any plant varies, and often the emergence of new species and hybrids acts as a catalyst to inspire more growers to specialise in a particular field. Primulas are becoming more widely grown every year, and as the demand increases the nurserymen make greater efforts to improve the range of plants available. This will, hopefully, result in an increase of varieties listed.

Many growers are now seeking to specialise, but they find they lack the basic information. It is intended to provide the amateur gardener with the facts needed to grow a wide selection of primulas successfully; to encourage the beginner; and to act as a comprehensive, though basic, reference book.

It is inevitable that any book on a specific subject will reflect the opinions and experiences of the author. The reader must make allowances for this and for the wide differences in climate that are to be found in the British Isles, and should adapt their growing techniques accordingly.

The members of the primula genus vary greatly in their cultural requirements. Many are good reliable garden plants, but others demand a cool, moist climate to prosper, and certain varieties need protection in winter. There is a place in most gardens for some representatives of this lovely and varied genus.

To many people it comes as a great surprise to learn that there are more than six hundred different species of primula, let alone the thousands of hybrids and cultivars. It would be impossible to include every primula that has ever been grown, and it must be remembered that many of the varieties that are listed in the older, and some, sadly, in not so old books, are virtually unobtainable. They may still be grown by the dedicated collector, but finding them is almost impossible, so space will not be wasted by describing them all in detail. Only a few of the most desirable and striking plants that the grower has some chance of obtaining, now or in the foreseeable future, will be included. There are equally good, if not better, varieties obtainable today, to replace the obsolete varieties of yesterday. New hybrids are appearing at such a rate that any book is forced to be incomplete by the time it is printed.

The *primulacae* genus is extremely large and diverse. Most of the species known will be listed in the appendix, along with the section to which it belongs. It the reader should be lucky enough to obtain a very rare plant, which is not fully described in the text, an educated guess as to a suitable means of cultivation can be made by determining the section from the alphabetical index, and then referring to the cultivation notes for that section in chapter 2. The list for further reading in the appendix will ensure that this guide is as complete as possible.

Many of the colour plates in gardening books tend to be of rare and difficult plants that are not generally available. This could be because the best photographs available are usually of plants that reflect some great achievement on the part of the grower. Unfortunately this attitude is of little help to the gardener who would like to see photographs of plants that are obtainable. Therefore the majority of the plates are of plants that are available, albeit with some diligent searching through the lists of specialist nurseries and the Society seed lists. Furthermore the plants illustrated in this book have been specifically selected to show the wide variation in form and colour occurring in this lovely genus.

Although many primulas are not strictly alpines, they are usually included in the lists of the specialist alpine nurseries, many of whom advertise in the gardening magazines and the bulletins of the specialist societies. Spring and autumn are the best times to find these in the classified columns, but do not forget the two or three line adverts; small nurseries and even private individuals will advertise there, and interesting rarities may be found. The Alpine Garden Society and the Scottish

Rock Garden Club circulate excellent seed lists to their members, and every serious collector is strongly advised to join one or both of these societies. Their addresses are included in the appendix.

Some of the primulas described only exist in the private collections of amateur growers and are rarely, if ever, offered for sale. This may be due to difficulty of cultivation or slowness of growth: some may only produce sufficient growth to be split into two plants every two or three years, and so it is realistic to realise that no nurseryman can keep sufficient stock plants in good health to offer such varieties commercially. There are many enthusiastic growers who have very fine collections of different sections of the genus, and their plants are often exhibited at the primula and auricula shows, and the shows of the Alpine Garden Society, the Scottish Rock Garden Club and the non-affiliated Rock Garden and Alpine Societies. The enthusiast is strongly urged to attend at least some of these shows, as pictures in books can never fully convey the beauty and delicacy of the Primula genus.

1
The History of the Primula

Primulas have been grown and recognised for hundreds of years, though like many other cultivated plants, they have enjoyed periods of popularity interspersed with periods of neglect.

Gardening books over the centuries give a fascinating insight into the type of plants being cultivated at different times, and by different social classes. It should be realised that plants were originally cultivated more for medicinal purposes than decoration, and so the earliest references to the primula were in herbals.

The first references to the cultivation of the primrose and cowslip were in Gerard's *Herbal* of 1597, when they were mentioned because of their medicinal value. Gerard was a well travelled gardener, and he listed the primulas that he grew in his garden at Holborn, including the Birds Eye Primrose *(Primula farinosa),* green primroses, 'hose in hose' cowslips and the double primrose. There are even earlier references to primroses and cowslips indicating that they were used as pot herbs. Even the charming *Primula scotica* was grown at the Chelsea Physic Garden by Philip Miller in 1753.

The coloured primroses were first documented by John Rea in 1665, and it seems probable that these were derived from *Primula vulgaris subsp. sibthorpii,* an eastern European variation of the common primrose, whose flowers were generally of mauve shades, although pinks, purples and crimson also occurred. It is thought that at some stage *Primula vulgaris subsp. heterochroma,* with an even wider colour range, was collected and bred into the primroses. This introduced a range of colours that were widely grown until the discovery of *Primula juliae* extended the colour range still further. Although the primrose has been in cultivation in this country since the end of the sixteenth century, it was not until the end of the seventeenth century that the first references are found to the polyanthus, and by the end of the eighteenth century the Gold-laced polyanthus was becoming popular.

The introduction of the auricula to cultivation followed a somewhat different, but parallel path. The wild species *Primula auricula* was first mentioned by Dioscorides in 50AD, and since then has suffered under an assortment of names, eventually in 1491 coming under the names *Primula artitica* or *Auricula ursa,* which literally translated means Bear's Little Ear, obviously referring to the shape of the leaves. In 1583 Clusius, a botanist and horticultural advisor, mentioned two auriculas that had been collected from the wild and these are thought to be the ancestors of the modern auriculas and pubescenses. One of the most fashionable spring flowering plants in the seventeenth century was the auricula and as early as 1659 many different varieties were to be found in the gardens of the wealthy.

By the latter half of the eighteenth century, and into the early part of the nineteenth century, many new species and natural hybrids of the *Auriculastrum* section were being collected in Europe and introduced into cultivation. Amongst the many plants introduced at this time were *Primula marginata* by Kennedy and Lee of Hammersmith in 1777, *Primula integrifolia* by Loddiges of Hackney in 1792, *Primula palinuri* from Naples in 1816, *Primula allionii* from France in 1818, *Primula minima* from southern Europe in 1819 and *Primula pedemontana* from the Piedmonte region of northern Italy in 1826.

At the end of the eighteenth century the first of the Asiatic primulas were introduced into cultivation. Professor Pallas sent seed of *Primula cortusoides* from Siberia in the 1790s, and in the same decade *Primula auriculata* was sent from Asia Minor and *Primula sibirica* from Siberia.

The 1800s saw the expansion of the seed firms who often financed the famous collectors, this brought about the introduction of many beautiful Asiatic primulas from China and Asia. There were several notable collectors, and many new plants were discovered and introduced into cultivation around this time. Amongst the first of these introductions were *Primula sinensis* from the gardens at Canton in China in 1820, and *Primula verticillata* which was brought from Arabia in 1826.

1830 saw the invention by Dr. Nathaniel Ward of the Wardian Case, which could be described as a portable miniature closed greenhouse. This was a very important step forward, because it meant that new plants could be transported from all over the world with a much better chance of survival. Joseph Hooker, the son of Sir William Hooker (the Director of Kew Gardens), was one of the first to use the Wardian Case, and during the 1840s was collecting plants in the Himalayas, Sikkim and northern India. Amongst his many introductions were *Primula involucrata, Primula stuartii, Primula gracilipes, Primula sikkimensis* and *Primula capitata.*

As well as the great plant collectors there were also the French missionaries to China, who were responsible for much of the early botanical work in that area. Noteworthy amongst their contributions were the collection of *Primula heucherifolia* from western Szechuan in 1869 by the Abbé David and the finding of *Primula poissonii* and *Primula secundiflora* by Father Delavay in Yunnan in the 1880s. One of the major introductions in the 1860s was the beautiful *Primula sieboldii* which Chevalier F. von Siebold brought back from Japan. It was a plant whose culture and tradition ran parallel to that of the Florists' auricula in Britain. A few years later saw the introduction of *Primula japonica* also from Japan.

New species were also being introduced from the Americas, noteworthy among these being *Primula parryi* from north-west America in 1865, *Primula rusbyi* from New Mexico and *Primula suffrutescens* from California.

Other interesting introductions at this time were from the Himalayas and included *Primula rosea, Primula floribunda, Primula prolifera* and *Primula reidii.*

In 1899 Veitch & Son, the nurserymen and seed merchants, sent Ernest Henry Wilson on his first journey to western China. This was the start of a flood of introductions, both of new species, and of species that had been lost in cultivation. Wilson travelled through much of Szechuan and Yunnan, and amongst the plants he collected were *Primula wilsonii* in 1902 and *Primula pulverulenta* in 1905.

In 1901 the book *Open-Air Gardening* by W.D. Drury was published, and among the recommendations for the rock garden were *Primulas cortusoides, denticulata, floribunda* and *marginata*; and for damp places *Primulas rosea, japonica* and *sikkimensis.* Thus started primula growing in gardens as is practised today.

Primula juliae was discovered in 1901, and by 1911 the first of many beautiful hybrids between it and the primroses and polyanthuses had been bred. These were originally called *Primula x juliana*, but have now been renamed *Primula pruhociniana*. No one could have imagined then the huge influence that one little primula would exert in the years to come: it is thought that the majority of the modern primroses contain at least a little *Primula juliae* blood, and the growing and breeding of these hybrids/cultivars as house plants is now big business, and billions of these lovely plants are raised annually to satisfy the market.

Many other new species have been collected in the last seventy years, and one of the most important of the great collectors was George Forrest. He spent twenty-eight years collecting plants in China from 1904 until his death in Yunnan in 1932. Amongst the many primulas he introduced were *Primulas forrestii* (1909), *nutans* and *helodoxa* (1916, W.Yunnan), *vialii* (1909, west Szechuan), *beesiana, bulleyana* (1908), *chionantha, sikkimensis, sonchifolia* (1910), and *aurantiaca* (1922). It is interesting to note that Forrest was commissioned by Bees of Chester to find new plants, and the lovely candelabras he collected, *Primula beesiana* and *bulleyana* were named after Bees himself, and Bulley, who owned the firm and distributed them.

Whilst Forrest was in China, Reginald Farrer and his companions explored the country north of Szechuan in Kansu, and the Tibetan border. In 1914 Farrer lists a vast range of primulas in his famous book *The Rock Garden* including Asiatic, European and American, and although many more Asiatic primulas were still to be collected it is obvious that many had already been introduced, though many did not survive long in the alien climate of English gardens.

Farrer died in upper Burma in 1920 and was succeeded by Frank Kingdom Ward, who collected in China, Upper Burma and Assam, Bhutan, Sikkim and Tibet until 1939. The introduction of *Primula helodoxa, Primula chungensis, Primula florindae* (1924), *Primula bhutanica* (1935), *Primula ioessa* (1936), and *Primula gracilipes* (1936–1938) were all attributable to Ward. In the 1930s Ludlow and Sherriff also re-introduced many species.

An interesting book published in 1941, *My Garden's Choice* by T.A. Stephens and A.T. Johnson listed *Primula auricula, Primula edgeworthii,* (which they described as a not too trustworthy novelty!), *Primula farinosa* and *frondosa, Primula involucrata, Primula juliae* (and its hybrids 'Pam,' 'Vulcan', 'Gloria', 'Merton Hybrid' and 'E.R. Janes'), *Primula marginata* and *marginata* 'Linda Pope', *Primula pubescens,* including 'Faldonside', 'The General', *alba,* 'Ruby' and 'Mrs. J.H. Wilson', *Primula rosea* and *Primula secundiflora.*

In the post-war years there have been further plant hunting expeditions, and many new and interesting species have been collected and re-introduced into cultivation. In the 1950s Stainton Sykes and Williams brought *Primula reidii williamsii* back from Nepal, and in 1960 the dainty little *Primula warshen-ewskiana* was first introduced from Afghanistan.

The collection and introduction of new plants has always been influenced by politics. There are still countries where the boundaries are closed to western foreigners, but every year new areas become accessible to explorers and every expedition increases the fund of knowledge in some way.

2
The Division of the Primula Genus into Sections

In order to present this book in a straightforward and comprehensible manner it is essential to understand the importance of subdividing this huge genus into manageable parts. Any system of classification can be likened to a library, where books are arranged in a specific order so that any title can be found easily. Separate areas are used for different subjects, and the books within each area are then arranged alphabetically under author, and then under titles, so any one can be found without having to search through thousands of different books.

Similarly the system of nomenclature for plants is a series of divisions, breaking down a large number of items into groups sharing similar characteristics, and then subdividing further on a secondary character, and carrying on subdividing until the sections are of a manageable size.

The naming of plants tends to overwhelm the uninitiated, especially when the experts reel off long streams of incomprehensible Latin and Greek names. It is really quite straightforward, and can be likened to a family tree.

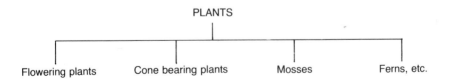

Flowering Plants are then subdivided into families, e.g. the *Primulacae* family, the *Rosacae* family, the *Liliacae* family and many others.

The *Primulacae* family is then subdivided into genera (the plural of genus).

Stylised primula flower of the classic primrose, *Primula vulgaris*.

The *Primulacae* family contains the genera primula, androsace, dionysia, soldanella, cyclamen, cortusa, dodecatheon and several others that are relatively unknown.

The primula genus is then divided into different sections, by grouping together plants with clearly seen similarities in leaf, flower form or general habit. For instance plants with the smooth leaves of the auricula are in the Auriculastrum section, and plants with the crinkly leaves of the primrose are in the primrose (Vernales) section. This is a gross oversimplification, but it indicates how plants can be classified.

The old, but still-used system of classification split the primula genus into thirty sections, some of which were split into subsections. This system was recommended by George Forrest and Sir William Wright Smith to the Fourth Primula Conference in 1928, and was based on the Pax System of 1905, having been updated to take account of new introductions in the intervening years. The Pax System of classification will be used throughout this book. The new system uses seven sections, and this may be more relevant from a botanical viewpoint but the old system is of more practical use to the amateur.

The primula genus is subdivided into thirty sections

Section 1: Cortusoides (Balf.f)

Section 2: Reinii (Balf.f)

Section 3: Pinnatae
(R. Knuth)

Section 4: Pycnaloba (Balf.f)

Section 5: Obconica (Balf.f)

Section 6: Sinensis (Pax)

Section 7: Malvacea (Balf.f)

Section 8: Carolinella (Pax)

Section 9: Vernales (Pax)

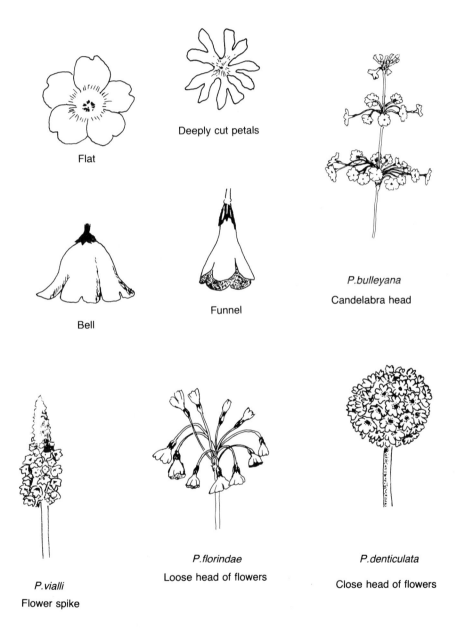

Flat

Deeply cut petals

Bell

Funnel

P.bulleyana

Candelabra head

P.vialli

Flower spike

P.florindae

Loose head of flowers

P.denticulata

Close head of flowers

The differing flower forms in the primula genus.

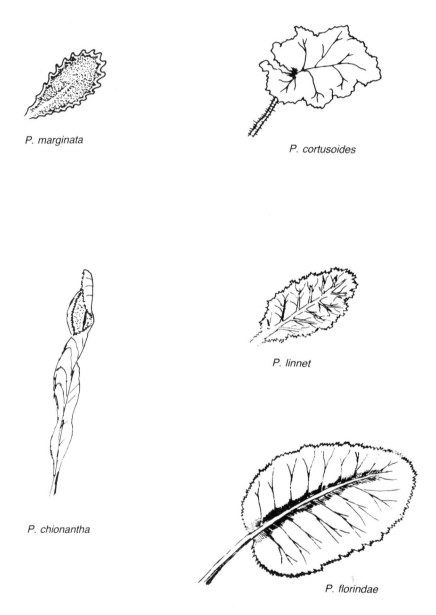

P. marginata

P. cortusoides

P. linnet

P. chionantha

P. florindae

The variations in leaf to be found in the primula genus.

Section 10: Amethystina (Balf.f)
Section 11: Cuneifolia (Balf.f)
Section 12: Petiolares (Pax)
Section 13: Malacoides (Balf.f)
Section 14: Grandis (Balf.f)
Section 15: Bullatae (Pax)
Section 16: Dryadifolia (Balf.f)
Section 17: Minutissimae (Pax)
Section 18: Souliei (Balf.f)
Section 19: Farinosae (Pax)
Section 20: Denticulata (Balf.f)

Section 21: Capitatae (Pax)
Section 22: Muscarioides (Balf.f)
Section 23: Soldanelloides (Pax)
Section 24: Rotundifolia (Balf.f)
Section 25: Nivales (Pax)
Section 26: Parryi (W.W.Smith)
Section 27: Sikkimensis (Balf.f)
Section 28: Candelabra (Balf.f)
Section 29: Auriculastrum (Pax)
Section 30: Floribundae (Pax)

The whole of the primula genus is now considered, and is first split into two divisions by looking at the way in which the young leaves grow, and is then further divided using other characteristics.

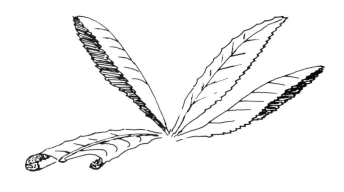

Young leaves folded inwards and outwards.

The Division of the Primula Genus into Sections

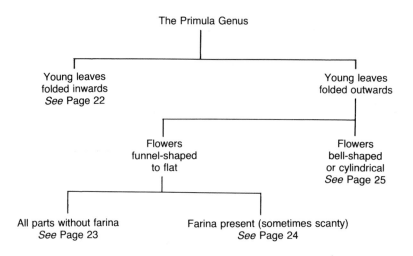

The Primula Genus

Young leaves folded inwards
See Page 22

Young leaves folded outwards

Flowers funnel-shaped to flat

Flowers bell-shaped or cylindrical
See Page 25

All parts without farina
See Page 23

Farina present (sometimes scanty)
See Page 24

The classification of primulas into their respective sections.

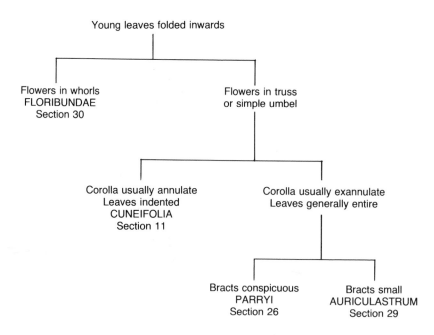

Young leaves folded inwards

Flowers in whorls
FLORIBUNDAE
Section 30

Flowers in truss or simple umbel

Corolla usually annulate
Leaves indented
CUNEIFOLIA
Section 11

Corolla usually exannulate
Leaves generally entire

Bracts conspicuous
PARRYI
Section 26

Bracts small
AURICULASTRUM
Section 29

Young leaves folded inwards.

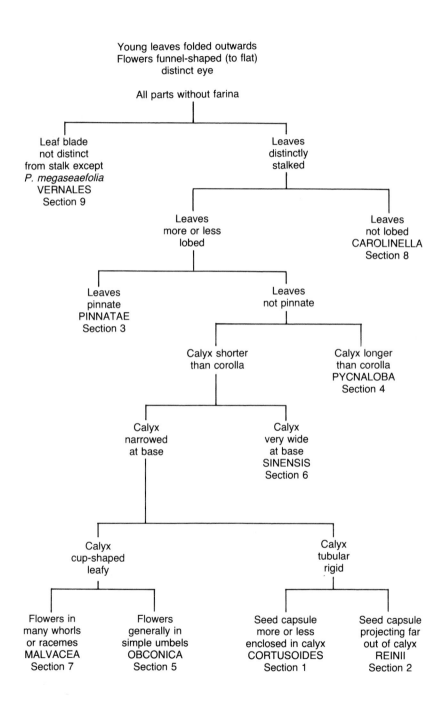

Young leaves folded outwards
Flowers funnel-shaped (to flat)
distinct eye

All parts without farina

Leaf blade
not distinct
from stalk except
P. megaseaefolia
VERNALES
Section 9

Leaves
distinctly
stalked

Leaves
more or less
lobed

Leaves
not lobed
CAROLINELLA
Section 8

Leaves
pinnate
PINNATAE
Section 3

Leaves
not pinnate

Calyx shorter
than corolla

Calyx longer
than corolla
PYCNALOBA
Section 4

Calyx
narrowed
at base

Calyx
very wide
at base
SINENSIS
Section 6

Calyx
cup-shaped
leafy

Calyx
tubular
rigid

Flowers in
many whorls
or racemes
MALVACEA
Section 7

Flowers
generally in
simple umbels
OBCONICA
Section 5

Seed capsule
more or less
enclosed in calyx
CORTUSOIDES
Section 1

Seed capsule
projecting far
out of calyx
REINII
Section 2

Young leaves folded outwards.

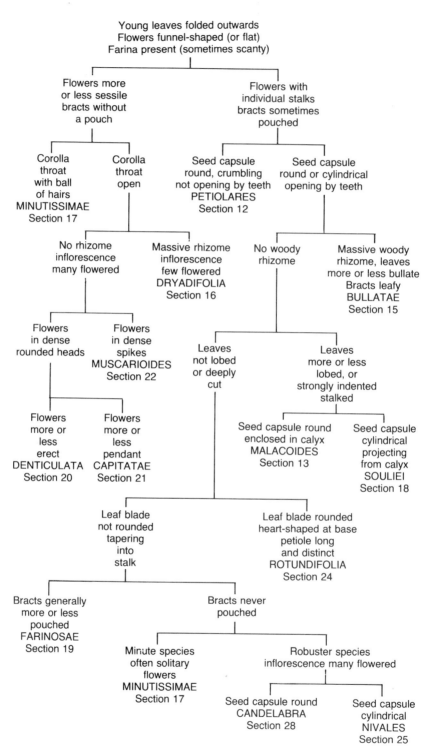

Young leaves folded outwards
Flowers funnel-shaped (or flat)
Farina present (sometimes scanty)

Flowers more or less sessile bracts without a pouch

Flowers with individual stalks bracts sometimes pouched

Corolla throat with ball of hairs
MINUTISSIMAE
Section 17

Corolla throat open

Seed capsule round, crumbling not opening by teeth
PETIOLARES
Section 12

Seed capsule round or cylindrical opening by teeth

No rhizome inflorescence many flowered

Massive rhizome inflorescence few flowered
DRYADIFOLIA
Section 16

No woody rhizome

Massive woody rhizome, leaves more or less bullate
Bracts leafy
BULLATAE
Section 15

Flowers in dense rounded heads

Flowers in dense spikes
MUSCARIOIDES
Section 22

Leaves not lobed or deeply cut

Leaves more or less lobed, or strongly indented stalked

Flowers more or less erect
DENTICULATA
Section 20

Flowers more or less pendant
CAPITATAE
Section 21

Seed capsule round enclosed in calyx
MALACOIDES
Section 13

Seed capsule cylindrical projecting from calyx
SOULIEI
Section 18

Leaf blade not rounded tapering into stalk

Leaf blade rounded heart-shaped at base petiole long and distinct
ROTUNDIFOLIA
Section 24

Bracts generally more or less pouched
FARINOSAE
Section 19

Bracts never pouched

Minute species often solitary flowers
MINUTISSIMAE
Section 17

Robuster species inflorescence many flowered

Seed capsule round
CANDELABRA
Section 28

Seed capsule cylindrical
NIVALES
Section 25

Young leaves folded outwards.

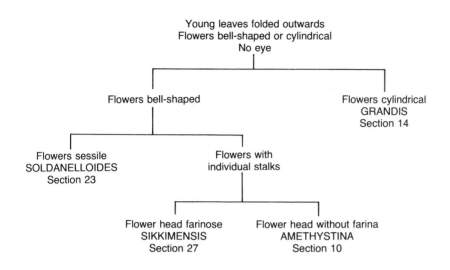

Young leaves folded outwards.

The larger sections are then divided into subsections in order to keep the system simple and manageable, and then the smaller sections and subsections are divided into species.

The primula is the largest genus in the *Primulacae* family, and
contains more than six hundred species, which can be found throughout the northern temperate regions, extending occasionally into the tropics, with one or two isolated species in southern South America. The majority of the species are to be found in the mountainous areas of central and southern Asia, from the Himalayas through to western China. A full list of sections and varieties within each section is detailed in the Appendix.

Interbreeding between different sections is rare, but not unknown, and some very beautiful hybrids between condelabras and sikkimensis have been produced. Many species within a section will interbreed, though this is less likely among the section Farinosae.

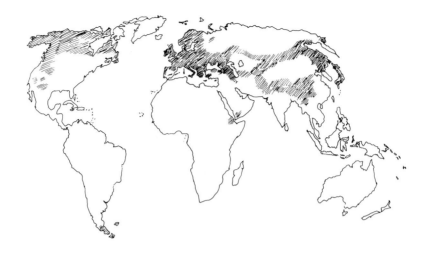

Map of the distribution of the primula genus.

DESCRIPTIVE LIST OF SECTIONS

It is essential to split the primula genus into its respective sections in order to describe the species in logical order. On reading this chapter it will soon become clear that only a few of these sections are represented in cultivation.

Section 1 Cortusoides
A group of small herbaceous plants with soft, hairy, lobed leaves, with attractive umbels of flowers held above the leaves. They are completely without farina, and in winter die back to small rhizomes. Distribution is from the Urals through Asia to Japan. This section contains some very distinctive and attractive plants, that are worthy of a place in any garden. Certainly not grown or appreciated as much as they deserve. *See* chapters 14 and 16.
CULTIVATION: As the species in cultivation are mainly woodland plants they are most suitable for peat beds, or for a moist position under small trees or bushes. Most species would grace the alpine house, especially the glorious cultivars of *Primula sieboldii*. Do label the planting position carefully as all this section die back almost completely for the winter. Some species can become dormant as early as July if they are allowed to become dry, with no real detriment to the plant, but early dormancy does prevent the plant from building up strong clumps.

26

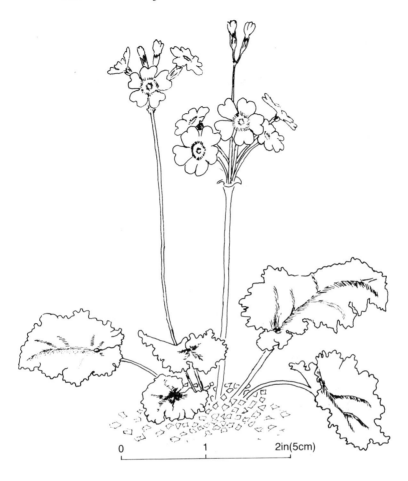

Primula cortisoides, a typical member of the Cortusoides section.

PROPAGATION: From seed, which is readily produced and does not seem to need frost action to germinate; or by the careful splitting of well-established clumps, preferably in spring.
AVAILABILITY: Quite easy from the specialist nurseries or the seed lists.

Section 2 Reinii

A small Japanese group, rare in the wild, where they occur in high meadows and rocky areas in the mountains. A few species may be found in private collections, but they present a challenge to the grower. Related to, and showing a certain similarity to the Cortusoides section, but in general are smaller plants with characteristic rounded lobed leaves on longish stalks. *See* chapter 16.

27

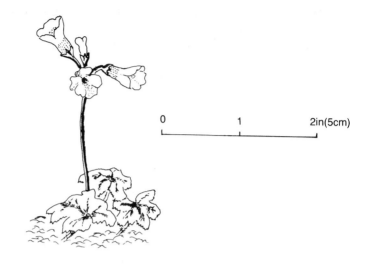

Primula takedena, a typical member of Reinii section.

CULTIVATION: Careful culture in the alpine house in a well-drained compost, and care with watering in winter offer the best chances of success.
PROPAGATION: Seed.
AVAILABILITY: Not readily available, but occasionally the odd plant is offered by the specialist nurseries or as seed from the seed lists.

Section 3 Pinnatae
A small Chinese group, rare in the wild and not in cultivation, they all exhibit a highly divided efarinose leaf, and are annual or dwarf herbaceous perennials of doubtful hardiness.
CULTIVATION: Cold (or even warm greenhouse).
PROPAGATION: One assumes seed.

Section 4 Pycnaloba
Only one species in this group, from China, rare in the wild and probably no longer in cultivation. It was described by Farrer as having flowers something like a multi-headed daffodil, and not being unduly difficult in cultivation providing it was allowed a winter rest, and given overhead protection from the rain.

Section 5 Obconica
The members of this group are not hardy, coming from the lower altitudes in China, the Himalayas and through to

Burma. They all have a well-developed rhizome and are without farina.

CULTIVATION: *Primula obconica* itself is of great importance as a house plant, or for a warm greenhouse. This plant is the most frequent cause of Primula Rash. *See* chapter 17.

PROPAGATION: Easy from seed.

AVAILABILITY: Most seed catalogues list a good colour range, and plants are regularly available from garden centres, flower shops etc.

Section 6 Sinensis

Is not hardy, and was first introduced into Britain about 1821 from China. It was very popular in the last century as a warm greenhouse primula. *See* chapter 17.

CULTIVATION: An easy and lovely plant for the frost-free greenhouse or as a house plant.

PROPAGATION: Seed.

AVAILABILITY: Not as popular as it used to be, but is still listed by many seed catalogues.

Section 7 Malvacea

Another group of non-hardy Asiatics, that have been fleetingly in cultivation, but have never survived for long.

CULTIVATION: Treatment as for the other warm greenhouse primulas would be safest.

Section 8 Carolinella

Very rare plants from the Yunnan, which have never been in cultivation. Being plants of the mountain forests one would expect them to need similar treatment as the Reinii, *see* section 2.

Section 9 Vernales

Is a very important European section, and contains primroses and polyanthuses. A well-documented section whose history dates back to the sixteenth century. *See* chapters 11 and 12.

CULTIVATION: Good rich border soil, humus-rich, and light shade during the hottest part of the day. Also of great importance as a house plant, *see* chapter 17.

PROPAGATION: Splitting in spring preferable, wild-collected seed for the species. The house plants are best renewed by buying new plants or growing from seed.

AVAILABILITY: Everywhere, in a vast range of colour and forms.

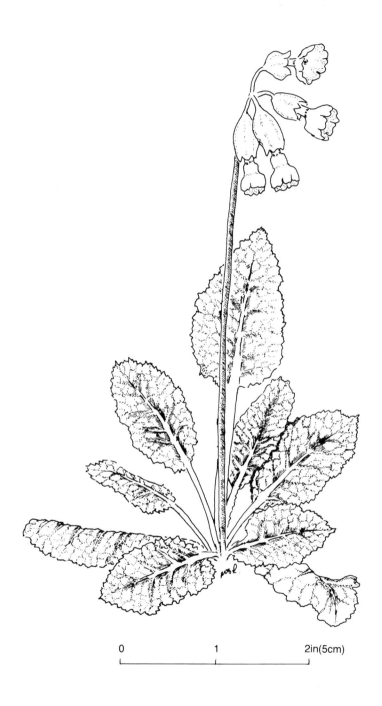

Primula veris, a typical member of the Vernales section.

Section 10 Amethystina
An Asiatic group from the eastern Himalayas and south-west China which has proved to be difficult in cultivation, possibly the odd specimen may be found in private collections. *See* chapter 16.

Section 11 Cuneifolia
Is a small section, closely related to the European auricula section, characterised by the wedge-shaped leaves. Found in areas bordering the northern part of the Pacific ocean, so it bridges the gap between the American and Asiatic primulas, and for the purpose of this book will be described in chapter 13 with the American primulas.
CULTIVATION: Alpine house, similar to the smaller members of the Auriculastrum.
PROPAGATION: Splitting or seed.
AVAILABILITY: Occasionally from the specialist nurseries, or from the Society seed lists.

Section 12 Petriolares
A very important and spectacularly beautiful section, emanating from the Himalayas, Tibet, northern Burma and the

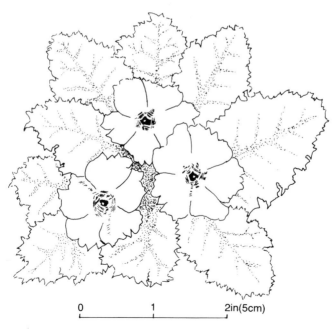

0   1   2in(5cm)

Primula aureata, a typical member of the Petiolares section.

mountains of western China. The second largest Asiatic section containing sixty or more species which are split into several subsections. Many of the plants have the appearance of exotic primroses. This section is characterised by its unique seed capsules, which are unlike those of any other section. On maturity the outside of the seed pod becomes transparent and then disintegrates, allowing the seed to be scattered. Although all the species are sound perennials, their lives can be short due to inadequacies of cultivation, as it is not easy to provide the cool, moist and buoyant atmosphere they crave.

CULTIVATION: Far from easy in cultivation especially in the warmer southern counties of Britain, *see* chapter 15 for a full discussion of the species in cultivation.

PROPAGATION: Very careful splitting or seed.

AVAILABILITY: Several of the specialist nurseries, especially the more northern, list a few varieties from time to time.

Section 13 Malacoides

Not unlike the Cortusoides in appearance, but not hardy. Only *Primula malacoides* is in cultivation, and it comes from marshy areas and rice fields of northern Burma and southern China. It is a beautiful house plant or greenhouse annual. *See* chapter 17.

CULTIVATION: Warm greenhouse or as a house plant.

PROPAGATION: Seed from the commercial seed catalogues.

AVAILABILITY: The better garden centres or flower shops, or grow from seed.

Section 14 Grandis

Only one species in this section, *Primula grandis,* which comes from the Caucasus, and has appeared fleetingly in cultivation, described as an unattractive plant, 1–3 feet (30–90cm) high, with loose umbels of long pale yellow tubular flowers.

Section 15 Bullatea

A section of woody evergreen perennials from Tibet through to south-west China, of which *Primula forrestii* is occasionally available in Society seed lists. *See* chapter 16.

Section 16 Dryadifolia

These small plants with characteristically lobed leaves are high alpines from the south-western Himalayas, which have briefly appeared in cultivation in the past. Highly desirable and hopefully they will be re-introduced in the future.

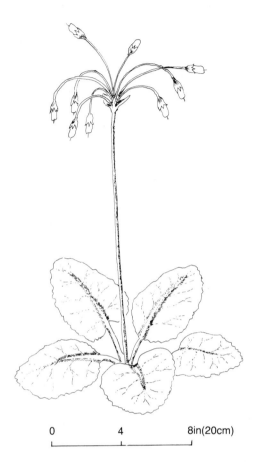

0   4   8in(20cm)

Primula grandis.

CULTIVATION: As for Section 2 Reinii would probably be most appropriate. *See* chapter 16.

Section 17 Minutissimae

A large section of very dwarf species, mainly from the Himalayas, that are very difficult to cultivate, although *Primula primulina (pusilla)* seed is occasionally offered, and is a pretty little thing that will survive with protection for a year or two.
CULTIVATION: Difficult, careful cultivation in a cold greenhouse, *see* chapter 16.
PROPAGATION: Seed.
AVAILABILITY: Try the seed lists, or occasionally the odd plant will be offered by specialist nurseries.

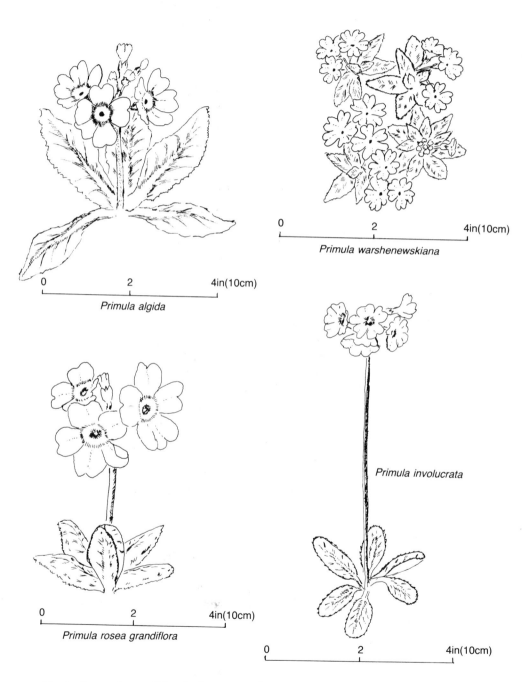

Primula warshenewskiana

Primula algida

Primula involucrata

Primula rosea grandiflora

Typical members of the Farinosae section.

Section 18 Souliei
High alpines from the eastern Himalayas through Tibet to western China. Difficult, and no longer in cultivation.
CULTIVATION: Probably as for Section 2 Reinii, *see* chapter 16.

Section 19 Farinosae
The largest section in the genus containing eighty or more species, mostly Asiatic, but several species occur in Europe, North America and even South America. It is certainly the most widespread section, and exceedingly diverse in its habits and appearance. *See* chapters 5, 13 and 14.
CULTIVATION: Very diverse, see the full discussion of all the subsections in the appropriate chapters.
PROPAGATION: Usually by seed, but good forms can be split.
AVAILABILITY: Many species from this section are readily available from specialist nurseries, garden centres, seed lists etc.

Section 20 Denticulata
A small section with a wide distribution in Asia. *Primula denticulata* is a popular and easy plant for the garden, coping with a wide range of conditions, and delighting the gardener with its large showy flowers every spring.
CULTIVATION: This well-loved 'Drumstick' primula is easy in any soil that does not become too dry, and delights the gardener in early spring with its large round heads in many shades of mauve, red, purple pink or white. The other species in this group are relatively insignificant, and require more careful treatment in a peat bed, *see* chapter 14.
PROPAGATION: By seed, splitting or even root cuttings.
AVAILABILITY: Stocked by most garden centres in the spring.

Section 21 Capitatae
From the eastern Himalayas, small plants with close heads of flowers in July above neat rosettes of leaves. Easily grown from seed, but not very permanent. *See* chapter 14.
CULTIVATION: Suitable for peat bed, peaty trough or the cold greenhouse.
PROPAGATION: Seed, or careful (and risky) splitting of a particularly vigorous plant.
AVAILABILITY: From the specialist nurseries, or the seed lists.

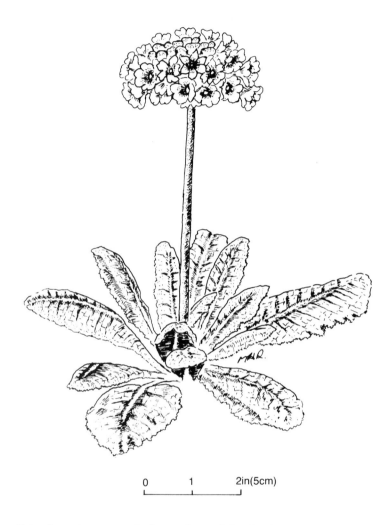

Primula capitata, a typical member of the Capitatae section.

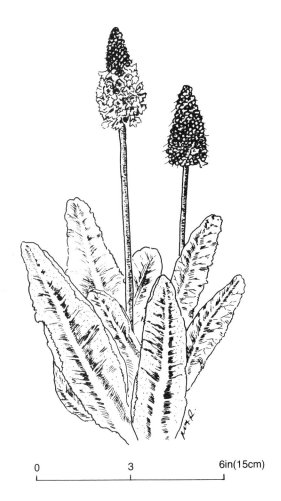

0   3   6in(15cm)

Primula vialii, a typical member of the Muscarioides section.

Section 22 Muscarioides

From the eastern Himalayas, Tibet and western China. The well-loved, if occasionally temperamental, *Primula vialii* belongs in this section, along with its smaller relatives, which are occasionally available. *See* chapters 14 and 16.

CULTIVATION: Peat bed or alpine house for the smaller, rarer species.

PROPAGATION: Seed, or by splitting a particularly large clump of *Primula vialii.*

AVAILABILITY: Occasionally offered by specialist nurseries.

0   1   2in(5cm)

Primula reidii, a typical member of the Soldanelloides section.

Section 23 Soldanelloides
A lovely section containing some beautiful species, often sweetly fragrant, characterised by the heads of bell-shaped flowers and soft hairy leaves. From the Himalayas and south-western China, they are well worth seeking out. *See* chapters 14 and 16.

CULTIVATION: Glorious plants for the peat bed or alpine house.

PROPAGATION: Seed.

AVAILABILITY: Occasionally from the seed lists, or established plants from the specialist nurseries.

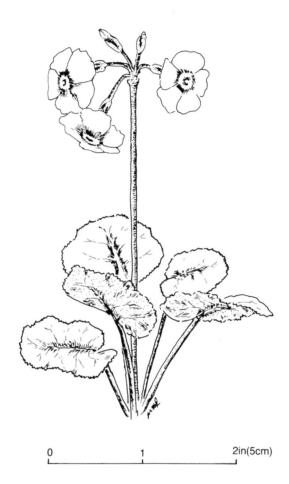

0   1   2in(5cm)

Primula rotundifolia, typical member of the Rotundifolia section.

Section 24 Rotundifolia

Contains some rare and difficult species from the Himalayas, occasionally seed is available of *Primula rotundifolia,* which makes an attractive specimen for the alpine house. *See* chapter 16.

CULTIVATION: Gritty compost that does not dry out, in the cold greenhouse.

PROPAGATION: Seed.

AVAILABILITY: Seed lists, rarely from specialist nurseries.

0   4   8in(20cm)

Primula chionantha, a typical member of the Nivales section.

Section 25 Nivales

An Asiatic plant of moist meadows that has a fairly wide distribution. They tend to be large plants with upright clumps of highly farinaed strap-shaped leaves. The Nivalids are fairly firmly in cultivation and are rewarding plants if the climate and soil are suitable. Some species appear to be very closely related, with possibly only geographical variations, and they hybridise very easily. Thus in cultivation it is very doubtful if any pure species still exist, and as they are normally raised from seed one waits until they flower before giving them a positive name. All very well for *Primula chionantha* which is white, but *Primula sinopurpurea* and *Primula melanops* are both mauve, with different colour eyes, and the seedlings often appear to have intermediate characteristics. *See* chapter 14.
CULTIVATION: Peat bed conditions, they will tolerate more sun in the north of Britain, but in a hot position they tend to attract aphids which can be lethal.
PROPAGATION: Easy from seed.
AVAILABILITY: Often from specialist nurseries, and a good range is usually included in the seed lists.

Section 26 Parryi

An exclusively American section, related to the Cuneifolia section and European Auriculastrum section. *See* chapter 13.
CULTIVATION: Varies with different species.
PROPAGATION: Seed or careful splitting.
AVAILABILITY: Occasionally from the seed lists.

Section 27 Sikkimensis

An important section from the Himalayas and adjoining areas, easy and vigorous plants given adequate supplies of water. This section is characterised by loose umbels of hanging bells, which are often sweetly scented. *See* chapter 14.
CULTIVATION: Easy in any moist to wet soil, the smaller members of this section are best grown in a peat bed.
PROPAGATION: Easy from seed, or split established clumps in spring, keeping the newly split plants well watered until they re-establish.
AVAILABILITY: Most specialist nurseries stock a few species, and occasionally from garden centres or seed lists.

Section 28 Candelabra

Are mainly robust plants from the eastern end of the Himalayas through to south-west China. From the loose rosettes of

41

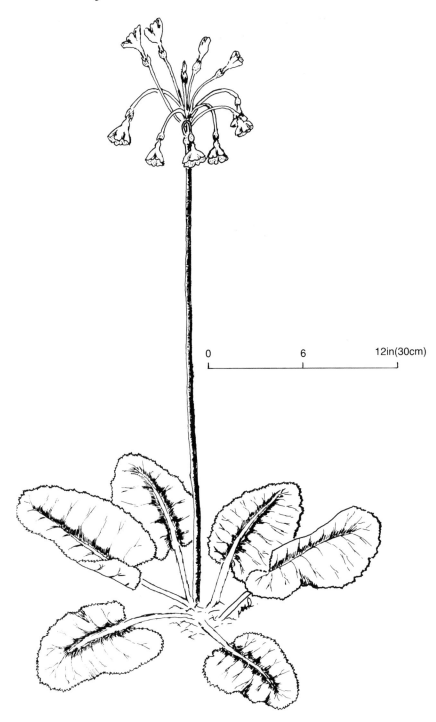

0   6   12in(30cm)

Primula florindae, a typical member of the Sikkimensis section.

large leaves emerge tall stems with the flowers in tiers, giving them their popular name of 'Candelabra Primulas'. The large display gardens that open to the public, e.g. Harlow Car Gardens in Harrogate, Ness Gardens on the Wirral and many in Scotland have impressive plantings of these lovely plants,

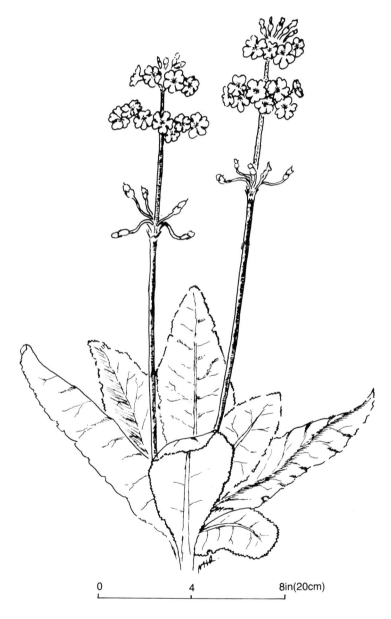

0   4   8in(20cm)

Primula bulleyana, a typical member of the Candelabra section.

which have interbred to give a wide range of colours. Please note, the species within this section hybridise very easily with each other, but the resultant plants are just as beautiful. A marvellously distinct section. *See* chapter 14.

CULTIVATION: Easy in any soil that stays moist, but is not waterlogged in winter.

PROPAGATION: From seed, or by splitting established clumps in spring, ensuring that the newly split plants are kept moist until well established.

AVAILABILITY: From specialist nurseries, seed lists or often from the pond plant section in garden centres.

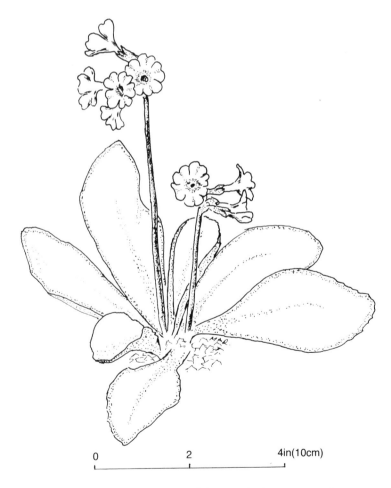

Primula auricula, a typical member of the Auriculastrum section.

Section 29 Auriculastrum

This section covers the majority of the European species, from the tiny *Primula minima* to the well-loved *Primula auricula,* and its ability to breed between species has led to the hundreds (or is it thousands?) of European hybrids.

CULTIVATION: Generally well-drained but not arid, or for the alpine house. A very large family which is covered thoroughly in chapters 6–10.

PROPAGATION: Usually by splitting.

AVAILABILITY: Easily available, all the specialist nurseries list several.

Section 30 Floribundae

Not hardy, but a hybrid between two members of this section led to *Primula* x *Kewensis,* which is a lovely plant for the warm greenhouse. *See* chapters 16 and 17.

CULTIVATION: House plant or warm greenhouse.

PROPAGATION: Seed, although a hybrid, the strain has been fixed.

AVAILABILITY: From seed catalogues.

3
Cultivation and Propagation

CULTIVATION

It is almost impossible to generalise about such a large genus. The only thing they all have in common is their hatred of dry conditions in the growing season, especially in spring and autumn. Primulas may be grown successfully in most gardens, providing note is taken of their specific requirements. In general the larger Asiatics enjoy a moist soil that is not water-logged in winter and does not dry out in summer, but with a certain amount of shade. The Europeans vary between good rich, moist soil for the primrose section, to rock garden, trough or cold greenhouse for the Auriculastrum section.

Although cultural instructions are included within the description of each section and species, an overall discussion of the general gardening terms is essential.

Rock Gardens
The general rock garden is defined as any garden bed in which rock plants are grown, usually in the sun, preferably well-drained, with rocks arranged to be pleasing to the eye or to the plants, and less frequently to both.

The soil can be infinitely variable, from lumps of clay, through to almost pure sand. The lucky few have a good, neutral, well-drained loam. It would be foolish to attempt to grow any primulas in a position that is consistently dry and arid. However, the majority of situations can be improved by the addition of humus rich materials, (peat, compost) and by the importation of loam. It is very easy to make special pockets for the primulas that require a specific soil type. A small area having all the conditions required by those primulas demanding peat bed conditions is easily created by using a suitably placed boulder to give shade, extra peat incorporated into that area, and a position near the base of the rockery that will keep the soil moist.

The clay soils can grow certain primulas to perfection, mix

some peat in and try the Denticulatas and the polyanthuses at the base of the rockery.

Recommended Plants:

Primula frondosa,
The larger pubescens hybrids,
Some auriculas.

Troughs and Similar Containers

These are very useful because of their versatility. They can be sited in sun or shade, and can be filled with the most suitable composts for the primulas desired. The only restrictions are on the size of the plants.

Conventionally the trough would be filled with a mixture of good soil, peat and grit, with a few small stones on the surface to give the plants a cool root run, to conserve moisture and, last but not least, to be aesthetically pleasing. A light airy position that is not sun-baked is required, as is regular watering.

If unsure of when to water, lift a stone, if it is nicely moist underneath then all is well. It is difficult to overwater in the spring and summer if your drainage is correct, but do ensure the watering is sufficient. It is a great mistake to just water the

A stone trough filled with alpines and primulas.

surface, as it will cause the roots of the plants to come to the surface in search of water, and if allowed to become dry the plants could well die. A good soaking once a week is far better than wetting the surface every day. As a general rule watering in the evening is more beneficial, unless there is any chance of frost, in which case watering in the morning is more sensible. These conditions are ideal for the small European species and hybrids, where they can be grown in conjunction with other small alpines, saxifrages, androsaces and the small treasures that could be overrun by larger plants in the rock garden.

Other troughs can be made with suitable composts for the smaller peat bed primulas, and situated in a shady position.

Recommended plants:

Many of the small pubescens hybrids,
Primula x *forsteri*,
Primula minima and other small European species,
Primula 'Blairside Yellow',
Primula marginata.

Scree Beds

A scree in nature is the loose rock fall at the foot of a cliff or gully in the mountains, and consists of rocks of all sizes, from several tons in weight down to fine silt. The artificial scree in gardening terms is a special bed, usually but not necessarily in full sun, that consists of a very free draining compost created by the incorporation of grit, with a surface dressing of grit. It is the ideal environment for the easier pubescens hybrids, and certain other hybrids.

Many gardening books describe in detail how a scree bed may be made. Their methods seem rather complicated and labour intensive. First consider the purpose of the bed. It is to emulate a natural scree, as found in mountainous areas, to provide perfect or near perfect drainage and a congenial home for the alpines that resent normal soil. If the bed is to be above the level of the surrounding garden, there is no point in digging out vast quantities of soil to provide so-called drainage; any form of raised bed is bound to drain freely if the soil composition is correct. If the area is badly drained, digging out the soil will just provide a sump to hold water. Far better to consider methods of raising the scree bed above the general level of the garden, or resiting the scree in a better drained position.

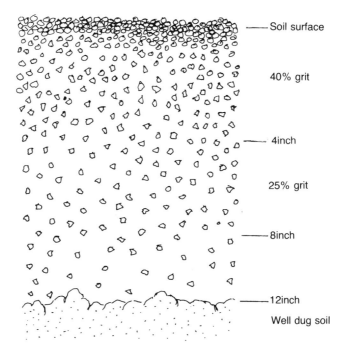

Cross section of a scree bed.

The aim is to have normal well-drained soil 9–12in (22–30cm) below the surface, about 25% grit 6in (15cm) down, and 40% grit 3in (7cm) down, with about 1in (2.5cm) grit on the surface.

Always consider the type of soil and adapt accordingly. If dealing with good garden soil, mix with grit as above. If very dry and sandy, it would be sensible to include some good moss peat into the mixture.

Recommended plants:

The small pubescens hybrids,
Primula auricula (true species),
Primula palinure (if obtainable) etc. etc.

Alpine House or Cold Greenhouse

An alpine house is an unheated greenhouse, with facilities for ample ventilation, where alpines and primulas can be grown in pots in order to enjoy their fragile beauty more easily.

Although there are many high alpines and difficult primulas that can only be grown successfully with the protection afforded by the alpine house, many are equally at home in the rock garden or troughs. They are grown under cover to protect the grower rather than the grown. It is lovely in the cold days of winter and spring to be able to enjoy the plants, and the winter sunshine can be a real tonic behind glass.

Certain primulas object to rain in winter and show their dislike by rotting when grown in the garden. In nature these plants are often covered in a mantle of dry snow, which protects them from frost. Also because they are at freezing point, the diseases that cause the rot are not present or at least inactive so there is less risk. The only way we can enjoy these plants is to grow them under glass. There are many other species and hybrids that are very attractive when grown in pots, even though they would grow well in the garden. It must be remembered that a plant does not need to be rare and difficult to be beautiful. Most growers enjoy a challenge, but discretion is the better part of valour to the novice. It is so disheartening to fail completely at the first attempt, and so be guided by the specialist nurseryman who will be more than happy to suggest plants suitable to a beginner. Certain growers enjoy the demands that a difficult plant provides, and hopefully the notes in the appropriate chapters will ensure success.

Pots: Clay or Plastic
All a matter of preference, remembering that different composts and watering are needed for the different types of pot. A good basic compost for use in plastic pots is comprised of one part John Innes No. 2, one part ¼in (6mm) grit and one part moss peat. This is a good starter, but do not hesitate to adapt this to suit your own growing techniques once you have acquired the 'feel' of the plants. Growers using clay pots usually use a compost that is basically John Innes No. 2 with the addition of a small percentage of grit and occasionally peat. Unless clay pots are plunged in damp sand, water evaporates from the sides of the pot as well as the surface of the compost and it is also lost through the leaves of the plant.

Many novices ask for advice about watering, they feel that there must be hard and fast rules. Yes, some plants do need more water than others, but there are so many variables. In general plants need more water in warmer weather, they also need more water in a position where there is a constant flow of air, because more water is lost through the leaves. They also need more water at their periods of maximum growth, and less when they are in a dormant or semi-dormant state. As experience is gained the grower will soon learn which plants will tolerate wide variations in watering and which have a very narrow tolerance and so need to have their watering monitored more carefully. Unfortunately this experience is usually gained the hard way – by losing the occasional plant.

Plants are alive, they are individuals and must be treated as such; some require more water and or food than others and an appreciation of this fact is the first step towards successful growing.

Recommended Plants:

The auriculas,
The Auriculastrum group,
The small Asiatics,
The list is almost endless.

Border
The conventional border often boasts a good humus-rich soil, such as that found in the vegetable garden, and is ideal for polyanthus and many of the primroses. The shade afforded by taller plants and shrubs can create ideal conditions with a modicum of thought.

Recommended plants for the drier sunnier border:

Border auriculas,
Alpine auriculas, both named and from seed.

Recommended list of plants for the moister, shadier border:

The Vernales primulas, primroses and relatives,
The more tolerant Asiatics such as
Primulas cortusoides, denticulata and *secundiflora* etc.

Shady Corners
These can be excellent for many of the Asiatic primulas and the Vernales section. The soil will probably need improving with moss peat to aid moisture retention, and if the shade is provided by trees there is a danger of the soil drying out too

much for most primulas. However if shade is provided by a tall fence or wall, and the aspect is northerly, an interesting and attractive bed can be planted, that will provide colour from early spring through to July.

Recommended plants:

> *Primula pruhociniana* hybrids, such as Primulas 'Wanda' and 'Lady Greer',
> The Vernales primulas,
> The easier Asiatics.

Peat Bed

This is the ideal environment for many of the smaller Asiatic primulas, and members of the Vernales section. The bed is best constructed facing north or north-west, with taller trees on the southern side to create light shadow in summer. This is a council of perfection and few gardens offer the ideal conditions. Do not despair, but remember the essentials, and choose the most suitable site: light shade from the sun in mid-summer, freedom from drips off overhanging trees, and a good peaty soil. A part of the garden which in summer is always much cooler, but is at the same time light and airy is suitable. The soil will need to be improved. If there is already a reasonably good neutral soil, up to one third by volume of good moss peat thoroughly incorporated will provide a good medium. However if the bed seems to be too wet and soggy in winter the addition of some grit to improve the drainage would be advantageous.

Peat blocks are ideal for edging, but seem to be rarer than the plants at present. Be careful with old wood from woods or anywhere where it has been outdoors; there is always a risk of honey fungus, which could prove lethal to the small shrubs that are so attractive planted in association with the primulas. Old railway sleepers can be very effective, as can well-weathered old second-hand wood, such as that sold by demolition firms. These are reasonably clean as regards pests and diseases – in the case of sleepers they have been soaked in oil and creosote for many years and the second-hand wood has been kept dry. If the garden is of a more formal nature, a low wall of suitable bricks, imitation stone etc can be very effective. Do not be afraid to experiment; as long as the soil is suitable and there is some shade the primulas will prosper. If the conditions are not quite perfect try the easier species first, and, as knowledge and understanding of the plants' needs improve, the collection can be increased to include other species that would most enjoy the environment.

Where peat is referred to, it needs to be good quality sphagnum moss peat that is normally sold compressed in bales, and will be labelled 'Moss Peat', not 'sedge' peat that is often cheaper. There is no point saving money on inferior materials to improve the soil, then spending a fortune on expensive plants just to lose them because the growing medium is unsuitable. Beware of garden centres and other purveyors of garden requisites assuring the customer that the product they have will do the job as well – it probably won't.

Recommended plants:

> Most of the Asiatics,
> The rarer members of the Vernales section,
> And a host of others.

Moist to Wet Areas round a Pond
Marvellous for the so-called 'Bog Primulas', that enjoy really wet conditions. A good soil where the pond overflows, and hence is permanently wet, is ideal, especially if the water is able to drain away. This soil can be further improved by the addition of peat, and if there is any suspicion of waterlogging add some grit. Excessive waterlogging can cause stagnant conditions, which are unsuitable – in fact can be lethal. With pond overflows it is possible to adjust the amount of water overflowing, and hence with some care to provide almost ideal conditions for the Candelabra and Sikkimensis groups. During winter there is usually sufficient rain to keep the average pond topped up, and it is only during spring and summer that the gardener needs to resort to the hose pipe.

Recommended plants:

> *Primula rosea,*
> *Primula florindae,*
> Candelabra primulas.

Streams and Natural Water Features
These can be given character by imaginative planting of the larger primulas; any gardener who sees the drifts of candelabra hybrids by the stream at Harlow Car Gardens cannot fail to be

thrilled by their impressive beauty. The Sikkimensis group have the added bonus of their scent, and the colour tends to be in the yellow range, which, planted alongside drifts of blue or black iris creates an entrancing feature.

Recommended plants:

Candelabra primulas,
Sikkimensis primulas,
Primula vialii.

The Bog Garden

This is usually taken to mean a very wet, almost waterlogged area, but it will be far more successful if the water is not allowed to become stagnant. The idea is to have a poorly-drained area, but where there is permanent movement of the water, for instance where a pond permanently overflows and the water takes time to drain. Often a small pool liner is used to hold the soil to create the best conditions. *Primula rosea* and *Primula florindae* are especially suitable.

PROPAGATION

In order to grow and enjoy any group of plants it is useful (but not essential) to be able to propagate them. It is always sensible to have spares so that there are replacements available for any plants that are lost. The ability to produce and rear young plants is very enjoyable and satisfying, and this way the grower is able to stock his garden with many of the lovely plants that are only available as seed from the Society seed lists.

Seed

An understanding of the processes that occur in nature is essential to the successful propagation of primulas from seed, so a brief discussion of natural selection is essential.

The reproductive methods of plants have evolved over thousands of years to ensure the best chances of survival for a particular species within its own environment.

Consider a seed pod full of seeds, which on ripening fall onto the ground – they will all have slightly different genetic characteristics. Some of these seeds will germinate immediately, and possibly be too small to survive the winter. Others will lie dormant until spring and then germinate and will thus have a full season to grow before the onset of the next winter; they will therefore be bigger, stronger plants that are able to survive the winter. It is clear that the seeds with the property of germinating immediately will not survive to produce seed and so will be unable to pass on that trait, whilst those that did not germinate until the following spring will survive to produce seeds with the property of delayed germination. Logical really, but if one considers carefully the environment of a plant's origin it becomes clear why certain genetic characteristics have become prevalent. It is all a question of survival of the fittest, and that applies to the seed as well as the plant.

This is only of importance where the plant has not been in cultivation for a long time, or where the seed has been collected from the wild. Often with species, strains and hybrids that have been in cultivation for many years, man has consistently grown on those plants that germinated fastest, and collected seed from them, and thus gradually eliminated the genetic characteristic that delayed germination.

Many primulas have their own inbuilt mechanism so that cross pollination is easier than self pollination; hence pin-eyed, where the stigma (the part of the female reproductive organ that is receptive to the pollen) is above the stamens (the male part that carries the pollen) and thrum-eyed where the stamens are above the stigma.

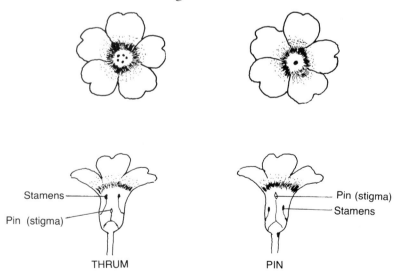

Pin and thrum-eyed primula flowers.

Do remember that the stigma is only receptive for a certain time, and the pollen is only ripe for a limited time.

One property of primula seed that is often ignored is the inhibiting factor of temperature. If primula seed is stored or sown at temperatures in excess of 70°F (20°C) the high temperatures can delay or even prevent germination, so care is needed in buying the seed. Many shops and garden centres keep their seed in very warm conditions, thus reducing significantly the growers' chance of success. It is advisable to always purchase seed directly from the seed firms.

This does not apply to all primula seed, both *Primula denticulata* and *Primula vialii* seed have been known to germinate at considerably higher temperatures, but it is a factor always worth considering.

The above comments do not apply to seed strains that have been in cultivation for many years, as the selection process has been based on colour rather than survival in the wild, hence the reduction of hardiness in the Pacific strains of polyanthus.

The seed of primroses and cowslips is notorious. It has evolved to delay germination over several years; a few will germinate the first spring, a few the second spring and so on. One explanation could be that occasionally all the seedlings that germinated in one spring could perish in a very hot summer, and the plants from the seed that germinated the second spring would survive to bear seed.

Stratification is the term used to describe a method of treating seed to help germination. Many seeds, especially those from Alpine environments, have evolved so that they will germinate in the spring, after they have undergone periods of alternate freezing and thawing in the winter. The action of the heavy rains of winter also appears beneficial. Fridges and freezers are often recommended as suitable alternatives, but this has been found to be far less effective than natural methods. Freezers are not recommended; the temperatures are too low and can damage the seed. The most effective way to treat seed that needs stratifying is to sow it in December in a gritty seed compost, cover with a thin layer of grit, and put it outside, uncovered, and forget it until March. Then it can either be left outside, watering when necessary, or brought into the greenhouse to germinate. It is important to find a place where the young seedlings will not be devoured by other forms of life.

Which species need stratification? Certainly all the Auriculastrum section species where the seed has been collected from the wild need it, as do plants that are not many generations removed from wild stock. It is usually unnecessary for the seed from hybrids and strains that have been in cultivation for many years. The wild members of the Vernales section need stratification, and may take several years to germinate, but the cultivated hybrids, given the right conditions, will germinate easily. *Primula scotica* and the Petiolarids benefit from the action of frost, but other members of the Farinosae section and the majority of the bog primulas do not appear to need stratification if the seed has been kept correctly. If in doubt it doesn't hurt to stratify the seed.

As a general rule the bog primulas would be best sown on a compost with a greater proportion of peat or a proprietory peat-based compost, but for the other primulas a compost comprising of one part John Innes Seed, one part moss peat and one part grit is suitable. Sow in January to March, cover with a light scattering of grit and put in a cool position outside. Do not cover with polythene, glass or anything – it can create more problems than it solves. The species that need stratification need to be sown in January. March is early enough for those species that do not require the action of frost to germinate. Keep a careful eye on the pots or trays of seed in dry weather, the germinating seed is extremely sensitive to dryness. Also protect from slugs.

The seed needs to be sown thinly. A standard seed tray of about 14 x 9in (35 x 22cm) will comfortably hold one hundred seedlings, and give the grower plenty of leeway as regards potting time. If there is the space for the seed trays it is wiser to sow thinly but if space is at a premium and it is desired to sow the seed in pots, there is no reason to sow all of a packet of seed at once as it can be stored.

If the grower collects his own seed it may be sown straight away or stored. It is always advisable to dry the seed after collecting, just pop it in an open bag with a name label, and hang it up for a few weeks, making sure the air can circulate round the seed and/or pods. It can be then cleaned and put in packets, clearly labelled with name and date, and stored for sowing at the right time. An airtight container (clean margarine tub) kept in the salad compartment of the fridge (spouse willing) is ideal.

Hybrids do not come true from seed, neither do named varieties, sometimes the seedlings from a particular hybrid are almost indistinguishable from the parent, but they are not the same, and must not be labelled as such.

Species bred in isolation do come true from seed, but it is often very difficult to guarantee the isolation. As a general rule the primulas do not interbreed between different sections, although there are exceptions. In particular the Farinosae do not interbreed within their own section, though again with a few exceptions.

Pricking out or potting up is best left until the small plants have at least four true leaves, though many authorities advocate transplanting when the seedlings are very small. This is all very well until you have a very hot day, where you are at work all day, and come home to find the seedlings scorched to death. In our experience it is better to leave the seedlings in their seed tray or pot until they are a reasonable size, but not cramped, select a cool moist day, then carefully pot up the number required into 3in (7cm) pots, water in and put in a shady place to establish. Once there is a well-established plant in the pot, it can be planted out, preferably before a period of cool, moist weather. Not being able to forsee the future one has to rely on inspired guess work, if the weather does turn hot soon after planting out, shading material draped over the plants will help considerably. Late August to October is very suitable, especially for the moisture lovers. If the primulas need to be kept outside for the winter they are usually safer planted than kept in pots, except for the Auriculastrum section, which are fairly tolerant.

To check whether a young plant is established first check if any roots are emerging from the drainage holes at the base of the pot. If none are visible, the root action can also be checked by 'knocking out'. This sounds drastic, but once you have mastered the technique it can be very useful. Do not try knocking out if the compost is snuff dry, it must be reasonably moist. Place the forefinger on the compost at one side of the young plant and the next two fingers on the compost at the other side, turn over, gently rap the top edge of the pot on a firm surface, and gently lift the pot off the compost with the other hand. This technique can be practised with a pot full of moist compost (without a plant) to gain confidence. If healthy white roots can be seen round the outside of the compost the plant is established.

Splitting

The majority of primulas are very easily propagated in this way, and with a modicum of care it will be successful throughout the year, excepting very cold periods. The splitting

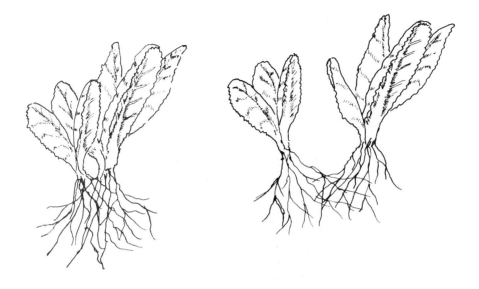

Illustrating the splitting of primulas.

itself is largely commonsense. It does help if the soil or compost is dryish, so that it falls of the roots easily, the more temperamental of the Asiatics require a great deal more care, as the newly split plants are very prone to scorch. A primula plant will have one or more rosettes of leaves on one or more thick basal stems. On closer examination, after knocking the soil off, it will be obvious where the plant can be cut in order to split it into several plants. Recommendations about specific methods for different groups are included in the appropriate chapters.

Cuttings

Most of the Auriculastrum section can be propagated from cuttings, and often this will result in a better-shaped plant than those obtained from splitting. An easy way to do this is take a seed tray half filled with the usual potting compost, fill up to the top with a good grit sand, smooth, and water thoroughly with a fine rose. Take the cutting off the plant, remove any dead leaves, dip in rooting powder, and push it in the tray, making sure all cuttings are labelled. The tray can be kept on the greenhouse bench or in a cold frame. Bottom heat helps and the tray needs to be kept dryish, though not snuff dry. If

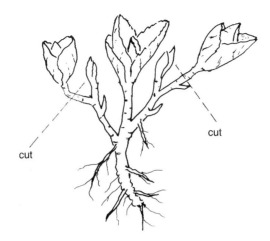

Primula cuttings.

this is done during the early spring months or in September it can be very successful. In the summer it is sensible to keep the trays of young cuttings well shaded.

Primulas from other sections can also be propagated in this way, but as it is more troublesome and takes longer it is rarely used unless in emergency. If all the roots decide to rot on a favourite Petiolarid (or any other primula), it is often possible to save that plant by cutting back all the rot to clean white roots or caudex, and treating the rosette as a cutting.

Root cuttings can be useful for good coloured *Primula denticulatas,* but splitting is easier.

Leaf cuttings are suitable for some of the Vernales section, but it is not particularly easy without the ideal conditions. It also can be very useful for some, but not all of the Petiolarids.

On close examination of the top surface of a single, reasonably mature leaf an incipient bud can be seen near the base of the midrib, and it is possible for this to develop into a plant. Various methods are used, and the one described is somewhat crude but will give a reasonable chance of success. Several leaves are carefully removed, one at a time, from the parent plant with a downward tug, making sure the incipient bud can be seen. The end of the leaf is dipped in a rooting powder containing a fungicide to help prevent rot. The leaves are then inserted horizontally into a seed tray containing a peat compost with a ½in (1 cm) layer of horticultural sand on top. This needs to be kept close and humid for several weeks either in a cool propagator or cold frame – often covering with cling film

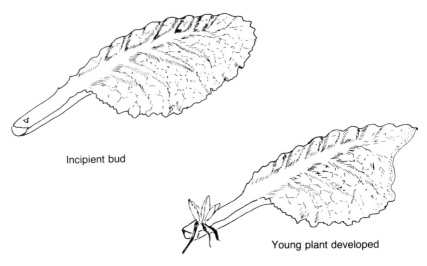

Incipient bud

Young plant developed

Typical leaf cutting.

will help. Spring is the best time, but beware of sun. The cuttings need to be shaded from the sun at all times and it is worth trying a few in autumn as well. The little bud will develop into a small plant with roots, which can then be potted up and grown on as described for seedlings.

Micropropagation (Meristem Culture)

Theoretically this could be of great importance. It is a complicated process that uses laboratory techniques to multiply small pieces of a plant, and so speed up the propagation process. In practise for it to be viable many thousands of plants need to be produced and sold. It has been of great use in the propagation of auriculas and double primroses, and has enabled anyone who wishes to grow a somewhat restricted selection of these lovely plants to do so. The other advantage of this method is that it reduces virus, and appears to endow the plants with greater vigour.

4

Introduction to European Primulas

Although these charming plants have been in cultivation for many hundreds of years, it is only recently that gardeners have begun to realise their full potential. The polyanthus and the auricula are old favourites, but the lesser known hybrids and cultivars have remained largely neglected by the general gardener. The European primulas are the most delightful and entrancing of all the spring-flowering plants, both for the garden and the cold greenhouse. There are plants to suit everyone, both easy and difficult, and there can be few other genera that can cover such a range of colour and form – not forgetting the added bonus of the scent.

The primulas of Europe are contained in three distinct sections, the Farinosae, the Auriculastrum and the Vernales. These will be discussed fully in the following chapters. Not only are they distinct in appearance, but they are also very different in their cultural requirements.

The Farinosae, otherwise known as the Bird's Eye Primulas, are small plants, often short lived, and as the name suggests the leaves are usually covered in farina, or meal. Some members of this section make excellent garden plants, while others are more suited to alpine house culture. Geographically it is a very widespread section, occurring in Europe, Asia and America.

The Auriculastrum section contains the auriculas, the pubescenses, the marginatas, the allioniis and literally thousands of hybrids, and the distribution of these species is limited to Europe. It must be remembered that the primula is still evolving, and many different species, though classed as separate, are little more than geographical variants; this being born out by the ease with which they interbreed. It is this faculty to interbreed that has brought about the vast numbers of named man-made hybrids that are present in our gardens today. The florists' and border auriculas and primula pubescens types are both descended from hybrids between the wild yellow *Primula auricula* and the red *Primula hirsuta* (formerly *Primula rubra*), which contain the ability in their genetic make up to produce flowers in a wide range of colours – not only the reds and yellows, but also a full range of mauve to purple.

The Vernales section contains the well loved primroses, polyanthus and all their relatives, which are also exclusive to Europe. The cultivars of *Primula vulgaris* have been in cultivation for many hundreds of years. The doubles are enjoying a surge in popularity at present, partly because of their greater availability due to modern methods of propagation.

5
The Farinosae Section
The Bird's Eye Primulas

This is the largest section in the primula genus containing eighty or more species, mostly Asiatic but several occur in Europe, North America and even South America. It is certainly the most widespread section, and exceedingly diverse in its habit and appearance. The European species nearly all belong to the same subsection, EU-FARINOSAE and are all fairly similar in appearance, as are their cultural requirements, with heads of mauve to pink flowers above rosettes of well-farinaed leaves. The exception is the yellow flowered *Primula luteola,* which is closely related to the well-known pink Asiatic, *Primula rosea.*

GENERAL CULTIVATION

In general the European farinose primulas like a gritty well-drained soil, but care must be taken to avoid drying out during the hot summer months. As with many other primulas too much heat and dryness in the summer can seriously weaken the plant, making it more likely to die in the winter. It must be remembered that these plants are often short-lived in the wild, only surviving one or two years, and that they replenish themselves annually from the copiously set seed. The more fragile members of this group are often better appreciated in a cold greenhouse, where culture is very straight-forward – a gritty compost, just damp in the winter, and plenty of water in the growing season. The smaller members of this section appear to benefit from root association which is best achieved by planting several plants together in a pan. In the garden or trough they can be planted with other small plants. It has been noticed that when there are several pots of a particular species, all potted up individually, it is usually the plant with a weed also present that grows away best, especially if the weeds are small grasses.

| 0 | 1 | 2in(5cm) |

Primula frondosa.

SEASONAL CULTIVATION

SPRING: The farinose resting buds start to open, and the flower heads emerge. Often the first flowers will open before the head of buds has risen above the leaves. In the alpine house increase watering, and gently feed with half strength liquid fertiliser once a week. The greenhouse will need shading, early to mid-April in the south, but in more northerly areas it will not be needed until mid-April or even later. If the plants are to be exhibited, be very careful not to mark the farina on the leaves by careless use of the watering can. After flowering, the more vigorous species that have several crowns may be split if desired.

SUMMER: As the season progresses the farina on the leaves gradually disappears. If the plants have set seed, and it is not required, remove the head at the top of the stem, to encourage the plant to use its strength in building up a good strong crown instead of directing its energies into the production of unwanted seed. Under glass carry on feeding until about the end of July.

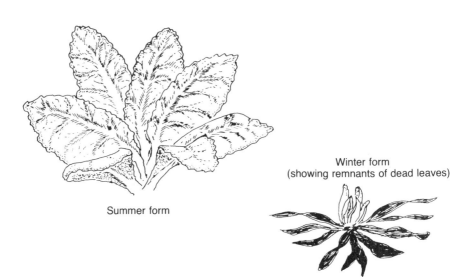

Summer form

Winter form
(showing remnants of dead leaves)

Summer and winter forms of *Primula frondosa*.

AUTUMN: The leaves die back to a tight resting bud, which is usually covered in farina, though this may well be washed off by rain or watering. It is sensible to remove the dead leaves when they come away easily. If they are left they provide the perfect home for botrytis and other moulds, which can spread through the whole plant in the moist and muggy days of autumn. Be careful that all dead and dying vegetation is disposed off. If it is left on the greenhouse floor it will only encourage more disease. In the garden the wind and rain will do the job adequately, but there is no point in encouraging disease under glass.

WINTER: The European members of this section spend the winter as small resting buds, heavily coated in farina. Under glass they need to be kept just moist, but not wet. In the garden the only danger is during periods of very hard frost. When the ground thaws after a prolonged period of frost, the plants need checking, as they are often lifted by the frost, and the roots are left lying on the surface. They will need to be carefully replanted *in situ.*

PROPAGATION

The freely set seed germinates well, usually without stratification. Some species may be split, but care needs to be taken, and it is advisable to keep the newly potted plants in a shady place until they are established. The members of the Farinosae group rarely hybridise so one can be reasonably confident that they will breed true, in fact the European members can be trusted completely not to interbreed.

RECOMMENDATIONS: A representative collection only really needs to contain *Primula frondosa,* and the charming, tiny native *Primula scotica.*

DESCRIPTIVE LIST OF
EUROPEAN SPECIES

Primula algida:
Very similar to the closely related *Primula farinosa* which it replaces in the Caucasus mountains and eastern Turkey, it could almost be classed as a geographic variant. It is more fully described in the chapter on Asiatic primulas.

CULTIVATION: Garden or cold greenhouse.
PROPAGATION: Seed or careful splitting.
AVAILABILITY: Occasionally available from the seed lists, or the specialist nurseries.

Primula darialica:

To be found on the northern slopes of the Caucasus and is closely related to *Primula algida*. It has often been confused with *Primula frondosa*, and many of the plants in cultivation are probably not the true plant.
CULTIVATION: Garden or cold greenhouse.
PROPAGATION: Seed or careful splitting.
AVAILABILITY: Listed by many specialist nurseries, but are they offering the true plant? Same comments apply to seed lists.

Primula farinosa:

The well-loved native 'Bird's Eye Primrose'. It is the most widespread of all primulas and occurs in upland pastures in Europe and Asia, and has a very close relative *Primula mistassinica* in Northern America. The 3–10in (7–25cm) stems carry heads of flat, mauve to pink flowers with a good yellow eye above rosettes of well farinaed leaves. It is easily grown once one realises that it is by nature a short-lived plant. However in cultivation it has a tendency to become over-tall and out of proportion, and thus loses the beauty and fragility of a plant in the wild.
CULTIVATION: Garden or cold greenhouse.
PROPAGATION: Easy from seed.
AVAILABILITY: It may be easily obtained as seed and plants can often be purchased from the specialist nurseries.

Primula frondosa:

A close relative of *Primula farinosa,* with all the good points and none of the bad. It comes from a small area of the Balkan mountains to the east of Sofia in Bulgaria, where it is found around and within woodland areas, often growing in rocky clefts, but, unlike *Primula farinosa,* rarely in turf. The leaves are heavily mealed, almost white in spring, but appearing greener as the summer progresses, because the rain tends to wash the farina off. The good heads of flowers are lilac-pink with a pronounced small yellow eye, usually about 6in (15cm) high, and it flowers March to May, depending on the severity of the winter, and whether the plants are in the cold greenhouse or outside. Like many of the primula family the old leaves die back in autumn leaving a tight farinose resting bud, which unfurls in spring to give loose rosettes of heavily mealed leaves. It is one of the most charming of the primula family and cannot be too highly recommended. Once one plant has been obtained it can be easily propagated from seed, or by careful division after flowering.

CULTIVATION: Easy in the garden, providing it is not allowed to dry out in the hot summer months. It will tolerate a reasonable amount of shade. *Primula frondosa* also makes a beautiful and eyecatching specimen for the cold greenhouse where it will delight the grower with its many good heads of mauve flowers. A very easy and rewarding plant for the show-bench.

PROPAGATION: Easy from the copiously set seed, which germinates well provided the seed has been looked after properly. Multicrowned plants are easily split, but it is sensible to establish the split plants in pots before exposing them to the rigours of the open garden.

AVAILABILITY: It is readily available from the specialist nurseries, some seed firms, seed lists, and it is also occasionally stocked by the better class garden centres and general nurseries.

Primula halleri (Primula longiflora):

A very distinctive member of the Farinosae group, and may be found in a variety of locations, from north-western Italy through to the Carpathians in Romania. It is to be found in stony alpine meadows with a high humus content, and in moist cracks in the rocks. It is usually found on limestone, but can also occur on the acid rocks. It is very similar to *Primula frondosa,* but of a rather more delicate appearance. The main distinguishing feature is the very long calyx tube.

CULTIVATION: Very similar to *Primula frondosa,* with a little extra care.

PROPAGATION: Easy from seed.

AVAILABILITY: Occasionally available from the specialist nurseries and usually in the seed lists.

Primula luteola:

Very different to the other European Farinosa primulas. It is found in the Caucasus mountains, and bridges the divide between the European and the Asiatic primulas. It is in the same subsection as *Primula rosea,* and is similar in form though not in colour. The 6–12in (15–30cm) stem carries loose heads of yellow flowers above upright rosettes of dark green efarinose leaves. It dies back to resting buds for the winter, and is a reasonably vigorous species.

CULTIVATION: Happy in any good garden soil that does not become too dry in summer. Sun or shade.

0   2   4in(10cm)

Primula halleri.

PROPAGATION: Easy from seed, or large established clumps may be split after flowering.

AVAILABILITY: Rarely from the specialist nurseries but is usually included in the Society seed lists.

Primula scandinavica:

To be found in the Norwegian mountains, and is closely related to the native *Primula scotica*. The little heads of flowers on 2–4in (5–10cm) stems are variable in colour, from darkish-mauve through to purplish-violet, and it is usually slightly taller than *Primula scotica*. It appears to be nearly as temperamental, and needs to be kept going by collecting the seed.

CULTIVATION: The cold greenhouse is recommended. It will stand any amount of cold, but the small resting buds tend to disappear from the open garden in winter. Charming in a trough as long as a steady succession is grown as a safeguard against losses.

PROPAGATION: From seed, stratification may help.

AVAILABILITY: Occasionally available from specialist nurseries, or the seed lists.

Primula scotica:

A little treasure from the northernmost coast of Scotland and the Orkneys, where it grows in moist pasture near the sea. The small heads of vivid purple flowers on 1–3in (2.5–7cm) stems are carried above flat rosettes of neat well mealed leaves in April and May, and often again in the summer. It disappears to a tiny mealy resting bud in the winter, when it is at most risk from the elements. Like many members of the Farinosae section it tends to be short lived. Well worth growing, and fit to grace the alpine house of the most discerning of growers.
CULTIVATION: Best in the cold greenhouse, despite the fact that it grows in damp meadows. A gritty compost, with copious water in the growing season appears to suit it best. It is usually grown in half pots, several plants to a pot for showing – as it is so small several are needed to look their best. It may also be grown, and is very attractive, in a trough, possibly planted in association with small saxifrages and *Gentiana verna*. The importance of collecting the seed to keep a succession of plants for replacements cannot be stressed too much.
PROPAGATION: In order to ensure its survival the seed must be collected regularly, and stratification appears to improve germination. Great care must be taken with the little plants as they can easily be lost when potted.
AVAILABILITY: Often available from the specialist nurseries or the seed lists.

Primula stricta:

A close relative of *Primula farinosa* from the Arctic and subarctic regions of Europe, Asia and North America. It is a very variable plant, with slightly smaller flowers, and only of interest to the avid collector.
CULTIVATION: As *Primula scandinavica*.
PROPAGATION: Seed.
AVAILABILITY: Try the seed lists.

6
The Auriculastrum Section

A daunting name for the section which contains the well-loved Auricula and its close relatives, and which are mainly characterised by the texture of their leaves. All the representatives of this section are to be found in Europe, and because of their remarkable ability to interbreed they have given rise to the thousands of hybrids that are in cultivation today.

A descriptive list of the species will follow, with the exception of *Primula marginata* and *Primula allionii* which will only be mentioned as they both merit a chapter to themselves.

GENERAL CULTIVATION

Generally this group require a gritty compost. For plastic pots the recommended compost is one part John Innes No. 2, one part moss peat and one part ¼in (6mm) grit, as described earlier. It should be well-drained yet with plenty of water in the growing season. The smaller species are far better grown under glass, where they can be attended to more closely or, failing that, a select trough. The larger species are good reliable garden plants. One of their most important characteristics is that they tend to be very long lived, providing they are looked after properly.

The species are all beautiful but some have never fully settled to captivity. Several are shy flowering, and whereas this can be an exciting challenge to some growers it can lead to frustration and despair in others. It has been noticed by several competent growers that all the European primula species flower better after a severe winter, and it would appear that a period of sub-zero temperatures in winter is essential to promote the formation of the full quota of flowers.

SEASONAL CULTIVATION IN THE GARDEN

All that is required is the usual general maintenance that one would extend to any beautiful plant in the garden. Provided they are planted in a suitable position it is only necessary to weed and keep the beds tidy. Any plants that are outgrowing their allotted quarters need to be lifted and split at the appropriate time, and occasionally checked for pests and disease.

SEASONAL CULTIVATION IN THE ALPINE HOUSE

SPRING: Enjoy the flowers. Dilute feed regularly, keep a close watch on watering for this is the period of maximum growth. Start shading the greenhouse when the conditions merit it. Remove the dead flower heads, at the top, unless the seed is specifically required. This is not essential but it will save the plant wasting its energies in producing worthless seed. After flowering is the best time for splitting the plants, or for taking cuttings.

SUMMER: All shading should be in place now. If the plants are kept outside for the summer, they should now be in their summer quarters. Keep a close eye open for pests. In the summer watering in the evening is far more beneficial to the plant. On a very hot day the occasional plant may wilt. First check how moist the compost is, and if it seems moist it is probably suffering from heat exhaustion rather than drought. It needs to be given a cooler, shadier position. Temporarily under the staging is as good as anywhere. Towards the end of August watering needs to be reduced and if the plants are in open frames they will need protecting from torrential rain.

AUTUMN: Any plants in pots should now be brought back into the alpine house. Under glass remove dead and dying leaves that come away easily. As autumn progresses keep an eye open for any signs of botrytis and if it should appear take appropriate measures. See the chapter on pests and diseases.

WINTER: Many of the Auriculastrum section will have now retreated into their contracted winter foliage of tight buds. This semi-dormant state is very variable between the different species; *Primula minima* almost vanishes, though a little speck of green is usually visible amongst the old brown

73

leaves. As long as the foliage is dry and clear of botrytis the dead leaves may be left. Watering should be minimal, a very slight amount of moisture in the pot is advised. In winter it is better to water in the morning and if any plant appears too dry, a five second dunk in an inch of water will suffice. Every year is different, and in mild winters, as experienced recently, more plants are lost from dryness than any other cause.

PROPAGATION

SPLITTING: Nearly all of the Auriculastrum section can be very easily propagated by splitting mature plants. It is advisable to allow the compost to become fairly dry before splitting. The plant should be knocked out of the pot, and the compost shaken off. If it refuses to come away easily gentle teasing with the fingers is usually effective. Close examination will show that many of the stems of the rosettes of leaves have roots attached, which may be separated and carefully potted into 3in (7cm) pots in the standard Auriculastrum compost. If there is an excessive amount of root it will need to be pruned with a sharp knife or pair of scissors. The root needs to balance the top growth – a rough guide is to cut the roots back to 3in (7cm) if potting in a 3in (7cm) pot. The newly potted plants need to be watered in thoroughly and put in a shaded position to establish – after the initial watering in, it is necessary to keep them just moist. If they are kept too wet there is a danger that the roots may rot. Establishment is usually quicker in early spring and late summer, when the plants and roots are at their most active.

CUTTINGS: This method has been described in chapter 3.

SEED: Although seed, which needs stratifying, is a perfectly easy method, it can lead to problems and disappointment, due to the ease with which the members of this section will hybridise with other members. The seedlings also tend to be very small and difficult to handle in the early stages, and it is recommended that they are grown on in their seed pots for a year before attempting to pot them up. Splitting is very easy, and reliable, and the only precaution is care in watering, and preferably light shade until the offsets are well established.

PESTS AND DISEASES: As many of the plants in this group are very small and slow growing, they tend to be kept in the same pots for two or more years. This can lead to a build up of root aphids/mealy bug, which, if undetected can lead to the loss of many rare and select plants. Undoubtedly dryness at the roots and hot weather can encourage an epidemic: the occasional root inspection by knocking out of the pot is advised and if necessary drench with a systemic insecticide containing dimethoate. Also see chapter 19.

AVAILABILITY: Many of these lovely species are not common in cultivation, but diligent searching of all the specialist nurseries, especially those advertising in the bulletins of the Alpine Garden Society, the Scottish Rock Garden Club and the Auricula Societies will yield untold riches. From the seed lists, there is also much satisfaction to be gained by raising rare plants from seed, and they can provide useful 'swapping material' to use in exchange for other rarities.

The subsections of the Auriculastrum section will be included in the glossary, and for ease of reference the species will be described in alphabetical order:

DESCRIPTIVE LIST OF SPECIES

Primula allionii (Subsection Rhopsidium):
This will be dealt with fully in chapter 8.
Primula apennina (Subsection Erythrodosum):
Reputedly an easy and hardy species. The lilac to magenta pink flowers are in loose heads on 1–4in (2.5–10cm) stems above rosettes of slightly serrated leaves. It is suspected by some authorities of being a geographical variant of *Primula villosa*.
CULTIVATION: Standard treatment for Auriculastrum species, but safer in the greenhouse as it is so rare in cultivation.
PROPAGATION: Careful splitting.
AVAILABILITY: Possibly available from the seed lists, and has been occasionally listed by the specialist nurseries.
Primula auricula(Subsection Euauricula):
One of the major parents of the vast numbers of beautiful hybrids that are in cultivation today. Also one of the only two yellow-flowered members of the Auriculastrum group, the other being *Primula palinuri*. It is to be found mainly in the mountainous limestone regions to the north of Italy. A very variable plant in the wild, it can be completely covered with white or cream farina, or with only a small amount on the edges of the leaves, sometimes hairy, sometimes not, leaves toothed or not toothed. It has been divided into several subspecies, but some authorities query whether they are true

subspecies or just variations within the plant, or varieties where the evolution has led to distinct differences in different areas. The following subspecies are usually acknowledged:

Primula auricula bauhini: is the typical form, and is very variable, but is characterised by the lemon-yellow scented flowers.

Primula auricula bauhini var. albocincta: has very thick farina on the leaf edges.

Primula auricula bauhini var. manocensis: is a variety to be found on the Bavarian moors north of Munich, the leaves are described as being narrowly oblong.

Primula auricula bauhini var. widmerae: comes from the Black Forest, and has thin textured, narrow leaves.

Primula auricula bauhini var. serratifolia: has serrated, toothed leaves.

Primula auricula ciliata (syn. balbisii): has no farina, tiny hairs on the edges of the rounded leaves and deep yellow scentless flowers.

Primula auricula ciliata var. obritsii: has no farina on the narrower leaves, and the flowers are scented.

CULTIVATION: It is an easy and rewarding plant, suitable for rock gardens or even the border. The smaller forms make lovely plants for the alpine house.

PROPAGATION: Propagation is safest by taking offsets, due to its tendency to hybridise with any other member of the Auriculastrum section within insect range.

AVAILABILITY: The pure species may only be obtained from the specialist nurseries, and then only occasionally. Alternatively look in the Society seed lists for wild collected seed. Beware of commercial seeds labelled *Primula auricula* (or *Auricula alpina*), as they are more likely to be mixed hybrids.

Primula carniolica (Subsection Brevibracteata):
Found in a small area in north-west Yugoslavia around the tops of low altitude limestone hills in light woodland and stony pastures, often inhabiting pockets in north-facing limestone rocks. The one sided head of pink to lilac scented flowers are on 2–10in (5–25cm) stems over rosettes of darkish green leaves. The farina round the eye is very distinctive, as is the lack of teeth on the leaves. Well worth growing (noting that it needs more shade than the other European primulas), but rarely available.

CULTIVATION: Standard, with extra shade in summer.
PROPAGATION: Careful splitting in spring.

AVAILABILITY: Try the seed lists, rarely from specialist nurseries.

Primula clusiana (Subsection Arthritica):
Comes from the limestone alps in northern Austria where it prefers to grow in grassy areas. The small heads of huge bright-pink flowers with a white eye on 1–4in (2.5–10cm) stems fade to lilac above compact rosettes of dark green shiny leaves, which are larger in cultivation than in the wild. Tends to be shy flowering, but one is unsure whether it is the nature of the plant or the skill of the grower which is at fault. In the wild only young plants are found. *Primula clusiana* 'Murray Lyon': is a selected very large flowered form, which in cultivation flowers even earlier than *Primula allionii*. It is thought by some experts to be a hybrid, possibly with *Primula minima*.

CULTIVATION: Gritty compost, cold greenhouse, but will tolerate conditions outside quite happily especially in a trough. Often pot-bound plants will flower, possibly a last effort in case they die! It is generally accepted that plants that have been shy of flowering, will, after some form of stress, flower freely which could be an inbuilt mechanism to ensure survival.

PROPAGATION: Careful splitting.

AVAILABILITY: Occasionally from specialist nurseries, but seed is often available from the seed lists.

Primula daoensis (Subsection Erythrodosum):
A pretty little thing from a relatively small area in the north of Italy, overlapping into Austria and Switzerland. It is always found on granite, and has similarities with *Primula hirsuta*. It is a very variable plant, characterised by the toothed wedge-shaped leaves. The small heads of pink to crimson nearly flat flowers sometimes have a white eye and are carried on 1–3in (2.5–7cm) stems above the rosettes of leaves. The flowers sometimes seem large in proportion to the leaves.

CULTIVATION: Standard treatment, in a gritty compost.

PROPAGATION: Careful splitting because of the dangers of interbreeding.

AVAILABILITY: Occasionally by specialist nurseries, or try the seed lists. As with all this section it is wiser to search in the part of the seed list devoted to wild collected seed.

Primula deorum (Subsection Cyanopsis):
Discovered in 1889 and is found in a small region south of Sofia in Bulgaria in wet grasslands above the tree line on non-limestone rocks. The one sided head carries up to ten rich crimson purple to violet purple funnel-shaped flowers on 2–

8in (5–20cm) stems above loose rosettes of shiny, leathery leaves. A beautiful plant but sadly rarely available.
CULTIVATION: Standard, grow in a cold greenhouse until stocks are sufficient to risk a plant on the rock garden.
PROPAGATION: Probably careful splitting, or wild collected seed.
AVAILABILITY: Try the seed lists.

Primula glaucescens (Subsection Arthritica):
Found in northern Italy, in an area between Lake Garda and Lake Como. It is a lime-loving plant to be found growing in limestone cracks, slopes and banks, showing a preference for moist shady positions rich in humus. The symmetrical heads of up to six pink to lilac flowers are on 1–6in (2.5–15cm) stems above the tight rosettes of dark green leathery, shiny, elliptic leaves, with a characteristic papery edge. Two subspecies have been described:
Primula glaucescens calycina: more vigorous, largest flowers and commonest.
Primula glaucescens longobarda: more graceful with smaller flowers.
CULTIVATION: Standard mix, possibly will be happier in slight shade. Cold greenhouse or trough.
PROPAGATION: Careful splitting in spring.
AVAILABILITY: Occasionally available from the specialist nurseries, or from the seed lists.

Primula glutinosa (Subsection Cyanopsis):
To be found in the eastern Alps, from northern Italy through Austria, roughly the same area as *Primula minima*. It is an elegant and beautiful plant with heads of bluish-violet flowers which will hybridise very readily with other members of the Auriculastrum section. Although abundant in the wild it is rare and difficult in cultivation.
CULTIVATION: Standard, cold greenhouse, and possibly on the rock garden when stocks allow, reputed to hate lime-stone.
PROPAGATION: Careful splitting, or try wild collected seed.
AVAILABILITY: Occasionally available in the seed lists. Listed in at least one of the specialists nurseries catalogues.

Primula hirsuta (rubra) (Subsection Erythrodosum):
A very widespread and important species, being one of the parents of a wide variety of hybrids including the auriculas and pubescens hybrids of today. It is found over a wide area of the Alps to the north of Italy and also in the Pyrenees, usually

in rocky crevices. It is an exceedingly variable species, probably still evolving, but typically has bright pink to red flowers (rarely mauve, lilac or white flowers) in symmetrical heads only just above the rosettes of mid-green sticky leaves covered with tiny glandular hairs. The leaves are usually toothed, either fine or coarse, and as is evident the description covers a multitude of variations. *Primula hirsuta* 'Boothmans' is a problem – no one is certain whether it contains some *Primula auricula* blood and is thus a pubescens hybrid, or whether it is a selected *Primula hirsuta*, but either way, it is certainly a lovely plant.

CULTIVATION: Easy following standard treatment, makes a lovely free flowering specimen for the cold greenhouse. Also charming for trough, scree or select position in the rock garden. Although fairly tolerant it resents excessive amounts of lime and topdressing with limestone chippings is to be avoided.

PROPAGATION: Splitting in spring, and establishing the small plants before planting outside.

AVAILABILITY: Wild collected seed is occasionally available from the seed lists.

Primula integrifolia (Subsection Rhopsidium):
Occurring both in the central region of the Alps north of Italy and also in the Pyrenees, usually in wet peaty conditions in meadows or at the side of streams, often over acid rocks, but also more rarely on limestone. A small plant with pinkish-lilac through to magenta flowers, with deeply cut petals and a very hairy throat giving the appearance of a white eye. The toothless leaves are edged with tiny hairs and form small tidy rosettes. Lovely in the wild but tends to be shy flowering in cultivation.

CULTIVATION: Gritty compost, but do make sure it never lacks water in the growing season.

PROPAGATION: Careful splitting or wild collected seed.

AVAILABILITY: Occasionally available from the specialist nurseries and seed lists.

Primula kitaibeliana (Subsection Rhopsidium):
A little-known species from Yugoslavia where it grows in north-facing pockets in cliffs, it is similar to *Primula integrifolia* but has larger leaves and bright magenta flowers.

CULTIVATION: If lucky enough to obtain this plant try the standard methods.

PROPAGATION: Careful splitting or wild seed.

AVAILABILITY: Seed sometimes offered in the seed lists.

Primula latifolia (viscosa) (Subsection Brevibracteata):
A lime-hating species which occurs locally in the Alps north and north-west of Italy, and also in the Pyrenees. It grows in shady and moist crevices and screes. The one-sided (hence the name) head of flowers has long corolla tubes. The Pyrenean form is the most vigorous, but the form from the Bernina area is much daintier. White forms do exist.
CULTIVATION: Standard treatment, if there are signs of chlorosis a dilute feed of sequestrene should help. This plant has been grown successfully outside, and is well worth trying if there are sufficient plants available.
PROPAGATION: Careful splitting, or wild collected seed.
AVAILABILITY: There is considerable doubt whether the named *Primula latifolias* in commerce are indeed true, or relics of previous nomenclature whereby *Primula* x *pubescens* was called *Primula viscosa*, which was the former name, now superseded by *Primula latifolia*. Wild collected seed from the seed lists is safest.

Primula marginata (Subsection Brevibracteata):
Described in full in chapter 7.

Primula minima (Subsection Chamaecalus):
To be found in the alpine regions to the north-east of Italy. It is a tiny plant to be found in humus-rich meadows, where it forms wide mats only one or two inches high. It crosses with other members of the Auriculastrum group very readily and it is often difficult to determine whether the species is true. Unfortunately the true species is often shy flowering in cultivation, but it has given rise to some spectacular natural and man-made hybrids which flower freely. (*See* natural hybrids at the end of the chapter). The flowers are a very bright magenta pink or more rarely white with the five petals cleft almost to the centre, giving the appearance of ten narrow petals. The flowers are very large in comparison to the leaves. It is fairly constant in form, so if a plant acquired under this name has broad overlapping petals it is probably a hybrid. The tight rosettes of bright green shiny leaves are serrated, and in winter are reduced to very small tight buds, surrounded by the dead remains of the previous year's leaves.
CULTIVATION: Fairly easy in a gritty compost, and is lovely, if frustrating, for a pot in the cold greenhouse, or in a select trough where it can be left to grow slowly and flower if and when it considers conditions suitable.
PROPAGATION: By careful division of an established clump, potting the small offsets and growing them on.

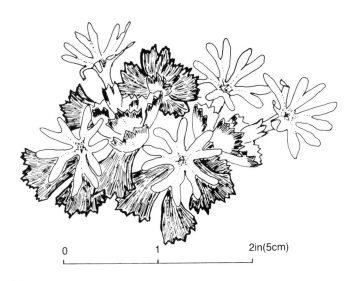

0   1   2in(5cm)

Primula minima.

AVAILABILITY: Occasionally available from the specialist nurseries, or try the seed lists. Wild collected seed is safer if the true species is desired, but still cannot be guaranteed to provide the pure species.

Primula palinuri (Subsection Euauricula):

Apart from the well known *Primula auricula* this is the only other yellow member of this section, and it comes from a very small area on the western coast of Italy south of Naples, where it grows high on the cliffs in sandy tufa or even pure sand. It is in cultivation, though relatively rare, and it appears to be the only primula that will stand being baked in hot weather. In the wild it often sheds its leaves in summer. Surprisingly it is easy to grow, and is one of the earliest of Europeans to flower, often in January under glass. The flowers are a very bright golden yellow, tubular with a funnel-shaped end which never opens fully, above loose rosettes of broad ovate saw-edged yellowish leaves (or is that poor culture!). Certainly no beauty, but its quiet charm will liven the garden or greenhouse in the depths of winter.

CULTIVATION: Easy, a gritty free-draining compost, or a well drained south facing bed in the garden.

PROPAGATION: From seed if it sets any, this is the exception that proves the rule as it does not seem to hybridise as readily as the other members of the Auriculastrum. It can also be

81

split, spring being the best time to attempt this, looking after the newly potted offsets carefully until they are established.
AVAILABILITY: Occasionally available in the seed lists, or from one or two specialist nurseries.

Primula pedemontana (Subsection Erythrodosum):
Is to be found in two small areas, one to the north-west of Italy south of Lake Geneva, and the other to the west of the Pyrenees in Spain. It usually grows in humus-rich soil above acid rocks in stony grassland, or in crevices in the rocks. It is suspected of being a variant of *Primula hirsuta*. The good heads of clear pink flowers with a white eye are on 1–6in (2.5–15cm) stems above shiny dark green leaves with tiny reddish hairs on the edges. White forms occasionally occur. Rare in cultivation.
CULTIVATION: Standard.
PROPAGATION: Careful splitting in spring.
AVAILABILITY: Occasionally from the specialist nurseries or try the wild collected seed in the seed lists. The beautiful white form is only present in private collections.

Primula rubra: see ***Primula hirsuta.***

Primula spectabilis (Subsection Arthritica):
To be found growing to the west of Venice around Lake Garda in rough stony grassland at the edge of cliffs. A very variable and beautiful plant. The funnel-shaped, slightly frilly flowers are pink to lilac, with the occasional white, in loose heads on 1–6in (2.5–15cm) stems, above untidy rosettes of large leathery, shiny leaves with smooth edges. Often flowers poorly in cultivation.
CULTIVATION: Gritty compost in a cold greenhouse, when you have sufficient plants try it outside on the rock garden.
PROPAGATION: Careful splitting, or wild collected seed.
AVAILABILITY: Try the seed lists.

Primula tyrolensis (Subsection Rhopsidium):
From a small area to the north of Venice, where it grows in moist shady positions in rocky cracks and meadows. It is a small plant, only 1–2in (2.5–5cm) high. It is closely related to *Primula allionii,* with almost flat flowers of rose to lilac shading and a white eye. There is an unusual, almost translucent quality to the deeply cleft petals, and tiny spoon-shaped leaves.
CULTIVATION: Careful culture in a cold greenhouse in a gritty compost.
PROPAGATION: Splitting in spring.
AVAILABILITY: Occasionally available from the specialist nurseries, or try the seed lists.

Primula villosa (Subsection Erythrodosum):
Found mainly in the Austrian Alps, but can be found locally in other Alpine areas on non-limestone rocks both in rocky pastures and in cracks in the rocks. This species is thought by some to be the same as *Primula pedemontana*. The almost flat flowers are pink to lilac with a large distinct white eye, up to 6in (15cm) high above loose rosettes of slightly sticky leaves with a reddish sheen. Well worth growing if it can be obtained.

Primula villosa cottia: is the form to be found in the Cottian Alps of north-west Italy, and is a smaller sturdier plant, with shorter flower stems and broader leaves. It flowers freely and in the garden requires a rich well-drained soil.
CULTIVATION: Standard.
PROPAGATION: Safer from splitting.
AVAILABILITY: Occasionally listed by the specialist nurseries, try and obtain wild collected seed from the seed lists.
Primula viscosa see **Primula latifolia.**
Primula wulfeniana (Subsection Arthritica):
Mainly found in the alps to the north-east of Venice, only on limestone rocks in meadow pastures. It is a dwarf plant that can form spectacular sheets of colour in the wild, but tends to be somewhat shy flowering in captivity. The pink to violet, white eyed, short stemmed flowers appear between the leathery unserrated leaves which are dark shiny green above and a lighter green below with a papery edge.
CULTIVATION: A small plant more suited to a cold greenhouse, or possibly trough culture, in a gritty compost with ample supplies of water in spring and summer, just moist in winter.
PROPAGATION: Careful splitting.
AVAILABILITY: Occasionally available from nurseries, or often listed in the seed lists.

THE NATURAL HYBRIDS OF THE AURICULASTRUM SECTION

(Not necessarily in cultivation)
In recent years there has been a great deal of interest in the Auriculastrum hybrids that are to be found in the wild, and several experts on these delightful small hybrids have collected better, more free flowering forms. A few of these plants are already on the lists of a few specialist nurseries, and no doubt more will become available in the next few years.

The standard policy amongst the botanists seems to be to differentiate between natural and artificial hybrids, even where they are of the same cross. This leads to confusion, as genetically they must be comparable. The artificial hybrids, even where they are known to be a straight cross between two species will be described in chapter 9.

A fairly brief list of the natural hybrids follows, with descriptions only of plants that are fairly widely grown, albeit only in private collections at the present.

Primula x *berninae*:
This is *Primula latifolia* x *Primula hirsuta*, and is intermediate between the two parents with fine purple flowers.

Primula x *berninae* 'Peggy Fell':
A particularly desirable named hybrid that was collected in the wild by the lady of that name. This plant was originally in circulation as a selected *Primula hirsuta,* but it is now thought to be a natural hybrid.
CULTIVATION: An easy vigorous plant for the alpine house or troughs.
PROPAGATION: By splitting or by cuttings.
AVAILABILITY: Occasionally listed by the specialist nurseries.

Primula x *berninae* 'Windrush':
A selected form found by the late Paul Rosenheim, and is a very compact and free flowering plant with rich red-purple flowers on 1–2in (2.5–5cm) stems. Well worth looking for, and makes a lovely pan for the cold greenhouse.
CULTIVATION: Normal culture for a small pubescens hybrid, probably better suited to cold greenhouse treatment, but will survive outside in a trough.
PROPAGATION: Careful division after flowering or cuttings as per *Primula allionii.* Limestone chippings not recommended.
AVAILABILITY: Occasionally from the specialist nurseries.

Primula x *biflora*
See *Primula* x *floerkeana forma biflora.*

Primula x *bowlesii*:
This is *Primula pedemontana* x *Primula latifolia* and occurs in a range of forms, some of which are reputedly very attractive.
AVAILABILITY: Present in a few private collections, and possibly may be available in the future.

Primula x *carueli*:
This is *Primula glaucescens* x *Primula spectabilis* and is again intermediate, but as the parents are very similar it can hardly be called distinct. Not available.

Primula x crucis:
This is *Primula marginata* x *Primula latifolia* a rare and beautiful hybrid of which a particularly fine form was *Primula* 'Blue Bowl', now sadly lost to cultivation.

Primula x discolor:
This is *Primula auricula* x *Primula daoensis* and very local in its distribution in nature, the hybrids showing a full range of characteristics between the two parents.
AVAILABILITY: Present in a few private collections, rarely offered commercially.

Primula x deschmanii:
See *Primula* x *vochinensis*

Primula x escheri:
This is *Primula auricula* x *Primula integrifolia* and is a rare plant in the wild that is not available in cultivation.

Primula x facchinii:
This is *Primula minima* x *Primula spectabilis* and is described as having large red flowers on short stems.
AVAILABILITY: Very rarely from the specialist nurseries.

Primula x floerkeana:
This is *Primula glutinosa* x *Primula minima* and the different forms have been named as: *Primula* x *floerkeana forma biflora* (often listed as *Primula* x *biflora*) for forms close to *Primula minima* – it is certainly present in several private collections: *Primula* x *floerkeana forma biflora alba* – is listed by one specialist nursery; *Primula* x *floerkeana forma salisburgensis* covers the intermediate forms, but is not available; and *Primula* x *floerkeana forma huteri* for plants close to *Primula glutinosa*, but is not available.

Primula x forsteri:
This is *Primula hirsuta* x *Primula minima* and is the most widely grown natural hybrid, its great advantage being its free flowering and ease of management. Messrs. Smith, Burrow and Lowe in their excellent book *Primulas of Europe and America* have proposed the following eminently sensible classification: *Primula* x *forsteri forma kellereri* for plants close to *Primula hirsuta; Primula* x *forsteri forma steinii* for plants of intermediate form; and *Primula* x *forsteri forma bileckii* (commonly *Primula* x *bileckii*) for plants close to *Primula minima*.

The above forms are usually available under the names *Primula bileckii*, *Primula steinii* and *Primula forsteri*, and usually *Primula bileckii* is the smallest, *Primula steinii* the middle and *Primula forsteri* the largest. However the plants available in commerce are all much closer to *Primula minima* than *Primula hirsuta* with typical shiny wedge-shaped leaves, and an abundance of relatively large dark pink, almost cerise flowers on 1–2in (2.5–5cm) stems. The flowers of *Primula forsteri* are of a slightly lighter shade than the other hybrids with slightly longer stems. It has given rise to the beautiful hybrid *Primula* 'Dianne', which is said to have some *Primula pubescens* blood, though this is not obvious from its appearance. *See* chapter 9.

CULTIVATION: Quite easy in a gritty compost, for cold greenhouse, trough or very select scree.

PROPAGATION: Splitting after flowering or by taking cuttings.

AVAILABILITY: Occasionally from the specialist nurseries.

Primula x heerii:

This is *Primula hirsuta* x *Primula integrifolia* and is an attractive though rare hybrid.

AVAILABILITY: Rarely from the specialist nurseries.

Primula x intermedia:

This is *Primula clusiana* x *Primula minima* and can be very good or very poor.

AVAILABILITY: Occasionally from the specialist nurseries.

Primula x juribella:

This is *Primula minima* x *Primula tyrolensis* and is a rare hybrid with distinctive little shiny leaves, very slow in growth and not very amenable to cultivation.

CULTIVATION: Not easy, best in a gritty compost in the cold greenhouse, conceivably would do better in a trough but it takes a brave man to plant a single rare plant outside, where it would be at the mercy of pests, pets and other predators.

PROPAGATION: Presumably splitting when it achieves any size.

AVAILABILITY: Present in a few private collections.

Primula x kolbiana:

This is *Primula latifolia* x *Primula daoensis*, but it is doubted whether this hybrid has occurred in nature.

Primula x lempergii:

This is *Primula auricula* x *Primula clusiana*, again of doubtful presence.

Primula x miniera:

This is *Primula allionii* x *Primula marginata*. This hybrid has been collected in the wild, and has been bred artificially to produce some very fine plants, for instance 'Sunrise' and 'Fairy Rose'.

Primula x muretiana:

This is *Primula integrifolia* x *Primula latifolia*, and is a very variable hybrid, and the flowers are usually brighter than either parents. Forms nearer *Primula latifolia* should be labelled *Primula* x *muretiana forma dinyana,* and those closer to *Primula integrifolia, Primula* x *muretiana forma muretiana.*

AVAILABILITY: Rarely from the specialist nurseries.

Primula* x *obovata:

This is *Primula auricula* x *Primula tyrolensis,* and is of doubtful existence.

Primula* x *pubescens:

This is *Primula auricula* x *Primula hirsuta,* and is a fertile hybrid in the wild, and occurs where the two species overlap. The natural hybrids should not be confused with the *Primula* x *pubescens* term as used in horticulture, where the exact parentage has been lost in the mists of time. These artificial hybrids will be discussed and described at length in chapter 9.

Primula* x *pumila:

This is *Primula minima* x *Primula daoensis,* and is a variable sterile hybrid that has been collected several times.

Primula* x *seriana:

This is *Primula daoensis* x *Primula hirsuta,* that has been collected only once.

Primula* x *truncata:

This is *Primula minima* x *Primula villosa.* This occurs where the two parent species overlap in Austria, but it is not common. It favours *Primula minima,* and plants in cultivation have rich, fairly dark pink flowers with a prominent white throat.

AVAILABILITY: Possibly from the specialist nurseries in the next few years.

Primula* x *venusta:

This is *Primula auricula* x *Primula carniolica,* and is thought to have been in cultivation at the turn of the century. This beautiful hybrid in its various forms is now rare in the wild due to over collection. Plants available in commerce in recent years have been incorrectly named. Hopefully it will be re-introduced.

Primula* x *venzoides:

This is *Primula wulfeniana* x *Primula tyrolensis,* and a rare hybrid, which is reputedly shy flowering in cultivation.

Primula* x *vochinensis:

This is *Primula minima* x *Primula wulfeniana* and is quite a common hybrid. A good selected form is available as 'Petzen Form', named after the mountain where it was collected in the western Karawanken.

AVAILABILITY: Occasionally from the specialist nurseries.

7
Primula marginata – its Cultivars and Hybrids

Primula marginata was first described in cultivation between 1777 and 1781, and is one of the most sought after of the primulas, not only for the beauty of its leaves but also for the blue of its flowers. Blue in all its shades is often a colour that is lacking in the garden and greenhouse, and the delicate flowers of the many cultivars of *Primula marginata* are a joy in early spring, giving colour before the main surge of the pubescenses and auriculas.

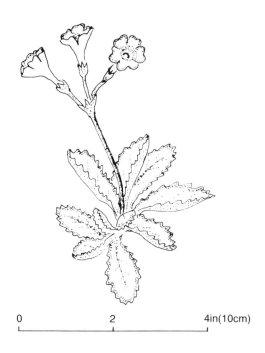

0   2   4in(10cm)

Primula marginata

Primula marginata is a low altitude species (800–2600m) which is mainly restricted to rock faces. It is found in the Maritime and Cottian Alps, which lie along the western Italy/south-east France border and also to the north of Nice – nearly always on limestone. Both in the wild and in cultivation it is highly variable and is characterised by the leathery toothed leaves, which when young are heavily coated in white or golden farina. On older leaves the farina tends to be restricted to the edges of the leaves. The teeth on the leaves are very variable, from very fine to almost fernlike. The woody stems increase yearly in length as the old leaves are lost, and can give a very untidy appearance. In cultivation it is sensible to replant more deeply at regular intervals. It is a long lived plant, both in cultivation and in the wild. The flowers are variable in shades of pale blue through to a mauve blue, or pink or white, and some even a deep striking violet. They flower very early, in March to April, and thus they are often better appreciated in the cold greenhouse. In size there is much variation, from 2–8in (5–20cm) or more, and under cover in the cold greenhouse the plants are always much larger, the flower stems longer and the growth faster.

GENERAL CULTIVATION

Primula marginata and its cultivars are all very hardy. They make excellent garden plants providing the drainage is right, and they are not allowed to become too dry in summer. They will grow well in the rock garden or trough, but having said that, they rarely achieve their full potential outside – the beautiful farina is usually washed off the leaves, and because they flower so early the delicate flowers are often ruined by spring rains. They will not grow well in a waterlogged position, and grit mixed in the soil where they are planted will help. It must be remembered that they are by nature very slow growing plants, and care needs to be taken to make sure other more vigorous plants do not overgrow and smother these little treasures.

They make lovely specimens for the cold greenhouse and need to be grown in a compost of one part John Innes No. 2, one part peat and one part ¼in (6mm) grit if using plastic pots. In clay pots a compost of four parts John Innes No. 2 to one part grit and one part peat is suitable. Annual repotting is advised, but sometimes a plant will make little or no growth and it is then better repotted into the same size pot. A top dressing of grit, or limestone chippings (as they are lime lovers), will enhance the appearance. As the surface dressing of grit tends to conserve moisture more care is needed with the watering, especially in July and August when it is very easy to overwater, causing root rot. Like many other members of the Auriculastrum some shade is appreciated in the hot summer months, and excess sun can cause yellowing of the leaves, which tends to upset the grower more than the plant.

SEASONAL CULTIVATION IN THE ALPINE HOUSE

SPRING: In late February, as the tightly furled winter foliage starts to open watering needs to be increased. Do be guided by the weather and the plants rather than the calendar. When the plants are seen to be in active growth they can be fed once a week with half strength balanced liquid feed. As the flowers fade remove the dead heads, unless seed is required. When flowering is finished the plants may be repotted into a slightly bigger pot, or split to provide extra plants. As the sun gets stronger the *marginata* primulas are happier if shaded.

SUMMER: Carry on watering when needed, and by the end of July greater care needs to be taken. Keep an eye on the plants; the occasional yellowing leaf is normal, especially if the plants are not shaded, but if the leaves suddenly start yellowing badly, check for Red Spider Mite. In very hot summers there is a slight risk of this pest attacking primulas, especially the Auriculastrum section, and if not dealt with promptly it can cause a great deal of damage. *See* chapter on pests and diseases.

AUTUMN: Shading is no longer necessary, and the compost needs to be kept just moist, but not wet. The outer leaves will be turning yellow, and may be removed if they come away easily. The inner part of the rosettes will probably be becoming tighter, with more farina. The plant is taking on its winter dormant state. Watering needs to be kept to the minimum.

WINTER: The plants are now dormant, keep an eye on the plants for botrytis. If the atmosphere is buoyant there should be little or no problem.

SEASONAL CULTIVATION IN THE GARDEN

SPRING: In the garden, there is little need for any maintenance, the plants may need replanting more deeply occasionally, and it is sensible to check periodically that more vigorous plants nearby have not grown over the *Primula marginatas*.

SUMMER: Normal garden maintenance, making sure that no vigorous neighbours have overgrown these small plants.

AUTUMN: Check the plants, and remove any dead leaves from trees that may have blown over the plants.

WINTER: The leaves will be tightly curled up on themselves. After periods of severe frost the occasional plant may need to be replanted.

PROPAGATION

SPLITTING: Is very easy, and an established clump can be easily split into several individual plants, each with its own roots, and these can be potted in a gritty compost and grown on until new root growth is apparent. *See* chapter 3 for further details.

CUTTINGS: Many authorities believe that a better shaped plant can be grown from cuttings rather than splitting. Cuttings can be taken in March and April or in the autumn, and inserted in sand above a gritty seed compost, as described in chapter 3. It is often better to allow the cut surface to dry before dipping in rooting powder and inserting in the tray or pot. Many growers tend to use one tray for several varieties, with a label between the varieties. This is a habit that can easily lead to confusion, and cultivars being wrongly named. It is far better to use a smaller pot or tray; try the 500 gm margarine tubs, with holes in the bottom for drainage. Never trust memory, always label plants and cuttings, and get into the habit of dating the label for future reference.

For example: *Primula marginata* Clears, 10 cuttings, 7/4/89.

SEED: It is well worth growing this attractive plant from seed, there are usually very few other primulas in flower at the same time as the marginatas, and also few insects to act as cross pollinators. The resultant seedlings can only be called *Primula marginata,* but they are usually all worth growing, and there is the chance of raising one that merits a cultivar name – the criterion for naming a new cultivar being that it is significantly different to any others in cultivation. Note that in order to name a significantly new cultivar, it is important that it be exhibited in the appropriate seedling class at a show, and be deemed worthy of naming by the judges. This procedure is essential, otherwise there would be an excessive number of named cultivars and hybrids in circulation.

A gritty compost is recommended, and a January sowing is probably the most sensible, as many of the Auriculastrum primula seeds benefit from stratification. Keep the tiny seedlings in their seed pot for a year, then pot up individually in March. They should flower the following spring.

AVAILABILITY

There are many cultivars in commerce and private collections, some distinct, others very similar, but they are all beautiful and well worth growing. There appears to be much confusion in the names, and many cultivars are wrongly named. There is now a National Collection in the care of Mr Michael Myers of Harrogate, and hopefully the names will be sorted so that it will be possible to check whether cultivars are correct or not. The descriptions following are as accurate as possible, but having never personally seen a few of the cultivars listed, even though they are definitely in cultivation, a certain amount of ambiguity has crept in. Some authorities are of the opinion that there has been too much indiscriminate naming over the years, but surely an enthusiast needs to know if he is purchasing a distinct cultivar or one he is already growing.

Most specialist nurseries stock a few *Primula marginatas,* and even if none are listed it is worth enquiring if a nursery has any available. They are not a plant that it is easy to produce in quantity as it takes time to build up decent sized stock plants, so there is rarely a surplus of these lovely plants.

Please note: a cultivar is a selected form of a pure species, not a hybrid, but, because it is a selected form it can only be propagated by vegetative means, not by seed. Any seedlings from a cultivar can only be labelled by the species name. For instance seedlings of *Primula marginata* 'Holden Clough' would be labelled *Primula marginata.* Even then care needs to be exercised as the plant could well have hybridized with another member of the Auriculastrum section. This is less likely with the marginatas but there is always the possibility.

DESCRIPTIVE LIST OF PRIMULA MARGINATA CULTIVARS

Primula marginata alba:
The plant usually offered under this name often causes disappointment as it is not really white, but a very pale, slightly muddy pink, which ages to nearly white. It is an attractive plant, just not quite what the name implies. However, better forms do exist, one of which has very distinct pale green leaves, and much whiter flowers, and hopefully this form will become more readily available.
AVAILABILITY: Several of the specialist nurseries.

Primula marginata 'Baldock's Purple'
(syn Baldock's Mauve):
A pleasant, fairly slow plant with light mauve purple, funnel-shaped flowers, the leaves being finely and evenly toothed.
AVAILABILITY: only in private collections.

***Primula marginata* 'Barbara Clough':**
Nicely rounded pinkish-lilac, fairly flat flowers with a white eye, showing farina around the eye, and yellowish farina on medium toothed leaves.
AVAILABILITY: Occasionally from specialist nurseries.

***Primula marginata* 'Beamish Variety':**
Raised by Susan Garnet Botfield around 1916, a friend of Farrer and Bowles. It is a very distinct form with rich purple, fairly flat pin-eyed flowers with a marked dusting of farina spreading from the centre of the flower. The leaves have medium sized teeth, fairly evenly spaced. There are reputedly two forms, one of which is said to exhibit farina on the edge of the petals – this is said to be the true plant, but as it can be slow and difficult to propagate, the more vigorous form without the farina on the petal edges is the form usually found in commerce.
AVAILABILITY: Occasionally from specialist nurseries.

***Primula marginata* 'Beatrice Lascaris':**
A very small slow growing cultivar, with neat rounded leaves and tiny teeth, lightly mealed, and small light mauve blue thrum-eyed flowers. It is very distinctive because of its size. There are said to be two forms in cultivation, only one of which flowers freely. Is this that the grower can not always provide the plant with the right conditions? I was once given a large pot full, because the owner was fed up with the lack of flowers, and it was literally kicked about the drive all winter, and gave a marvellous display the following spring. Never, of course to be repeated. Since then clusters of really tiny flower buds have been

93

noticed on several occasions, in the leaf axils in February–March, but these buds have never developed into proper flowers. It could be one of those plants which will abort the flower buds if conditions are not exactly to their liking. It is suspected of being a hybrid by some authorities.

AVAILABILITY: Listed by several specialist nurseries.

Primula marginata 'Caerulea':

The flowers are small, pin-eyed, funnel-shaped and slightly frilly and of a good clear blue with virtually no eye. The leaves are attractively toothed and well coated in farina, especially in winter. A very attractive plant for trough or alpine house. It is a rather slow growing cultivar, that tends to be confused with *Primula marginata* 'Holden Clough', which is fairly similar.

AVAILABILITY: Listed by several specialist nurseries.

Primula marginata 'Clear's Variety':

Good heads of large light pinkish mauve flowers, slightly funnel-shaped on somewhat tall stems. The largish leaves have fairly coarse teeth and are well covered in farina. An excellent and distinct variety that regularly graces the show bench. It is possible that it should really be called 'Clares Variety' after the old nursery of that name.

AVAILABILITY: Occasionally from specialist nurseries.

Primula marginata 'Correvon's Variety':

Thought to be similar to *Primula marginata* 'Holden Clough'.

AVAILABILITY: Occasionally from specialist nurseries.

Primula marginata 'Crenata':

This could well be the same plant as 'Laciniata'.

AVAILABILITY: Only in private collections.

Primula marginata 'Dark Seedling':

A lovely violet form, well worth growing.

AVAILABILITY: Occasionally from the specialist nurseries.

Primula marginata 'Drake's Form':

Neatly serrated, fairly narrow, very distinctive leaves, and large light mauve blue pin-eyed slightly funnel-shaped flowers, with a light dusting of farina around the eye. There appear to be other cultivars in circulation under this name – one which is said to be a large vigorous form with large rounded leaves. This is not 'Drake's Form'.

AVAILABILITY: Several of the specialist nurseries.

Primula marginata 'El Bolton Form':

Found in the 1970s by Alec Stubbs in Grassington on an old rock garden that had been planted by Backhouse of York in the 1920s. It was named after a nearby Old Peoples' Home, and distributed by Charlie Johnson of Waincliffe Nursery,

Halifax. It could be an old cultivar or a seedling. Whichever is the case it is a fine cultivar and worthy of any collection.
AVAILABILITY: Several of the specialist nurseries.
Primula marginata **'Elizabeth Fry':**
An old variety that appears to have lost its vigour.
AVAILABILITY: Occasionally from specialist nurseries.
Primula marginata **'Gold Leaf'**
Both this variety and *Primula marginata* 'Gold Plate' originate from Ingwersen's and boast very attractive and distinct foliage, heavily coated in golden farina. Very similar to *Primula marginata* 'Holden Clough.'
AVAILABILITY: Only in private collections.
Primula marginata **'Gold Plate':**
The large leaves are spoon-shaped and well serrated. Probably more suited to greenhouse culture.
AVAILABILITY: Only in private collections.
Primula marginata grandiflora:
A loose term used to describe several plants with supposedly larger flowers.
AVAILABILITY: Only in private collections.
Primula marginata **'Highland Twilight':**
A large flowered cultivar, with mid purple pin-eyed flowers, of a shade between 'Beamish' and 'Pritchard's'.
AVAILABILITY: Occasionally from the specialist nurseries.
Primula marginata **'Holden Clough':**
A beautiful variety, the clear light blue funnel-shaped flowers are carried in loose heads above the well toothed leaves that are covered in copious amounts of golden farina. As mentioned earlier it is possible that some of the plants in circulation as 'Holden Clough' are in fact 'Caerulea'. It is a fairly compact plant without any vices, and is often exhibited at both the alpine and the primula shows.
AVAILABILITY: Occasionally from specialist nurseries.
Primula marginata **'Inschriach Form':**
A compact cultivar with pin-eyed nearly flat flowers of good light blue above neatly serrated rounded leaves well coated in farina. A fairly vigorous cultivar, larger than 'Drake's Form'.
AVAILABILITY: Only in private collections.
Primula marginata **'Ivy Agee':**
A large very distinct plant with large heads of almost flat, mid mauve blue slightly frilled, thrum-eyed flowers with a well defined farinaed eye. It was raised by Mrs Ivanel Agee in America. Well worth growing in garden or greenhouse, and makes a lovely specimen for the show bench.

AVAILABILITY: Should become more readily available in the future due to its vigour.

Primula marginata 'Jenkin's Variety':
Sometimes listed as Dr. Jenkins', a typical marginata.
AVAILABILITY: Rarely from specialist nurseries.

Primula marginata 'Kesselring's Variety':
A smallish plant with neatly serrated leaves, and nearly flat, rich mauve pin-eyed flowers with a well defined white eye. It is indistinguishable from *Primula marginata* 'Pritchards Variety', although some authorities say that one flowers earlier, they are probably now so mixed up that it is impossible to separate the two cultivars.
AVAILABILITY: Occasionally from several specialist nurseries.

Primula marginata 'Laciniata':
Sky blue, funnel-shaped, thrum-eyed flowers, with a delicate dusting of farina round the eye. The leaves on this plant are incredibly deeply cut and serrated, giving it an unmistakable appearance. A superb form if only if could be obtained.
AVAILABILITY: Only in private collections.

Primula marginata 'Lilac Form':
A seedling from Beamish, free flowering with lilac mauve flowers.
AVAILABILITY: Rarely from the specialist nurseries.

Primula marginata 'Longifolia':
A form with longer than normal leaves, and typical marginata flowers.
AVAILABILITY: Rarely from the specialist nurseries.

Primula marginata 'Maritime Form':
A lovely delicate light blue form, with evenly toothed leaves, possibly collected in the Maritime Alps!
AVAILABILITY: Rarely from the specialist nurseries.

Primula marginata 'Millard's Var':
An attractive cultivar, very similar to 'Pritchard's' and 'Kesselring', but with slightly larger pin-eyed flowers with a better defined eye, with very neatly serrated leaves.
AVAILABILITY: Occasionally available from the specialist nurseries.

Primula marginata 'Miss Savoury':
Reputedly a seedling from *Primula marginata* 'Caerulea' distributed by Ralph Heywood. Other sources indicate it was collected in the Savoie Mountains, and Miss Savoury is a corruption of the place of origin.
AVAILABILITY: Only in private collections.

Primula marginata 'Mrs Carter Walmsley':
Very similar to *Primula marginata* 'Sharpe's Var.', and has golden farina.
AVAILABILITY: Only in private collections.

Primula marginata 'Pale Blue Form':
A very attractive cultivar with quite large, flattish flowers of a good pale blue.
AVAILABILITY: Only in private collections.

Primula marginata 'Peter's Var':
Named after Peter Hill of Paradise Nurseries who distributed this attractive form.
AVAILABILITY: Only in private collections.

Primula marginata 'Pinkie':
Reputedly similar to 'Clears'.
AVAILABILITY: Only in private collections.

Primula marginata 'Pritchard's Variety':
Loose heads of light mauve flattish pin-eyed flowers, and appears identical to 'Kesselring'.
AVAILABILITY: The most generally available of all the marginatas, and can be obtained from many of the specialist nurseries.

Primula marginata 'Rosea'
This cultivar has been exhibited on the show bench, but not much appears to be known about it. It has been seen in Edinburgh Botanic Gardens, as was the following plant, and is possibly a form collected in the wild.
AVAILABILITY: Only in private collections.

Primula marginata 'Rubra':
A plant has been seen on the show bench, certainly more red than pink.
AVAILABILITY: Only in private collections.

Primula marginata Sharpe's Var':
The plant that has been seen bearing this name is very similar to *Primula marginata* 'Pritchard's', with flattish mauve pin-eyed flowers with a white eye.
AVAILABILITY: Only in private collections.

Primula marginata 'Shipton Form':
This has the most frilly flowers of any known cultivar. It also has extremely attractive well farinaed broad, almost round, neatly toothed leaves.
AVAILABILITY: Only in private collections.

Primula marginata 'small flowered form':
Thrum-eyed with separated petals, quite attractive.
AVAILABILITY: Only in private collections.

***Primula marginata* 'Thrumeyea':**
Supposedly thrum-eyed, hence the name, an attractive cultivar with light mauve blue flowers.
AVAILABILITY: Occasionally from the specialist nurseries.
***Primula marginata* 'Violet Form':**
An attractive plant with fairly dark violet-blue flowers.
AVAILABILITY: Occasionally from the specialist nurseries.
***Primula marginata* 'Violet seedling from Beamish':**
The same plant as the preceding one? The fairly flat rich mauve purple flowers are delicately powdered in farina above small neatly toothed leaves.
AVAILABILITY: Occasionally from the specialist nurseries.
***Primula marginata* 'Waithman's Variety':**
A good deep mauve, presumably raised by Reginald Kaye of Waithman Nursery in Silverdale.
AVAILABILITY: Occasionally from the specialist nurseries.

THE HYBRIDS OF PRIMULA MARGINATA

It is very difficult to classify many of the Auriculastrum hybrids with certainty, so the plants included in the following list will be those that appear to contain a good percentage of marginata genes. The hybrids between *Primula marginata* and *Primula allionii* will be described with the other allionii hybrids at the end of the following chapter, as often their cultivation requirements are closer to that of *Primula allionii*.

***Primula* 'Blue Wave':**
Darkish blue flowers with wavy edges, farinaed eye, leaves slightly farinaed.
AVAILABILITY: Occasionally offered by the specialist nurseries.
***Primula* 'Gordon':**
An outstanding hybrid bred by John Mercer of Bradford, and is the result of seedlings raised by crossing *Primula marginata* 'El Bolton' with *Primula pubescens* 'Bewerly White'. The large purple flowers with a bright white eye contrast beautifully with the toothed leaves well covered in farina. It is a distinctive and lovely plant even when not in flower. This variety does not produce many offsets, so is not as yet available.
AVAILABILITY: Only in private collections.

Primula 'Herbert Beresford':
Large well-formed flowers with a white eye, was bred by
Alec Stubbs of Grassington. An excellent variety for the show
bench.
AVAILABILITY: Only in private collections.
Primula 'Hyacinthia':
A lovely plant, bred from *Primula marginata* 'Beamish' by Mr
G.H. Berry in 1943. The rich green leaves are lightly serrated
with only a very small amount of farina on the edges of the
leaves. It produces good heads of large hyacinth blue, almost
flat flowers, with a whitish eye, on 6in (15cm) stems.
AVAILABILITY: It has been micropropagated and is stocked
by several of the specialist nurseries.
Primula 'Janet':
A very old variety with flowers of a true pale blue with leaves
that are lightly covered in silver farina. The flowering stems
have a tendency to fasciate, which is a type of deformity
whereby two or more parts of a plant merge almost but not
completely together. Despite that it is a very worthwhile
plant, for either the rockery, trough or cold greenhouse.
AVAILABILITY: Occasionally from the specialist nurseries.
Primula 'Liane':
Bred by John Mercer, and is the sister plant to 'Gordon', with
dark reddish mauve flowers.
AVAILABILITY: Only in private collections.
Primula 'Linda Pope':
Appears to have first been mentioned in 1911, and was raised
by Birmingham Nurseryman Mr Pope, who named it after
his daughter. A beautiful plant with large heads of flowers on
6–8in (15–20cm) stems. The flat, almost blue flowers have a
prominent white eye. The leaves have large rounded teeth and
are very distinct from the other marginatas. An excellent plant
for the select rock garden, and not only does it make a
magnificent specimen for the alpine house, but is also frequently
exhibited on the show bench where it regularly wins prizes.
AVAILABILITY: From the specialist nurseries.
Primula 'Lilac Domino':
A seedling of 'Linda Pope', and of a similar form though
much smaller and with less farina on the leaves.
AVAILABILITY: Only in private collections.
Primula 'Marven':
(*Primula marginata* x *Primula* x *venusta*). Rich purple blue
flowers, with a distinctive very dark eye, surrounded with a
ring of farina. The good heads of fairly small flowers are

carried on a 6in (15cm) stem. The leaves are neat and covered in farina. This is not the easiest plant to keep in good health, probably due to old age and overpropagation. It has been in cultivation since before Farrer. Cold greenhouse treatment is recommended and great care with the watering in autumn and winter.

AVAILABILITY: Rarely from the specialist nurseries.

Primula 'Rhenaniana':

Thought to have been found in the wild, and is probably a hybrid of *Primula marginata*. It has coarsely serrated farinose leaves and mauve flowers with a white eye. Not outstanding.

AVAILABILITY: Only in private collections.

Primula 'White Lady':

An attractive plant, that could be described as a white flowered version of 'Linda Pope'. This vigorous plant has large flattish thrum-eyed flowers, nicely ruffled, in drumstick type heads. There appears to be two forms of this plant in cultivation, one of which seems identical to 'White Linda Pope'.

AVAILABILITY: Rarely from the specialist nurseries.

Primula x 'White Linda Pope':

A white seedling from Linda Pope named in 1970. The original is believed lost, but occasionally sister seedlings under the same name are available. The plant around at the moment under that name is very slow to give offsets.

AVAILABILITY: Only in private collections.

8
Primula allionii –
Cultivars and Hybrids

For any gardener with suitable facilities, the beautiful cultivars of *Primula allionii* are a luxury not to be missed. These pretty plants flower in early spring, and the number of flowers that can be produced by such a small plant is incredible. Quite often the large flowers will completely obscure the leaves, giving rise to a perfect dome of colour. Such beauty is not to be bought cheaply, and attention to detail in cultivation is essential, or these pretty little primulas will die.

Primula allionii occurs locally in south-eastern France and across

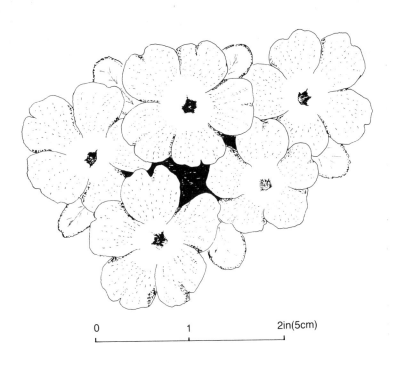

| 0 | | 1 | | 2in(5cm) |

Primula allionii.

the border into Italy. It is only found in a relatively small area but there it is abundant, and grows on limestone cliffs, mostly quite open, but sometimes under overhanging rock. This small plant has relatively large flat flowers in shades of pink, or rarely white.

Though not the easiest of plants to grow, it is so free flowering that it is worth every effort. There are many named forms, some virtually inseparable, others gloriously distinct, but they are all worth growing, and give the grower a wealth of colour in February and March through into April. The small rosettes of sticky leaves are often hidden by the large pink flowers.

CULTIVATION

This is slightly different to the other primulas so will be discussed more fully. *Primula allionii,* its hybrids and cultivars are invariably grown in the alpine house. Once again it must be stressed that every serious grower needs to develop his own methods of cultivation, and the purpose of this book is to guide the grower on different ways on which to base his system. This is not a rule book to follow to the exclusion of other good ideas. Common sense is a vital ingredient of all composts and growing regimes, think about the reasons for different methods and do not be afraid to adapt – every grower accumulates ideas. The discussions at any show or meeting place of gardeners can yield many new ideas that can often be adapted to improve growing methods. Read, listen and learn, and always remember that pot culture is alien to plants. *Primula allionii* is, by its very nature, a cliff hanger (as is its cultivation in mild foggy winters!). Contrary to popular belief, plants that grow in crevices have access, by means of their long probing roots, to abundant supplies of water. This water percolates through the rocks and contains very weak solutions of food, and it isn't chlorinated, fluorinated or in any way contaminated. Despite the addition of chemicals to tap water it is still better for the plants than the green, disease-ridden liquid that is to be found in the water butts of many growers.

The grower tends to forget that many plants in the wild are untidy, often with dead and dying rosettes, certainly not suitable for the show bench. In cultivation every effort must be made to keep the plant healthy and happy, so that it always presents an attractive picture.

Shading is essential for *Primula allioniis,* and they must be kept as cool and airy as possible in the summer months. The shading needs to be in place by early April, and should be removed in September.

When growing in plastic pots the standard compost for the Auriculastrum section is recommended, with up to 10% extra grit incorporated. The more grit there is in the compost the less food is available, and the more water is needed. Do not overpot. If the root system is excessive the roots may be carefully pruned. Many growers prefer clay pots where a John Innes No. 2 with about 10% extra grit, plunged in sand is recommended. It regulates the moisture content in the pot, and it helps keep the roots at an even temperature. Most of the *Primula allioniis* are happiest in shallow pans.

The plant is normally purchased in a very small pot, 2½in (6cm), and it is important that the condition of the roots be checked. On knocking the plant carefully out of the pot, thick white roots should be visible on the outside of the compost; beware of black or brown roots as these indicate root rot, in which case it would be sensible to repot immediately. The compost to be used depends on the time of the year. In late summer and autumn a conventional gritty compost is recommended, mixed with one third of its volume as extra grit. After first carefully cutting off any dead or decaying roots, and dusting the cut surfaces with Flowers of Sulphur the plant may be repotted into a suitably sized clean pot. In the spring repotting and aftercare is fairly straightforward, following the instructions for any of the smaller members of the Auriculastrum section, but a good top dressing of ¼in (6mm) limestone chips is essential. These supply the lime that appears to be essential to keep this plant in good health, and they also keep soggy compost away from the neck which is the most vulnerable part of the plant.

SEASONAL CULTIVATION OF THE ALPINE HOUSE

SPRING: The *Primula allioniis* flower from late February through into April, and the mound of perfectly formed flowers completely obscures the leaves. Though not easy they are amongst the most rewarding of plants. Gentle feeding is recommended, and will improve the colouring of the flowers. After flowering is finished it is sensible to carefully remove the dead flower heads, and now is a good time to repot, as the roots will be entering their period of maximum growth. It is sound policy to repot these plants every year, even if there is insufficient growth to necessitate a larger pot, this ensures an open airy compost. Plants need air round their roots as well as food and water, and old compost has far less air space than new compost.

SUMMER: Shading is strongly recommended, and make sure watering is adequate, but not excessive.

AUTUMN: Watering needs to be restricted, and a careful watch kept on the plants for any signs of mould. A fungicidal spray is very effective.

WINTER: This is the dangerous period, and any dead and decaying leaves must be removed to prevent the rot spreading into the plant. This a time consuming task, and a small pair of tweezers are essential. Like all members of the Auriculastrum section the lower leaves of each rosette die away every year. The *Primula allionii* cultivars have small rosettes that are densely leaved, which result in many dead leaves in winter. The removal of the dead leaves is best done little and often. Invariably the odd rosette will be detached with the dead leaves – this can be cleaned and used as a cutting. The plants need to be kept almost dry, in nature they grow on cliffs and high enough above sea level for the temperatures to be at or below freezing; thus there are none of the spores of botrytis and similar about. In cultivation there are regular mild spells, when the moist air can carry lethal doses of plant diseases. By keeping the plants dry there are little or no decaying leaves to give these diseases access to the plants. Do not allow drips or splashes to fall on the leaves.

PROPAGATION

SPLITTING: The *Primula allioniis* can be split like the other members of the Auriculastrum, the late summer to early autumn is safest, when the new roots are coming down. Sometimes it is necessary to split the plants in spring but it can be very difficult to keep the newly potted plants cool enough for them to establish and losses are likely to be higher.

CUTTINGS: In late autumn (November is suitable), take the cuttings making sure the cut is clean, and any roots are carefully removed, dip in hormone powder, and insert into trays of normal Allionii compost with ½in (1cm) coarse sand on top. Keep on the bench in the greenhouse over winter, the new roots will start growing anything from 4–6 weeks later. Pot up in early spring (February – March) into 2½in (6cm) pots, not forgetting the top dressing of limestone chips. Grow on in a cool shady environment, and keep just moist.

SEED: If seed is set, and it is often not found until the plants are split in autumn, it is well worth sowing, using the instructions in chapter 3. The resultant seedlings are very tiny and need to be grown on under glass. The plants raised are often very attractive, whether pure *Primula allionii* or hybrids. As *Primula allionii* flowers so early it is less likely to have hybridised as there are no other primulas in flower.

AVAILABILITY

No apologies are made for including descriptions of plants that are not available commercially. It is very likely that over the next decade many more of the cultivars that are presently in cultivation, will be propagated and distributed.

Although only a few varieties are available from the alpine nurseries at present, with increasing popularity it is conceivable that they will become more readily available in the near future. The *Primula allionii* cultivars are slow and demanding plants, and must be worth more than other plants. One of the problems is that many growers find it difficult to come to terms with the size of the plant that they purchase. The main criterion of a good plant is a healthy established root system, not the quantity of leaves and rosettes. A pot full of a *Primula allionii* indicates either overfeeding or an old, root bound specimen, both of which could cause problems to the inexperienced grower.

DESCRIPTIVE LIST OF PRIMULA ALLIONII CULTIVARS

Primula allionii **'Agnes':**
Pale pink thrum–eyed flowers with a large rounded white eye. AVAILABILITY: Not normally available, only present in private collections.
Primula allionii alba:
Collected in the wild by Clarence Elliott in 1926, and is reputedly the only white form to have been collected. The flower is of medium size and is in proportion to the leaves.

This plant tends to flower slightly later than the other *Primula allionii* cultivars. Other white cultivars are in cultivation, but they are all slow and often difficult to manage.
AVAILABILITY: Not normally available.

Primula allionii 'Anna Griffith':

Reports vary as to the exact origin of this distinctive and slow variety, but it is believed to have been collected from the wild. It was given to Anna Griffith, and rescued from her collection, after her death, by Mrs. K.N. Dryden. It is a small plant and slow in growth. The small, very pale pink thrum-eyed flowers with irregularly cleft petals are freely produced, and the delicate appearance of a plant in full flower is unforgettable.
AVAILABILITY: Though scarce it is becoming more readily available from the specialist nurseries.

Primula allionii 'Apple Blossom':

A large flowered variety with mauve flowers shading to a white centre, and raised by Mr. F. Barker. Late flowering, the flowers are long lived making it an excellent exhibition variety.
AVAILABILITY: Occasionally available from the specialist nurseries.

Primula allionii 'Austen':

Clear medium sized pin-eyed flowers of a slightly lighter shade of red purple than 'Crowsley's'.
AVAILABILITY: Occasionally available from the specialist nurseries.

Primula allionii 'Avalanche':

Raised by Mr Joe Elliott. It has slightly funnel-shaped, pin-eyed cream to white flowers, and can be difficult even for an allionii!
AVAILABILITY: Rarely available from the specialist nurseries.

Primula allionii 'Broadwell Strain':

Raised at Mr Joe Elliott's Broadwell Nurseries, and has a medium sized thrum-eyed flower of rich purple.
AVAILABILITY: Rarely available from the specialist nurseries.

Primula allionii 'Celia':

Raised by H.M. Earle from seed off *Primula allionii* 'Viscountess Byng' in 1939. Early flowering with large thrum-eyed flowers two shades lighter than 'Crowsley's'.
AVAILABILITY: Rarely available from the specialist nurseries.

Primula allionii 'Clarkes':

A typical *Primula allionii*, not particularly distinct.
AVAILABILITY: Occasionally from the specialist nurseries.

Primula allionii 'Crowsley Gem':
Pin-eyed flowers in a darker shade of purple than 'Crowsley's', with a starry white eye.
AVAILABILITY: Rarely offered.

Primula allionii 'Crowsley's Variety':
Collected by Dr R. Bevan in 1928 and has certainly stood the test of time. The small rich crimson purple pin-eyed flowers are funnel-shaped and do not lie as flat as other cultivars, but the colour is so strong it is a must for every serious collection. It is a slow small plant in comparison with other *Primula allioniis*.
AVAILABILITY: Occasionally available from the specialist nurseries.

Primula allionii 'Diana':
A fairly new cultivar raised by H.M. Earle in 1975, late flowering, and similar to 'William Earle'.
AVAILABILITY: Not available commercially.

Primula allionii 'Elizabeth Baker':
Raised by Gwen Baker of Wolverhampton. It has large pin-eyed flowers of pale mauve pink shading into the large white eye.
AVAILABILITY: Rarely available from specialist nurseries.

Primula allionii 'Elizabeth Earle':
Raised by H.M. Earle in 1949. The good mauve pink thrum-eyed flowers with a small white eye are of the classical primrose format; the petals only overlap slightly and are not wavy.
AVAILABILITY: Rarely available, but present in many private collections.

Primula allionii 'Elliott's Var':
Raised by Mr Joe Elliott of Broadwell Nursery. The large, pale pink flowers have a white eye shading into the pink, and the size of the flowers sometimes appears too large for the leaves.
AVAILABILITY: Occasionally available from the specialist nurseries.

Primula allionii 'Fanfare':
Collected by Mr. Frank Barker in the maritime Alps. The thrum-eyed mauve pink flowers are large and slightly frilly with a small white eye. It is a very free flowering variety with up to five flowers per scape. The leaves are fairly dark in comparison with other cultivars, and are very wavy. One of the first to flower.
AVAILABILITY: Rarely available at present, but is expected

to be available in the future, at a price. Present in many private collections.

Primula allionii 'Frank Barker':

Also known as 'XXX', this is a seedling raised by Frank Barker, and is the parent/grandparent, along with *Primula allionii alba,* of the many excellent cultivars raised by K.R. Wooster. The medium sized thrum-eyed flowers are a light mauve purple with a round white eye.

AVAILABILITY: Rarely available.

Primula allionii 'Gerard Parker':

A seedling from 'Appleblossom' with large pale mauve pink thrum-eyed flowers.

AVAILABILITY: Rarely available.

Primula allionii 'G.H. Berry':

Rich mauve purple thrum-eyed flowers with a distinct crumpled appearance.

AVAILABILITY: Rarely available.

Primula allionii 'Hartside':

Fairly rich coloured flowers, similar to, but darker than *Primula allionii* 'Pennine Pink', which was also raised by the Huntleys of Hartside. A worthwhile acquisition.

AVAILABILITY: Occasionally available from the specialist nurseries.

Primula allionii 'Hartside No 12' and 'Hartside No 15':

These are further good seedlings from the Hartside stable. Mr N. Huntley did not consider them worthy of naming, but 'Hartside No 12' is a rather fine form, which has been awarded prizes at the shows.

AVAILABILITY: Occasionally from the specialist nurseries.

Primula allionii 'Hocker Edge':

Originated at the nursery from which it derives its name. One of the easier cultivars with rich mauve purple pin-eyed flowers with a white eye.

AVAILABILITY: Rarely available, but present in private collections.

Primula allionii 'Horwood':

Raised by K.R. Wooster, and has large mauve pink pin-eyed flowers, with a small round white eye.

AVAILABILITY: Only present in private collections.

Primula allionii 'KRW 5/7':

Presumably one of Mr K.R. Wooster's seedlings. The enormous mauve pink thrum-eyed flowers are slightly wavy, with a round slightly ill-defined eye.

AVAILABILITY: Occasionally available from the specialist nurseries.

Primula allionii **'Margaret Earle':**
A seedling of *Primula allionii* 'Superba' and was raised by H.M. Earle in 1947. The lovely large thrum-eyed flowers have wavy petals of a distinct blueish mauve, and is easily pleased, floriferous and early. This variety is said to prefer a deep pot, rather than a pan.
AVAILABILITY: Rarely available, but present in several private collections.

Primula allionii **'Marion':**
Clear lilac pink pin-eyed flowers with a distinct large clearly defined round white eye. A distinct cultivar very worthy of a name. Tends to flower a week or so earlier than other varieties.
AVAILABILITY: Occasionally available from the specialist nurseries.

Primula allionii **'Marjorie Wooster':**
Very large thrum-eyed flowers of pale mauve pink.
AVAILABILITY: Rarely available.

Primula allionii **'Martin':**
A pleasant selected cultivar with small flowers. Relatively vigorous and easy.
AVAILABILITY: Occasionally from the specialist nurseries.

Primula allionii **'Mary Berry':**
A late flowering cultivar with rich crimson purple flowers with a star-shaped white eye, and was raised by the late Mr Gerard Parker. Tends to be mat forming rather than the usual mound. Much sought after because of the rich colour but larger specimens can be temperamental.
AVAILABILITY: Occasionally available from the specialist nurseries.

Primula allionii **'Mrs Dyas':**
An old variety, separated petals, mauve pink, medium star-shaped white eye.
AVAILABILITY: Occasionally available from the specialist nurseries.

Primula allionii **'Nightingale':**
An attractive form with large rich pink flowers. Selected by Stuart Boothman and identical with the variety 'Stuart Boothman' or 'Boothman's var'.
AVAILABILITY: Only present in private collections.

Primula allionii **'Norma':**
A slow, late flowering thrum-eyed variety with large mauve purple flowers with a white eye.

AVAILABILITY: Rarely available. Present in private collections.

Primula allionii 'Nymph':

A thrum-eyed white form raised by K.R. Wooster.

AVAILABILITY: Present in private collections. Rarely, if ever, available.

Primula allionii 'Pennine Pink':

One of several raised by Neil Huntley of Hartside Nursery Gardens in recent years. This attractive cultivar has medium sized, rounded flowers of a rich pure pink.

AVAILABILITY: Occasionally available from the specialist nurseries.

Primula allionii 'Picton's':

Presumably raised by Percy Picton, has very small slightly frilly thrum-eyed flowers with pinkish edges merging into the large white central area. A very attractive and distinctive variety.

AVAILABILITY: Occasionally available from the specialist nurseries.

Primula allionii 'Pinkie':

Raised from seed in 1951 by Mr. K.R. Wooster. This distinct cultivar has small primrose-shaped flowers of a delicate, pure true pink, very different from the other *Primula allionii* cultivars, and a cream eye. A very dwarf form with completely sessile flowers that appear often almost a month earlier than the other cultivars.

AVAILABILITY: Only in private collections.

Primula allionii 'Praecox':

Originated at the Six Hills Nursery, and, as its name suggests is very early flowering. The thrum-eyed flowers are mauve pink and funnel-shaped.

AVAILABILITY: Occasionally available from the specialist nurseries.

Primula allionii 'Pygmy':

Light mauve pink thrum-eyed flowers that lie flat on the leaves. Raised by K.R. Wooster.

AVAILABILITY: Rarely available.

Primula allionii 'Snowflake':

Raised by K.R. Wooster, and has large glistening white thrum-eyed flowers. The petals are overlapping and it tends to flower late in the season. Probably the easiest of the white flowered cultivars.

AVAILABILITY: Occasionally available from the specialist nurseries.

Primula allionii 'Stephen':
Rich mauve pink thrum-eyed flowers, unmarred by any
shading. It was collected in 1980 by J.C. Archibald.
AVAILABILITY: At present only in private collections, but
hope springs eternal!

Primula allionii 'Stuart Boothman':
Originated in Stuart Boothman's private collection and is said
to be the same plant as 'Nightingale', after the name of his
nursery.

Primula allionii 'Superba':
Raised by Frank Barker from plants he collected in the wild.
Large mauve pink pin-eyed flowers with huge wavy petals
make this a beautiful and distinct variety. Prefers a deep pot.
As it sets seed easily it is the parent of many good named
varieties.
AVAILABILITY: Rarely available.

Primula allionii 'Tranquillity':
Medium sized, pale flat flowers with a white eye, and an
almost satin sheen to the petals. A good distinct variety with
narrow leaves that was raised by the Huntleys at Hartside
Nursery Garden.
AVAILABILITY: Occasionally available from the specialist
nurseries.

Primula allionii 'Viscountess Byng':
Raised by Frank Barker, and has large thrum-eyed flowers of
a rich purple red, with wavy petals and a large clearly defined
white eye. It can be temperamental. There are other *Primula
allionii* varieties masquerading under the same name!
AVAILABILITY: Occasionally available from the specialist
nurseries.

Primula allionii 'William Earle':
A seedling of 'Viscountess Byng' raised in 1949 by H.M.
Earle. The large mauve pink thrum-eyed flowers have wavy
petals and a small ill-defined eye.
AVAILABILITY: Occasionally from the specialist nurseries.

THE HYBRIDS OF PRIMULA ALLIONII

These lovely plants all possess some of the characteristics of
Primula allionii and unless indicated otherwise require alpine
house treatment similar to the pure cultivars described previously.

Primula allionii 'Alexina':
A relatively vigorous hybrid, with large leaves and trusses of rich purplish crimson pink flowers with a good white eye. The colour is similar to *Primula allionii* 'Crowsley's', but slightly paler. This hybrid was raised by the Huntleys of Hartside, by crossing their *Primula allionii Seedling No 10* back on to 'Ethel Barker'.
AVAILABILITY: Occasionally from the specialist nurseries.

Primula allionii x Primula 'Linda Pope Alba':
Mr Joe Elliott raised twelve to fifteen seedlings from this cross, at least five of which are in cultivation. They are very attractive compact plants, with flowers ranging from white to a very rich good pink with a distinctive white eye. Very worthwhile.
AVAILABILITY: Occasionally from the specialist nurseries.

Primula 'Beatrice Wooster':
This has leaves very similar to *Primula allionii,* but larger. Very free flowering with heads of clear pink, white-eyed flowers. This rewarding plant is the result of the crossing of *Primula allionii* with *Primula* 'Linda Pope' by K.R. Wooster in 1947. One of the best, will succeed in the garden in a trough but is doubly rewarding grown in the cold greenhouse. Highly recommended for the novice.
AVAILABILITY: From several specialist nurseries, the most widely grown and known of the *Primula allionii* hybrids.

Primula 'Clarence Elliott':
A seedling raised by Joe Elliott from some seed off 'White Linda Pope' in 1982. Up to seven large rich mauve pink flowers with white throats and slightly wavy edges to the petals, are carried on the 2–3in (6–8cm) stem over the cushion of typically allionii leaves. Cultivation and propagation as for *Primula allionii.*
AVAILABILITY: Only in private collections.

Primula 'Ethel Barker':
This is *Primula allionii* x *Primula hirsuta,* raised by Mr. Frank Barker pre-1937. Good solid heads of large carmine pink white-eyed flowers on short stems over broad toothed leaves.
AVAILABILITY: Rarely from specialist nurseries.

Primula x 'Fairy Rose':
Raised by K.R. Wooster in 1947, from crossing *Primula allionii* with *Primula* 'Linda Pope'. A very desirable plant with large rose pink, thrum-eyed flowers with a small white eye, and jagged toothed leaves.
AVAILABILITY: Only in private collections.

Primula 'Hemswell Ember':
(Formerly ABY2), this is the best of four seedlings raised by
Michael Robinson of Martin Nest in 1984, produced by
crossing *Primula allionii* with *Primula* 'Blairside Yellow'.
Neat rosettes of allionii-type leaves, and short stemmed
flowers of flame pink with a rich yellow centre that merges
into the petal colour.
AVAILABILITY: From one or two specialist nurseries.

Primula 'Hemswell ABY4':
From the same cross as the preceding plant, but is larger
and more vigorous. Short stems carry loose heads of pale
pink, yellow-eyed flowers.
AVAILABILITY: Occasionally from the specialist nurseries.

Primula 'Joan Hughes':
A hybrid between *Primula allionii* and *Primula* 'Linda Pope'
raised by Jack Drake. Tight rosettes of leaves and distinctive
heads of magenta pink flowers on short stems.
AVAILABILITY: Slow to offset so rarely offered.

Primula 'Lismore P79/7':
(*Primula allionii* x *Primula pubescens* 'Harlow Car'). Brian and
Judith Burrow of High Bentham have raised some lovely
hybrids in the late 1970s and 1980s, which are at present being
distributed under their breeding code numbers. 'Lismore 79/
7' is a lovely plant, with huge white flowers, delicately edged
in a purplish pink, over typically allionii foliage.
AVAILABILITY: Occasionally available from the specialist
nurseries.

Primula 'Lismore P79/10/2':
This is *Primula allionii* x *Old red Dusty Miller* then back crossed
on to *Primula allionii,* that is ¾ allionii. An attractive plant
with dark reddish pink flowers and a yellow eye, over typical
allionii foliage.
AVAILABILITY: Occasionally from the specialist nurseries.

Primula 'Lismore 79/26':
(*Primula allionii* x *Primula pubescens* 'Harlow Car') Deep pink
flowers and a large white eye.
AVAILABILITY: Occasionally from the specialist nurseries.

Primula 'Lismore . . . ':
There are several more excellent allionii hybrids in circulation
bred by the Burrows of Lismore, identified with numbers.
AVAILABILITY: From a few specialist nurseries.

Primula x *loiseleurii* 'Lismore Yellow':
An attractive light yellow hybrid raised by Mrs Judith
Burrow by crossing a white *Primula allionii* with *Primula*

auricula. To get the best results this plant needs to be grown hard, and thus should not be overfed. It needs a gritty compost, and enjoys being potbound. Erratic watering can also be the cause of the flowers being out of character.

AVAILABILITY: Often available from specialist nurseries.

Primula x 'Margaret':

Clusters of full, flat, rich mauve pink flowers, and is a hybrid between *Primula allionii* and a *Primula* x *pubescens*. A lovely plant that is well worth acquiring if ever offered.

AVAILABILITY: Only in private collections.

Primula x miniera: (*Primula allionii* x *Primula marginata*)

It is debatable whether the plants in cultivation with this name are natural or artificial hybrids. These hybrids tend to be rather variable, some are good, others are rather washed out shades.

AVAILABILITY: Occasionally from specialist nurseries.

Primula x miniera 'Sunrise':

This hybrid between allionii and marginata was bred by Jack Drake, is very eye catching, and always creates interest and envy when seen on the show bench. Somewhat temperamental, as befits its beauty, a decent sized plant is quite likely to die for no apparent cause.

AVAILABILITY: Only in private collections at present, but it is conceivable it may reach a specialist nurserymen's list in a few years time.

9

The Smaller Hybrids of the Auriculastrum Section

(Including those popularly called Pubescenses)

The pubescens primulas and the auriculas, as known today, have evolved from *Primula* x *pubescens,* a naturally occuring hybrid between *Primula auricula* and *Primula hirsuta (rubra)*. It is thought that these lovely plants were first introduced into cultivation by Clusius about 1580, and quickly became popular. It is likely that there was further hybridising with other members of the Auriculastrum section giving rise to the vast range of hybrids in cultivation today.

Although both the pubescenses and the auriculas are descended from basically the same stock, their breeding has diverged along two different paths. This chapter will cover the smaller members. The larger hybrids of the Auriculastrum, known as auriculas, will be discussed in the following chapter. There is a certain amount of overlap, and it is sometimes difficult to decide whether a plant is a large pubescens hybrid or a small border auricula. A useful way is to look at the plant, those nearest *Primula auricula* in size and form are usually classed as auriculas, and the smaller hybrids with more affinity to *Primula hirsuta* come under the name 'Pubescens hybrids'.

Although it is very difficult to classify the hybrids of this section with any degree of certainty, it does contain many of the most attractive and rewarding of the smaller primulas. Also included in this chapter will be included any small man made hybrids of the Auriculastrum section.

These little primulas are of great value to the gardener, they are relatively easy to grow and they are an ideal size for the smaller gardens of today. In general they are very free flowering and also make lovely and amenable specimens for the cold

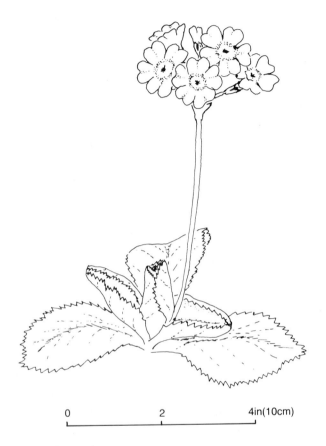

0   2   4in(10cm)

A typical *Primula* x *pubescens*.

greenhouse, and will brighten the benches from late March through into May.

The distinction of hybrids for the garden and hybrids for the cold greenhouse is very arbitrary – all the plants described here will make lovely specimens for the greenhouse and many are ideal for the garden.

CULTIVATION

ROCK GARDEN: It is not generally realised how easy these small hybrids are to please, and how much colour and joy they

can bring to the spring rock garden. They flower from the end
of March through into May in every shade except pure blue,
and many are delicately scented. Over the years they will
grow into good clumps, 12in (30cm) or more across, and
provide splashes of solid colour in the garden in the spring.

The majority of these small hybrids are tolerant of a wide
range of conditions and are exceptionally hardy, surviving
anything the British weather can provide, from the severest
frosts to the most persistent rain. All that is required is the
provision of good drainage, which is essential in wet areas,
but less important in areas of low rainfall. Like the majority of
primulas they will not tolerate drought in spring and summer.
Most of the pubescenses are remarkably tolerant of root
disturbance and are naturally very long lived plants.

Many of the members of the Auriculastrum section, including the pubescenses and other small hybrids, have the habit of
shedding leaves in autumn and winter, leaving sections of
thick stems standing proud of the soil. There are two remedies.
One is to dig up the plant with a large root ball, put it to one
side, then dig the hole a few inches deeper and replant the
plant, adding an extra layer of soil round the neck of the plant,
so that the rosettes of leaves are fairly close to the soil level.
The alternative is easier, but is not as tidy – it consists of piling
a mound of soil around the neck of the plant.

TROUGHS: These hybrids are very suitable for growing
in troughs, in association with other small alpines, such as the
Kabschia Saxifrages and *Gentian verna*. A lightly shaded
position suits them best. The smaller varieties are most
suitable, but any can be used, the more vigorous hybrids will
need digging up and splitting more regularly. The pubescenses
will stand a greater degree of starvation than other primulas,
but their growth will be much slower – all very well if they are
being grown in a confined area such as a trough. In any case
the food content in a trough is often quite low, and this will
inhibit their growth quite markedly. A good admixture of
grit is recommended and a surface dressing of grit will help
these little plants feel at home.

SCREE: All the varieties described as being suitable for
growing outside are very suitable for the scree, providing the
conditions are not too hot and dry.

ALPINE HOUSE: The small hybrids of the Auriculastrum
section are the perfect and most suitable of all plants for the
novice to grow in the cold greenhouse. They cannot be too
highly recommended. They are easy, no-nonsense plants,

ideal for the beginner, and perfect for showing. They are easily grown in the standard Auriculastrum compost, and will provide a range of colour in the spring months. Annual repotting is advised, preferably after flowering. Do not over-pot, a plant growing in a 3in (7cm) pot will need to be potted up into a 3½in (9cm) pot, and so on. Overpotting can cause stagnant conditions, which will lead to root rot and possible death. Some growers plant several plants to a pot to produce a large speciment for showing more quickly. This practice is frowned upon in some circles, but if done skilfully it is very difficult to tell if in fact it is a large plant or not. Watering needs to be liberal in the peak growing periods, which are spring and early summer. For the rest of the year the compost needs to be kept just moist, although in winter it will not harm the plants if they are on the dry side. Keeping them snuff dry for months on end will lead to problems. The preceding comments refer to the majority of the small hybrids, but there are some which are more particular, and need a method of culture approaching that used for the *Primula allionii* cultivars, as described in chapter 8. This will be discussed in the description of the individual plants.

SEASONAL CULTIVATION IN THE COLD GREENHOUSE

SPRING: When the leaves start to unfurl towards the end of February the water needs to be increased steadily, and as soon as they appear to be growing well a half strength liquid feed will be beneficial, although not essential. These little plants grow and prosper with the minimum of attention, but the occasional feed will result in bigger, better coloured flowers. If the plants are required for showing be careful not to get water on the flowers, as this will result in the marking and premature aging of any flowers that are splashed. If they have farina on the leaves be careful not to splash them either. After they have finished flowering they can be repotted, and if the space is needed they can be moved to their summer quarters. A lightly shaded cold frame without lights, or any cool corner where they will not get neglected is sufficient. It is advisable to make sure they are not in contact with the bare earth, or assorted pests will gain entry through the drainage holes. If they are to be kept in the alpine house, shading is recommended from about mid-April, possibly later in the north and earlier in the south. Although splitting is feasible at any time of the year, the best results and quickest establishment are from splitting straight after flowering.

SUMMER: Under glass keep the plants shaded and moist, and watch for pests and diseases.

AUTUMN: Bring the plants back under cover, and remove any shading. Any dead and dying leaves that come away easily can be removed carefully. Enjoy the odd autumn flowers in October when there is little else to decorate the greenhouse.

WINTER: In the winter the leaves roll up tightly on themselves, waiting for the warming up of spring. Watering needs to be reduced, and treat for botrytis and other moulds if it becomes necessary. Keep the greenhouse well ventilated at all times. Frost will not harm these plants, but stagnant moist air will.

SEASONAL CULTIVATION IN THE GARDEN

SPRING: Maintenance is minimal, just enjoy the flowers. If for any reason a plant is looking unhealthy and does not appear to be growing as it should in spring it can be dug up, any rotten roots cut away, and the remaining pieces treated as cuttings. If some roots remain those pieces can be potted up and grown on as described in chapter 3.

SUMMER: Regularly check that the smaller hybrids are not being overgrown by vigorous neighbours.

AUTUMN: The plants in the garden need to be checked to make sure they are not covered with autumn leaves.

WINTER: Curl up in a warm chair with the specialist nurserymen's lists.

PROPAGATION

SPLITTING: These plants are easily split at any time of the year, and can then be potted and established. If extra plants are needed from large show plants, that do not need splitting, a few cuttings can be taken as described in chapter 3, or if the plant is allowed to become fairly dry, it is quite easy to get hold of a small rosette near the edge of the plant and wiggle it until it becomes loose, and pull it out complete with roots.

This offset can then be potted and grown on in the standard Auriculastrum compost.

CUTTINGS: Use the procedure as described in chapter 3.

SEED: Is not recommended unless the grower wishes to grow on lots of seedlings in the hope of raising one that might be distinct. The seedlings make passable garden plants, but when there are so many good named varieties about it is not really worth the effort.

PESTS AND DISEASES: Always watch for vine weevil. Root aphids/mealy bug can be a problem but are easily treated. *See* chapter 20.

AVAILABILITY

Nearly every specialist alpine nursery lists a few of these charming plants. The newer and slower varieties are now becoming more readily available.

It must be realised that many varieties described in books are virtually extinct, some possibly gone forever. The following lists will be as comprehensive as possible, but new varieties are continually being introduced, some of which do not really merit being named and it is impossible to describe every new hybrid.

Many modern amateur and professional breeders are using 'stable' names, often related to the area they come from, or the name of the nursery. Watch out for the following:

Primula 'Aire . . .'
Primula 'Hemswell . . .'
Primula 'Hurstwood . . .'
Primula 'Lismore . . .'
Primula 'Stradbrooke . . .'
Primula 'Wharfedale . . .'

DESCRIPTIVE LIST OF PUBESCENS AND OTHER ARTIFICIAL HYBRIDS

Primula x *pubescens* 'Alba':
(Pubescens group)

This is often seen at the primula shows but very rarely offered for sale. A very beautiful plant with congested heads of pure white flowers on 3in (7cm) stems (almost like a miniature *P. denticulata*) and fairly large neat rosettes of pale green leaves. The alpine house would be safest if the grower is fortunate to obtain this little treasure.

AVAILABILITY: Offsets very slowly, only present in private collections, but work is being done to develop a seed strain similar to this plant.

Primula x 'Appleblossom': (Pubescens group)

A small hybrid with loose heads of mauve pink fading to pale pink flowers on 3in (7cm) stems. the large creamy white eye is very distinct when newly opened, but becomes less obvious as the pin-eyed flowers fade. Rosettes of neat rounded pale leaves. Attractive and different.

AVAILABILITY: Occasionally from specialist nurseries.

Primula x 'Barbara Barker':

A hybrid between *Primula* 'Linda Pope' x *Primula* 'Zuleika Dobson' (a cultivar now sadly lost). It has plain green leaves with distinctive white notched edges, and pinkish lilac flowers nearly 1in (2.5cm) in diameter with white eyes, carried several to a 2in (5cm) stem. A lovely hybrid with attractive foliage that contrasts well with the rich dark pink flowers.

AVAILABILITY: Occasionally from the specialist nurseries.

Primula x 'Belluensis': (Pubescens group)

This is almost identical to 'Freedom', the only difference is that 'Belluensis' has a suspicion of a paler eye. The two varieties now seem to be completely confused in commerce, and possibly one should bow to the inevitable and call them all 'Freedom'!

AVAILABILITY: Rarely from specialist nurseries.

Primula x 'Bewerley White': (Pubescens group)

This was the name given to a batch of seedlings, so there are several variations on the theme. It should not be confused with 'Cream Viscosa' which is an old variety. The plant most commonly available as 'Bewerley White' is pin-eyed and has quite compact leaves well powdered in farina, and loose heads of creamy flowers on 4in (10cm) stems.

AVAILABILITY: From specialist nurseries, but many of the plants sold under this name are indistinguishable from 'Cream Viscosa', and are probably not 'Bewerley White'.

Primula x 'Blairside Yellow':

This temperamental little beauty is a perfect microform of the wild *Primula auricula*. On close examination of the small rounded slightly sticky leaves one wonders if it is in fact a hybrid, with *Primula allionii* being one of the parents. It bears good pollen but it does not seem to want to carry seed to maturity, if viable seed is set, and that is doubtful, it usually aborts within a few weeks. The 1–2in (2.5–5cm) stems carry small heads of rich bright yellow flowers, above the neat rosettes of rounded leaves. Many authorities maintain that it is losing its vigour, but like many of the Florists' auriculas, if it is kept well fed and shaded in the hot summer months it will grow well and prosper. Recommended for the cold greenhouse, but when enough plants are available, it is well worth trying in a trough.

AVAILABILITY: Occasionally from the specialist nurseries.

***Primula* x 'Blue Rufus':**
This goes after the style of 'Rufus', but with bluish flowers. Said to be rather a disappointing plant.

AVAILABILITY: Rarely from the specialist nurseries.

***Primula* x 'Boothman's Var':**
(Pubescens group)
A dark reddish purple with a slightly starry small white eye, thrum-eyed, and is a vigorous and easy variety fairly readily obtainable. This is one of the best, not temperamental and equally lovely in trough, garden, scree or alpine house. A well grown specimen is a joy to behold, and quite worthy of any show bench. No skill is needed to grow and flower well. Also to be found listed as *Primula rubra* 'Boothman's Var' or *Primula hirsuta* 'Boothman's Var'. An excellent plant for the novice.

AVAILABILITY: Stocked by several of the specialist nurseries.

***Primula* x 'Carmen':**
(Pubescens group)
Rich crimson red flowers, and is very similar to 'Boothman's Var'. If space is limited there is no point growing both plants.

AVAILABILITY: Occasionally from the specialist nurseries.

***Primula* x 'Christine':**
(Pubescens group)
A very fine and distinctive variety. It is unfortunate that many of the plants masquerading under this name are in fact either 'Boothman's Var.' or something very similar. The true plant has very rich pink thrum-eyed flowers, that fade slightly to a dark old rose. The veins on the petals tend to be slightly raised giving a textured appearance. The leaves are pale green, evenly and lightly serrated. Suitable for a trough, or makes a

lovely pan in the alpine house. Exceedingly floriferous, and very suitable for exhibiting.

AVAILABILITY: From several of the specialist nurseries.

Primula x 'Cream Viscosa':
(Pubescens group)

Fairly readily available under an assortment of incorrect and misleading names, this plant is a pubescens, it is not a *Primula viscosa* (now renamed *Primula latifolia*) hybrid. Before the different species in the Auriculastrum group were properly sorted and reclassified the pubescens hybrids went under the name *Primula viscosa*, hence the term 'Cream Viscosa'. Anyhow, whatever name it is purchased as, it is an attractive free flowering hybrid, and very tolerant of a variety of conditions. It has loose heads of slightly funnel-shaped cream thrum–eyed flowers above loose rosettes of longish serrated pale green leaves. Many of the plants under the name 'Bewerley White' are probably 'Cream Viscosa'. Excellent for the novice.

AVAILABILITY: This is one of the most easily obtained of this group, from many specialist nurseries.

Primula x 'Crichton Red':

A strong growing plant of a similar size to 'Rufus', with dusky deep red flowers.

AVAILABILITY: From the occasional specialist nursery, seems to be more widely grown in the south.

Primula x 'Crimson Velvet':
(Pubescens group)

Often listed as *Primula* x *viscosa* 'Crimson Velvet' or *Primula* x *latifolia* 'Crimson Velvet'. There is considerable controversy about how this plant should be named, some authorities think that it contains a great deal of *Primula latifolia* (formerly *viscosa*) blood, others maintain that it is pure Pubescens. A truly beautiful and vigorous plant. The huge rounded heads of dusky rich crimson flowers on sturdy 6–8in (15–20cm) stems are very sweetly scented, with strong overtones of lemon, and it can be identified by its scent alone. Lovely in the border or rock garden, and spectacular on the show bench. A good beginner's plant.

AVAILABILITY: Often listed by the specialist nurseries.

Primula x 'Dianne':

A *Primula* x *forsteri hybrid*, though with what is uncertain. It is slightly larger than *Primula* x *forsteri,* and has large rich crimson flowers. A lovely plant for a trough or a pan in the alpine house. Highly recommended both for ease of culture and freedom of flowering.

AVAILABILITY: Occasionally offered by the specialist nurseries.

Primula x 'Faldonside':
(Pubescens group)

An old variety with large distinct leaves that tend to look yellowish and slightly unhealthy. The small, dark, rich red, frilly thrum-eyed flowers are slightly funnel-shaped, and have an ill-defined white starry eye. As with 'Blairside Yellow' it seems to grow better under cover, shaded in summer and with a fair amount of food.

AVAILABILITY: Only occasionally from the specialist nurseries.

Primula x 'Fiona':
(Pubescens group)

Like a miniature 'Harlow Car' with almost white flowers. It was bred by Barry Atack, who named it after his daughter.

AVAILABILITY: Only in private collections.

Primula x 'Freedom':
(Pubescens group)

A relatively vigorous and easy plant, with loose heads of almost flat pin-eyed flowers of a pure mauve purple shade and very distinctive darkish green serrated leaves. One of the earliest of the pubescens to flower. Some of the pubescens grow more quickly with the extra warmth provided by a greenhouse, 'Freedom' does not seem to be one of these. Lovely for trough, scree, or rock garden, and makes an incredibly free flowering specimen for the alpine house. Another highly recommended variety that cannot fail to delight the grower.

AVAILABILITY: Most specialist nurseries stock this plant.

Primula x 'Gnome':

Small red slightly frilly funnel-shaped flowers, messy yellow eye, slightly farinaed. Slight farina on the outer edge of the leaves. Can be very temperamental to grow, and is more suited to the alpine house. In fact it looks just like a very small version of 'Old Red Dusty Miller'.

AVAILABILITY: Rarely available but worth searching for as the almost brick red colour is very distinctive.

Primula x 'Harlow Car':
(Pubescens group)

Originally raised at Holden Clough. Creamy white thrum-eyed flowers with the merest hint of pink on ageing. If selfed the resultant seedlings are very similar to the parent, and it has been described as breeding true from seed, which is incorrect.

The true plant can often be identified by its habit of producing a small extra petal in the middle of the flower. It has good heads of very large well formed flowers, and a well grown plant is a marvellous sight. It seems to produce much better specimens when grown under glass. In very cold areas the growth rate outside is very slow, and it can rot off in very cold, wet winters. The majority of gardeners however will find it a thoroughly garden worthy plant. Recommended for the novice. An excellent plant for the show bench.
AVAILABILITY: Occasionally from the specialist nurseries.

Primula x 'Harlow Car Seedling':
(Pubescens group)
A lovely plant with huge heads of creamy flowers and large rosettes of slightly farinaed leaves. Quite rare because it does not produce many offsets.
AVAILABILITY: Only in a few private collections.

Primula 'Harmony':
See *Primula* 'Yellow Rufus'.

Primula x 'Henry Hall':
This is synonymous with *Primula* 'Freedom'. According to hearsay the nurseryman who bred 'Freedom' distributed it in England under the name 'Freedom' and in Scotland as 'Henry Hall', though certainly there is no discernible difference.
AVAILABILITY: Rarely from the specialist nurseries.

Primula x 'Hurstwood Midnight':
(Pubescens group)
Loose heads of thrum–eyed flowers of a lovely dark velvety purple with a slightly star-shaped cream eye.
AVAILABILITY: Only in private collections, but should become more readily available.

Primula x 'Joan Gibbs':
Handsome reddish purple pin-eyed flowers.
AVAILABILITY: Occasionally from specialist nurseries.

Primula x 'Joan Danger':
Dusky purplish red flowers on 4in (10cm) stems. Somewhat similar to the preceding plant.
AVAILABILITY: Rarely from the specialist nurseries.

Primula x 'Kath Dryden':
(Pubescens group)
A lovely light yellow thrum-eyed variety with lightly farinaed leaves, similar to 'Cream viscosa'.
AVAILABILITY: Not in general cultivation as yet, but as it is relatively vigorous and easy going it should become available in a few years.

***Primula* x 'Mary Curle':**
(Pubescens group)
Described as having broad, pale green toothed leaves and large heads of reddish purple flowers. The author has neither grown nor seen this variety, but as it was awarded the Award of Merit in 1964 one assumes it is still in existence.
AVAILABILITY: Only in private collections.

***Primula* x 'Miles Rough':**
(Pubescens group)
Bred by John Mercer of Bradford, and is a seedling from 'Faldonside' with small bright red flowers with a good white eye, flower size is compensated for by the quantity produced.
AVAILABILITY: Only in private collections.

***Primula* x 'Moonlight':**
(Pubescens group)
Loose heads of well proportioned thrum-eyed flowers of a light primrose shade. The leaves are not serrated. A very pretty free flowering plant, but does not seem destined for the garden, more for the cold greenhouse and the show bench.
AVAILABILITY: Rarely from specialist nurseries.

***Primula* x 'Mrs G.F. Wilson':**
Slightly larger than 'Mrs J.H. Wilson', certainly distinct, with a more yellowish eye, the plant seen under this name looks more like a border than a pubescens. Some nurseries, especially in the south, are selling a plant identical to 'Mrs J.H. Wilson' with this name.
AVAILABILITY: Rarely from the specialist nurseries.

***Primula* x 'Mrs J.H. Wilson':**
(Pubescens group)
Good compact heads of bright light purple pin-eyed flat flowers with a large fairly well defined slightly star-shaped cream eye. A lovely easy variety, fairly often offered. One of the most fragrant of the pubescenses, and makes nothing short of a spectacular specimen for the alpine house and show bench. Equally at home in the rock garden, trough or scree. The colour of the flowers is vivid, and in the twilight is almost luminous. An old variety that was mentioned by Farrer in 1914. An excellent plant for the novice.
AVAILABILITY: Occasionally from the specialist nurseries.

***Primula* x 'Mrs J.H. Wilson Seedling':**
(Pubescens group)
Very similar to 'Mrs J.H. Wilson', with darker larger flowers of the same shade, and a more pronounced eye. Rarely offered as it produces less offsets. Although the flower form is similar

the rosettes of lighter green leaves are much larger. It is not as easy going as its parent, and will rot off if conditions are not perfect. If a plant could be obtained it is worth the extra care needed to keep it in good health.

AVAILABILITY: Only in private collections.

Primula x 'Old Rose':
(Pubescens group)

Raised by R. Milne Redhead formerly of Holden Clough Nursery. An attractive variety with dark pink flowers.

AVAILABILITY: Rarely from the specialist nurseries.

Primula x 'Pamela':

Pretty white eyed lilac flowers, probably a marginata hybrid.

AVAILABILITY: Only in private collections.

Primula x 'Pat Barwick':
(Pubescens group)

A very attractive hybrid bred by Mr Ron Cole of Scunthorpe, who named it after his wife's maiden name. The flat flowers are very pale cream, with a touch of salmon pink, and are carried in good heads over tidy rosettes of toothed leaves. Lovely for the alpine house.

AVAILABILITY: Rarely from the specialist nurseries.

Primula x 'Pink Freedom':
(Pubescens group)

Free flowering pink form, is almost identical to 'Freedom', but for the slightly smaller pinkish flowers.

AVAILABILITY: Rarely from the specialist nurseries.

Primula x 'Ruby':
(Pubescens group)

Small wine red flowers with a white eye.

AVAILABILITY: Occasionally from the specialist nurseries.

Primula x 'Rufus':
(Pubescens group)

Larger than the other pubescenses. It carries huge heads of bright scarlet red flowers, the colour darkens slightly towards the centre of the flower and there is a light ring of farina around the rich yellow eye. This darker ring emphasises the eye making 'Rufus' a very distinct and beautiful variety. The thrum-eyed flowers are large and flat. The leaves form large rosettes and are a light bright green. If there was room for only one *Primula* x *pubescens* in a collection, this would probably be the hybrid chosen. Regularly wins prizes at all the shows, and cannot be equalled for its good temper and vivid colour. Lovely in the garden, better still in the alpine house. Strongly recommended for the novice.

AVAILABILITY: Occasionally available from the specialist nurseries.

***Primula* x 'Sid Skelton':**

This carries a mass of small flat beautifully shaped pale blue thrum-eyed flowers with a very small white eye. Not one of the easiest, and seems to sulk after being split. A good pan is a wonderful delicate sight.

AVAILABILITY: Only in private collections.

***Primula* x 'Sonya':**

Compact round heads of cream flowers with an attractive pale mauve shading towards the edge of the petals. The light green leaves have a very distinct appearance in winter. This charming variety needs the protection of an alpine house, it has a tendency to rot in very wet weather.

AVAILABILITY: Rarely from the specialist nurseries.

***Primula* x 'Sugar Icing':**

A large leaved pubescens with lovely very pale mauve flowers with a creamy eye.

AVAILABILITY: Only in private collections.

***Primula* x 'The Cardinal':**

An old variety with brick red flowers.

AVAILABILITY: Rarely from the specialist nurseries.

***Primula* x 'The General':**
(Pubescens group)

Rich scarlet red thrum-eyed flowers with overlapping petals and a bright yellow star-shaped eye. Worth searching out for its bright cheerful colour. One of the slower varieties, but fine in a trough or the alpine house. An old variety mentioned by Farrer in 1914.

AVAILABILITY: Occasionally from the specialist nurseries.

***Primula* x 'Victoria':**

Neat mealed leaves with very few serrations, like a miniature Dusty Miller. The flowers are a dark rich red, almost with a touch of maroon. Not one of the easiest varieties to keep in good health, possibly losing its vigour from overpropagation, or even old age.

AVAILABILITY: Difficult to obtain, mainly in private collections.

***Primula* x 'Wedgwood':**

An interesting pubescens of unknown origin. Very solid heads of a light mauve blue, above pale green serrated leaves, looks almost border size and certainly makes up in vigour what it lacks in form.

AVAILABILITY: Occasionally listed by specialist nurseries.

***Primula* x 'Wharfedale. . .':**
There are some really lovely little hybrids in the Wharfedale Series, bred by Alec Stubbs of Grassington, which will hopefully become more readily available in the next few years.
AVAILABILITY: Rarely available from the specialist nurseries.

***Primula* x 'Winifred':**
Large pin-eyed flowers of a good mauve purple, with a slightly starry white eye.
AVAILABILITY: Rarely available from the specialist nurseries.

***Primula* x 'Yellow Rufus':**
This has been renamed 'Harmony', and is a most attractive plant, after the style of 'Rufus', but with yellow flowers.
AVAILABILITY: Only in private collections.

10
The Larger Hybrids of the Auriculastrum Section
(Popularly known as Auriculas)

There is a great deal of confusion regarding the name 'Auricula'. An auricula is a member of the primula genus, originally *Primula auricula* itself, but nowadays by popular usage it has come to mean any hybrid of *Primula auricula* with similar leaves and form as the original. The term Auricula alpina is totally incorrect, and either refers to *Primula auricula* or a mixed strain of indeterminate hybrids in varying colours of the size and form of *Primula auricula*.

In recent years, thanks to the production of auriculas by micropropagation, many more growers have found that it is now fairly easy to acquire a small collection of named alpine, show and double auriculas, and there are several nurseries that offer a good range of these lovely and exotic plants. Unfortunately there are very few of the old border auriculas available in commerce. Hopefully time will remedy this and once again it will be easy to find a selection of these charming plants to grace the garden.

THE FLORISTS' AURICULA

(Alpines and Shows)
The Auricula is part of our heritage, and was introduced into Britain about 1580 by the Flemish weavers who were escaping from religious persecution in the Netherlands. Seven varieties were listed in Gerard's *Herbal* as early as 1597 and exhibiting was recorded in the eighteenth century. It is believed that it was during this time that the mutation of part of the petal into a leaf like 'Edge' first appeared. Auricula growing was very popular in the nineteenth century with growers travelling many miles to exhibit at the auricula shows; the main centres

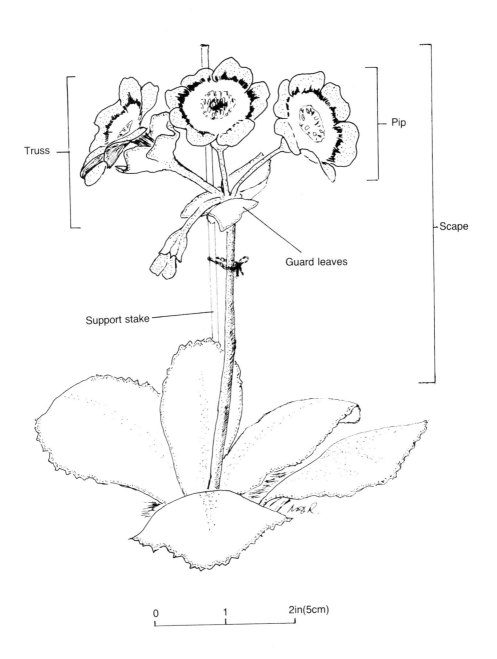

Truss

Pip

Scape

Guard leaves

Support stake

0   1   2in(5cm)

A typical auricula.

of growing being south and west Yorkshire, Lancashire, Cheshire and London. The Florists' flowers became less popular in Victorian times, but the dedicated few continued growing and showing and this continued interest culminated in the formation of 'The National Auricula Society' in 1872. During the First and Second World Wars the breeding of auriculas almost ceased, but in the last fifty years the growing of the Florists' auriculas has become more popular, helped in no small way by both the advent of micropropagation, and the breeding and distributing of new varieties by the dedicated modern Florists.

Nowadays there are three distinct societies in Britain, with some sub groups, namely 'The National Auricula and Primula Society Northern Section'; 'The Midland Section' and 'The Southern Section'. Each of these societies holds two shows per year, for the Northern Section the Primula Show is held on the first Saturday in April and The Auricula Show on the first Saturday in May.

CULTIVATION

This is basically very simple remembering the essentials: good drainage, moisture retention, and plenty of fresh air.

The Florists' auriculas are usually grown in an unheated greenhouse. They can also be grown in an unheated conservatory or porch – but they need plenty of light, especially in winter. Cold frames are also suitable, but extra work is involved in spring and autumn e.g. taking the frame lights off on good days and when watering, and replacing them to protect the plants from heavy rain.

Every grower of the Florists' auricula has definite ideas on composts and watering. The recommendations in this chapter are to provide a starting point from which the novice grower can develop suitable methods of cultivation. Gardening is not an exact science – and every garden or greenhouse has its own microclimate. In general auriculas are easy plants to grow, but considerable skill and devotion is needed to achieve top show-quality flowers, either for personal benefit or to stage at the auricula shows.

It is worth trying the easier of the Florists' auriculas in the garden, especially the alpines. They need a gritty, loamy soil containing some humus – free draining in winter but not arid in summer. It must be remembered that too hot and sunny a position can weaken the plant, making it less able to cope with the rigours of winter. One grower grows 'selfs' very successfully in a trough outside, and another grower has a border of green edges in the garden! The auriculas are perfectly hardy and can be grown outside if the conditions are right. It is, however, foolish to experiment with a single valuable plant, far better to grow it on for a while in the greenhouse until there are sufficient offsets, and then try one of them outside. Do also remember the paste on the selfs and edges will be ruined by rain if grown outside.

If the auriculas are being purchased from a nursery, take careful note of which compost they are grown in. It is not always easy to wean an auricula from a purely peat-based compost into a loam-based compost, and vice versa, and casualties often occur in the process. The sensible course is to repot a young plant which has been raised in either pure peat or loam-based compost into one that has equal ratios of peat and loam, with the appropriate amount of grit. After establishing the plant in that compost it can then be transferred to the preferred one.

If newly purchased plants are from a source suspected of being infected with Vine Weevil (*See* chapter 20), carefully dispose of all compost in a sealed bag in the dustbin, wash the roots thoroughly, and repot in your own compost.

Pot culture in plastic pots: A good basic compost would be one part John Innes No.2, one part moss peat and one part ¼in (6mm) grit (from a builders merchant, and washed). This will produce a healthy plant with a good root system, but not show quality flowers.

Pot culture in clay pots: If clay pots are preferred, a sensible compost to start with it four parts of a good John Innes No. 2, with one part grit and one part moss peat and enough water in summer to prevent the compost drying out, but much less in winter – too much water and the roots will rot.

SEASONAL CULTIVATION

SPRING: Feeding is recommended when growth starts in spring. The tightly furled leaves of winter will start to unfurl, and the whole appearance of the plant subtly changes as growth starts – it becomes a fresher green and loses the dullness of winter. Early March, or even earlier in the south is about the right time to start feeding – it all depends on the weather. If the weather is still very cold and dark it is advisable to delay feeding. Any proprietary balanced liquid feed, at half the recommended strength, once a week is suitable. The fertilizers that come in a soluble powder or crystal form are more economical. The edges, from the time the flower truss appears, need a feed higher in nitrogen, to develop fully. Watering from March on needs to be ample but do not allow the plants to become too dry or too wet, or the flowers will suffer. Shading is recommended from mid to late April, depending on the weather. If the weather at this time is predominantly dull and cloudy it may not be necessary to shade until well into May.

After flowering it is sensible to remove the dead flower heads to prevent the plant using its energies in producing unwanted seed. The flower heads are removed by cutting off at the top of the main stem, not at the bottom. If they are cut near the base disease can enter and rapidly spread into the crown of the plant. The dead stems must only be removed when they are completely dry, and can be pulled from the plant easily with a quick sideways tug.

SUMMER: Carry on feeding as in spring until about the end of July. Auriculas prefer to be kept fairly cool in the summer months, either an open shady frame outside (with facilities to cover the plants during periods of persistent rain) or in a greenhouse shaded with latting, blinds, net curtains or the whitewash type shading. Shading is essential, for without it the plants will tend towards a semi-dormant state, with yellowing of the outside leaves and a generally poor appearance. Watering needs to be ample in June and July, but by August and September more care should be taken.

AUTUMN: During October to February keep watering to the minimum. At all times be careful not to splash water on the leaves as it spoils the very attractive meal.

In the late summer to autumn, as the weather becomes cooler there is a secondary period of activity, nowhere near as vigorous as in the spring, but with active root growth and the occasional flush of autumn flowers. Many growers worry as to whether to allow the autumn flowers to develop. It is all a question of preference – it is pleasant to enjoy a few auriculas in the autumn, but some very experienced growers maintain that allowing the plants to flower in October will prevent them from flowering as well as they might in the spring.

It is recommended that a careful eye be kept on the plants in autumn and winter. Remove dead and dying leaves with a gentle tug. If there is evidence of botritis spray with a fungicide, or water in a systemic fungicide. Certain fungicides are suspected of causing distorted flowers, but often this is preferable to losing the plant. In the autumn the flowers start to develop as the central leaves become furled up on themselves in preparation for winter as the plants enter a semi–dormant state.

WINTER: A small amount of water may be needed during mild and sunny periods, but be careful as the plants seem to survive better on the dry side, and there is then less chance of fungal attack to the roots or leaves, both of which can be fatal.

POINTS TO REMEMBER

1) Different varieties need different treatment to grow them to perfection.
2) Too much food can cause root rot (as can too much water in winter).
3) 2½in (6cm) or 3in (7cm) pot for young plants, 3½in (9cm) pot for mature plants.
4) Some growers use a peat-based compost very successfully, but great care is needed in watering in winter or you will end up with no roots at all due to rot.
5) Edges are more demanding than selfs and fancies, which in turn are more demanding than alpines. Generally it is sensible to learn to grow the selfs and alpines before attempting the edges.
6) If vine weevils are a problem it is better to repot later in the year, so that the old compost can be disposed of along with any weevil eggs that have been laid in the compost.

PROPAGATION

SEED: Auriculas do not breed true from seed, and so seed is not used unless the grower is interested in breeding new varieties. This will be discussed further in chapter 17. As the seed is not generally required it is sensible to remove dead flowers by nipping off the flower at the top of the footstalk. This saves the plant from wasting strength in producing useless seed. Do not remove the old flower stalk at the base as this may cause rot, but allow it to dry off gradually. When completely dry it should come away easily.

The seed of show auriculas may be purchased and is excellent if it is realised that the chances of raising a good variety are slight. Breeders of show and alpine auriculas raise many hundreds of seedlings (the seed coming from deliberate crosses) and they will be lucky to raise one or two worthy of naming. Remember that it is only permissible to name new auriculas when invited to do so after the variety has won a class at an auricula show.

SPLITTING: Mature auriculas can often be split to yield several plants – this is best done after flowering (April/May) and before the end of July – to enable the plant to establish before autumn and winter. Pot the young plants into the compost recommended, but do not overpot (i.e. do not put a plant with a small root system into a large pot). A rough guide is to hold the plant in the position at the top of the pot that it would occupy if it were planted, and if several roots touch the sides and/or bottom of the pot, but do not look cramped, you have the right-sized pot. If a plant has excessive roots in comparison with the rosettes of leaves, prune the roots with a sharp pair of scissors or a knife.

Offsets can be taken from the mother plant without knocking

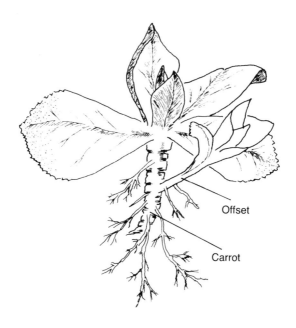

Offset

Carrot

Diagram of an auricula before splitting.

it out of the pot. If a gritty, loamy compost is used, allow it to dry out. The offset can be gently pulled out of the pot without disturbing the main plant. Sometimes the offset will have no roots. The easiest method to root it is to push it down the side of a pot of normal auricula compost, keeping the compost only slightly damp until it is established, and potting it up when it has sufficient roots.

CUTTINGS: Are believed by some experts to give a better plant. The method to be used is the same as for the rest of the Auriculastrum section – *See* chapter 3.

AVAILABILITY

The auriculas that have been micropropagated are much more readily available, and there are many good varieties to form the basis of a representative collection.

There are a few excellent nurseries specialising in auriculas, and several of the specialist alpine nurseries list a few varieties. It must be remembered that each auricula only gives a specific number of offsets per year, and nurserymen are not magicians. It is impossible to provide enough of every variety to satisfy the customers, especially the slower green edges.

Auriculas are sold differently by the various nurseries. Some provide bare root offsets and some small plugs – both ready for potting. Other nurseries send established plants in 3in (7cm) or 3½in (9cm) pots. Prices also vary, but considering the cost of these lovely plants a century or two ago, they are very good value these days.

Note: Many of the varieties listed in the older books are no longer in cultivation. Some of the new varieties that win prizes at the shows are not readily available. Every auricula show has seedling classes, and raisers of varieties that win these classes are invited to name them – thus every year many new varieties emerge, some of which will stand the test of time while others will disappear into obscurity.

This book does not contain a full list of all the varieties available as there is insufficient space. The varieties listed are those most likely to be obtainable or to be seen on the show bench. The best of the more recently bred plants are included.

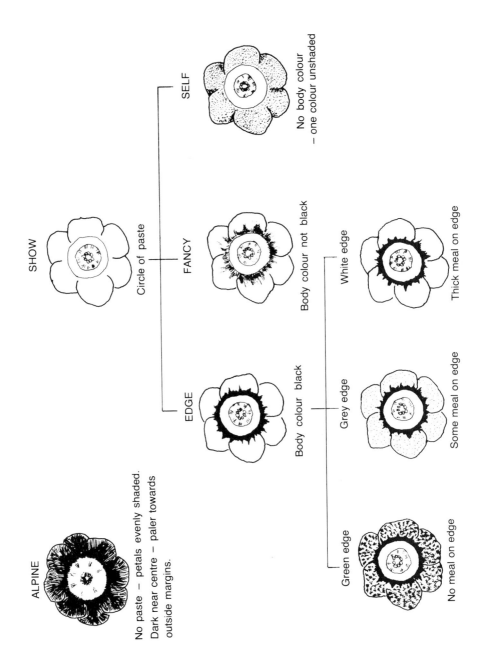

SHOW

SELF

No body colour
– one colour unshaded

Circle of paste

FANCY

Body colour not black

White edge

Thick meal on edge

EDGE

Body colour black

Grey edge

Some meal on edge

Green edge

No meal on edge

ALPINE

No paste – petals evenly shaded.
Dark near centre – paler towards
outside margins.

Classification of show and alpine auriculas.

ALPINE AURICULAS

The origins of the alpine auriculas began between 1861 and 1871, when many new varieties were raised by the work of Charles Turner of Slough. This work was continued by the Douglases of Great Bookham. The alpines were first shown in Manchester in 1873 at the inaugural show of the National Auricula Society.

The quiet beauty of the alpine auriculas is often overshadowed by the exotic appearance of the show varieties, but they cannot be too highly recommended either as plants for the alpine house or the garden.

There is no meal on either the flowers or the leaves. The centre is cream, white or gold, and the petal colour is darker near the centre, shading evenly to a paler shade at the petal edge.

LIGHT CENTRED ALPINES

(Having a bold cream to white centre)

'Adrian': Purple shaded to light blue, this is an excellent variety, and good for showing. Has been micropropagated.

'Ann Taylor' Raised by Mr Taylor from Blue Alpine seed from the 'House of Douglas'. A pure white centre, round, true and clean, with strongly shaded light blue petals, early flowering and not the easiest to grow well.

'Anwar Sadat' Derek Telford so admired the late President of Egypt that when he heard of his assassination he named this Auricula in his memory. A good variety, in blue to mauve shades.

'Argus' An excellent white centred variety, in shades of crimson red, bred about 1890 by J.J. Keen of Southampton. It still wins top prizes when grown well. Vigorous and easy enough the the garden. Micropropagated, and so fairly readily available.

'Beatrice' Strongly shaded in blue to light blue, but not of great merit for the show bench. A lovely variety nonetheless.

'Blue Bonnet' A fine old variety bred by J. Douglas (mid-1930's) in medium blue shades.

'Comet' Red shades, and similar to Argus.

'C.W.Needham' A lovely plant raised by Percy Johnson and first shown in 1934, with distinctive evenly serrated leaves. Shading is not distinct, with dark blue tending to purple.

'Craig Vaughan':   Cream centre and velvety purple shaded petals.

'Elsie May':   Deep plum purple shades, bred by Derek Telford and named after his mother. Micropropagated, and so fairly readily available.

'Frank Crosland':   A justifiably popular variety in shades of dark blue to pale blue. This variety was raised by C.F. Faulkner about 1930.

'Geordie':   Best described as an improved 'Gordon Douglas', raised by Derek Telford and named after his brother-in-law.

'Gordon Douglas':   Creamy-white centre and deep violet blue shaded to pale blue flowers. It benefits from shading. This variety seems to have lost much of its vigour.

'Jeannie Telford':   Bred by Derek Telford who named it after his wife, it is similar to 'Lisa', and is an excellent variety for showing.

'Joy':   Rich velvety crimson and delicately shaded. A good variety for the show bench. It was raised by Percy Johnson in 1931.

'Joyce':   Purple blue shades.

'Kerkup':   Shades of light mauves.

'Lady Daresbury':   An old variety bred by C.F. Faulkner (about 1930), with large well-formed flowers strongly shaded in rich wine red to pale cerise.

'Lisa':   A lovely and reliable variety bred by Derek Telford in 1978, it is strongly shaded in wine to pink. Micropropagated, and so fairly readily available.

'Margaret Faulkner':   This is a classic for showing, and a delight in shades of purple. It was first shown in 1961.

'Mark':   Another of Derek Telford's introductions (1972), very large flowers strongly shaded in wine purple to pink.

'Mrs Hearn':   Small well-shaped flowers with a pale cream centre, and shaded grey blue to Cambridge blue. Another of J. Douglas's (1930s).

'Paragon':   An old variety in shades of mauve.

'Phyllis Douglas':   An old variety in purple blue shades.

'Rabley Heath':   Purple shades and bred by Allan Hawkes.

'Rowena':   Purple-mauve, and an old and popular variety that regularly shows well.

'Roxburgh':   An old Douglas variety. True white centre, and prettily shaded deep violet to violet mauve.

'Sandra':   Shades of mauve blue, and a very refined flower.

'Thetis':   Dark blue shaded to mid-blue. Bred by G. Douglas, about 1947.

'Valerie':   Dark red shaded, and a good variety for showing.
'Vee Too':   Bred by Allan Hawkes, and is a fine plant for showing. Could be likened to a darker shaded 'Phyllis Douglas'.
'Vulcan':   One of the Douglas auriculas in blue shades.

GOLD CENTRED ALPINES

(Having a rich gold centre)

'Andrea Julie':   Raised in 1972 by Derek Telford. The russet orange edging contrasts well with the rich gold centre. Only holds its best condition for a few days so timing is crucial if showing. Micropropagated, and so fairly readily available.
'Applecross':   Good red shades, introduced by Mr D. Edwards in 1968, it is the sister plant to 'Sandwood Bay'. A good variety for showing. Micropropagated, and so fairly readily available.
'Blossom':   Bred by Mrs S. E. Auker (1960) this is a beautifully shaded crimson variety, and is very reliable for showing.
'Bolero':   A fine orange red variety bred by C.F. Hill of Birmingham.
'Bookham Firefly':   Introduced by the 'House of Douglas' this fine variety has certainly stood the test of time. The bright, well defined centre contrasts well with the glowing crimson shading to maroon edging. Micropropagated, and so fairly readily available.
'Bright Eyes':   Dark red shades. A very good new variety bred by Derek Telford.
'Brown Bess':   From H. A. Cohen (1963), in brown to light brown, and strongly shaded, a lovely distinctive flower.
'C.F. Hill':   An orange brown variety bred by Allan Hawkes.
'Chocolate Soldier':   Brownish red, and raised by Derek Telford.
'Cranborne':   Dark red shades. Bred by Emlyn Jones.
'Doreen Stephens':   Bright red shades. Another lovely introduction by Derek Telford.
'Elizabeth Ann':   Bred by Jim Sherwood. A good variety for breeding.
'Elsie':   Maroon to light brown shading. Lovely and eye-catching, but not recommended for showing as the petals tend to curve backwards.

'Finchfield':   Dark brown orange shades. Bred by Gwen Baker of Wolverhampton in the 1980s.

'Frank Faulkner':   First shown in 1951 and has stood the test of time. The true bright gold centre and brilliant colour caused a sensation when first shown.

'Galen':   Lovely dark orange brown shades. Bred by Ron Cole of Scunthorpe in the 1980s.

'Gay Crusader':   A startling bright plant from Les Kaye, it can only be described as orange red shaded to orange. Performs well on the show bench.

'Goldwin':   Dark red shades. Bred by Allan Hawkes.

'Gypsy':   Dark crimson and well shaded. G. Douglas c.1950.

'Ida':   Raised by J.F. Ballard and first exhibited in 1966. It produces a good truss of beautifully chestnut shaded flowers.

'Janie Hill':   Bred by C.F. Hill, and named after his granddaughter. Orange red shades.

'Kim':   Attractive orange brown shades.

'Largo':   A fine gold centre bred by Allan Hawkes, with rich brownish shaded petals.

'Lee Paul':   Derek Telford classes this lovely plant as the best he has ever raised. Bred from 'Sirius', it has a bright gold centre without corrugation, and is strongly shaded yellow, with very flat pips. Excellent for the show bench.

'Lewis Telford':   A good new variety from Derek Telford, similar to 'Blossom', but a much better habit.

'Ling':   A fine variety bred by Les Kaye of Stocksbridge. The name is derived from a broken label 'Seed/ling'. A plant was given to a friend who admired it, and it was then propagated and distributed.

'Merridale':   This excellent plant was raised from seed out of the same pod as 'Finchfield' by Gwen Baker. Orange brown shades.

'Olton':   Was bred by Fred Edwards, and is named after a suburb of Birmingham.

'Prince John':   A very distinct variety, the large gold centre contrasts with the maroon to crimson shaded edging. A reliable plant for the show bench. One of the most important varieties from J. Douglas (pre-1927). Micropropagated, and so fairly readily available.

'Rodeo':   C.F. Hill bred this orange brown shaded alpine.

'Rondo':   An attractive gold centre bred by C.F. Hill.

'Sandwood Bay':   Bright orange red, shading to the edges and a vivid gold centre. Raised by D. Edwards in 1971. Micropropagated, and so fairly readily available.

'Sam Hunter':   Red shades, bred by Derek Telford and named after his colleague in Ulster.

'Shergold':   Very dark red shades bred by Allan Hawkes.

'Shotley':   Bred by Derek Telford in red shades.

'Sirius':   A strikingly beautiful plant raised by Frank Jacques. Cream/maroon shades. Very distinctive and good on the show bench.

'Snooty Fox II':   An excellent variety bred by Derek Telford, out of 'Andrea Julie'. The colour is similar to 'Finchfield', orange brown shades.

'Tally Ho':   A good gold-centred, orange brown shaded flower bred by C.F. Hill.

'Tarantella':   Raised by Derek Telford, the sister plant to 'Snooty Fox II'.

'Ted Roberts':   Introduced in 1977 by J. Allen, with maroon to crimson shading. For exhibition purposes, it is advisable to thin the flowerbuds. Micropropagated, and so fairly readily available.

'Verdi':   A very fine variety introduced by H.S. Lennie in 1943. It produces a classical flower, flat and well proportioned in shades of reddish brown to golden brown. An excellent show plant.

'Winifred':   (More correctly 'Winnifred'), this was bred by Frank Faulkner and is a lovely rich red variety that always shows to advantage, and is superb when grown well.

A good representative starter collection for the cold greenhouse, including varieties that show well would include:

Light Centres: 'Adrian', 'Argus', 'Mark', 'Rowena', 'Sandra' and 'Elsie May'.
Gold Centres: 'Applecross', 'Blossom', 'Prince John', 'Sandwood Bay', 'Sirius' and 'Winifred'.

EDGED AURICULAS

About 1740 the edged auricula was born, when a mutation occurred whereby the edges of the petals had mutated to leaf, and this, depending on the amount of meal, could be white, grey or green. Very shortly, because of the work of the hybridists many edged auriculas were available, and because the paste and meal were spoilt by the rain, these were generally grown under cover.

The body colour should be black, smooth on the inside and feathering out into the 'Edge'. The colour or type of the edge depends on the amount of meal that overlays the edge. Green edges are completely devoid of meal, grey edges have a light sprinkling of meal and white edges have a heavy coating of meal. Thus one can see how there is considerable overlap between the grey and white edges, and many varieties can be in either class depending on cultivation. The paste referred to is the ring surrounding the yellow tube (the hole in the middle) which is covered in a thick layer of crystalline farina.

GREEN EDGES

(Having no meal on the edge or leaves)

'**Bob Lancashire**':   Raised in 1984 by Jack Wemyss-Cooke by crossing 'Chloe' with 'Geldersome Green'.
'**Chloe**':   One of the finest greens, first shown in 1967 and bred by Mr F. Buckley of Macclesfield.
'**Chloris**':   Said to be a temperamental variety that breaks up into small rosettes easily, and is difficult to flower.
'**Dr Duthie**':   Quite old, and a pleasant green edge.
'**Fleminghouse**':   Bred in 1967 by Mr J. Stant. This excellent variety has the flattest pips of all. It is often described as performing better in the north. Not only has it the breeding to be best in show, it is fairly easy to keep in good health and will give great enjoyment to the novice grower. Micropropagated, and so fairly readily available.
'**Geldersome Green**':   This plant flowered, was named and died. All the plants in circulation under this name are in fact 'Geldersome Green No. 2'.
'**Geldersome Green No. 2**':   Bred by Jack Ballard, and a reliable reasonably vigorous variety.
'**Gild Green**':   Thought to be an abbreviation of the above and the same plant.
'**Greenheart**':   Raised by F. Buckley (1967), but probably losing its vigour.
'**Green Mouse**':   A good vigorous plant, but not good enough for showing.
'**Green Parrot**':   Fairly easy to grow, but rarely seen on the show bench.
'**Gretna Green**':   Raised by Mr Buckley, not one of the most reliable but can be good.

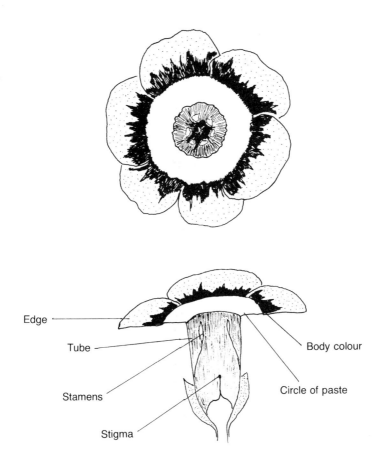

Flower of a show edged auricula.

'Orb': Bred by Dr D.A. Duthie, and is a fine dark green that is not temperamental.

'Praque': Raised by David Hadfield. Reckoned one of the best, with large well proportioned pips which come flat and round, and builds up a good truss.

'Roberto': Bred by Dr Newton. Not so reliable, but with skilful growing and a bit of luck can make a fine large truss of beautifully formed pips.

'Serenity': Raised by J. Ballard (1957). Not a good show variety, but relatively easy to grow and offsets well. An excellent plant for beginners.

'Superb': Bred by Mr Buckley but difficult to achieve perfection. Lighter green pips.

'Tinkerbell':   Raised by Clive Cookson in 1932 and is a difficult variety with long narrow leaves. Tends to look half dead in winter, often hanging on with one miserable root.

GREY AND WHITE EDGES

(Having meal on the edge and the leaves)

'Almondbury':   A grey bred by Derek Telford, but not the best for showing.

'Brookfield':   A pleasant plant, which could be a winner if grown well.

'C.G. Haysom':   White edged, and raised by R. Loake in 1962. A good reliable plant. Micropropagated, and so fairly readily available.

'Clare':   A very fine grey edge raised by Peter Ward. Classed as the best, but liable to distort if overfed.

'Colbury':   An old unreliable variety.

'Elegance':   Grey, not one of the easiest, and hardly show class.

'Elsie Sowden':   An old variety that seems to have lost vigour.

'Emery Down':   A grey edge, not often grown.

'Falsefields':   Thought to be a plant that was incorrectly circulated as 'Fairfield', and was thus renamed.

'George Rudd':   A very fine old grey, raised in Halifax by Thomas Woodhead and introduced in 1882. Appears to be losing vigour.

'Grey Friar':   Bred by Mr Buckley, but has now been superseded by better plants.

'Grey Lag':   Good foliage, and is a reasonable plant for showing.

'Helena':   This can be very good when grown well.

'James Arnott':   A very good white, with attractive toothed foliage, which can be excellent. Micropropagated, and so fairly readily available.

'J.W. Midgeley':   An old white edge.

'Lovebird':   A lovely reliable old variety raised by J. Douglas in 1932. Very neat refined foliage, and grey edged flowers. It is micropropagated, and so it is fairly readily available.

'Manka':   Bred by Jack Ballard. A difficult plant to keep healthy.

'Margaret Martin':   Very unreliable, but occasionally it can be excellent.

'Queen's Bower':   Raised by C.G. Haysom, (1947), not the easiest plant to keep healthy, and not of show quality.

'Rosalie Edwards':   This can be good, but is very fickle.

'St Boswells':   An excellent plant bred by Ron Cole, with very attractive foliage.

'Sherwood':   Pleasant, easy grey edge, but just short of show class.

'Snowy Owl':   This can be either white or grey edged.

'Teem':   This well known plant was raised by T. Meek, and first shown in 1957. An elegant plant, it can be classed as either grey or white, and is a good variety for showing.

'The Bride':   Either grey or white edged, bred by Buckley, with the richest jet black ground of any. Rivalled only by 'Teem', but often ruined by the whole flower, centre paste and ground becoming a pentagon. Responds well to good growing. White edges are in short supply, and this variety can be one of the best.

'Walhampton':   A good white edge, from C.G. Haysom (1946). A bit straggly and difficult to flower well, but very useful for breeding.

'Warwick':   Thought to be one of the best, this very refined plant was bred by Peter Ward, and grown well it can be unbeatable. Attention must be paid to feeding and thinning, and it is somewhat late flowering.

'White Wings':   White edge, raised by J. Douglas in the 1930s. Can be very good or very bad, and is certainly a test of skill to show well. A good plant for the novice.

'Yorkshire Grey':   A fine new variety bred by Allan Hawkes.

FANCIES

These are show auriculas which do not conform to any of the previous classifications; they are usually edges (grey, white or green) with the body colour not in black, but for example red or yellow.

'Coffee':   Bred by Gwen Baker. Milky coffee colour with a grey edge.

'Colonel Champneys':   Violet with a light grey edge.

'Green Isle':   Red body with a green edge.

'Grey Monarch':   Golden yellow with a grey edge.

'Hawkwood':   Red with a grey edge.
'Rajah':   Red with a green edge. Micropropagated, and so fairly readily available.
'Rolts':   Red with a green edge, and vigorous enough for the garden.
'Spring Meadows':   Yellow with a green edge.
'Stubbs Tartan':   Red background and huge flat flower.
'Sweet Pastures':   Yellow with a grey edge.

A good starter collection of show edges could include: 'Fleminghouse', 'C.G. Haysom', 'Lovebird', 'James Arnott' and 'Rajah'.

THE SELFS

The selfs probably date from the early part of the nineteenth century, but it is very difficult to sort out from the literature whether the alpine (previously called a self) or the self is being referred to. In recent years the selfs have become more popular and widely grown.

   The selfs are show auriculas where the body colour is even from the edge of the paste to the margin of the petals, there is no shading and no edge. A wide range of colours is available, and they are subdivided into red, yellow, blue, dark and other selfs.

RED SELFS

'Alfred Niblett':   From H.A. Cohen in the early 1960s.
'Alice Haysom':   Raised by C.G. Haysom (1935), a bright cardinal red, with good form, but the paste is a bit coarse.
'Cherry':   Bred in 1968 by Dr D.A. Duthie. It has good form, and if debudded is an excellent variety for the beginner. Aptly named, the colour is cherry red, a colour that is loved or hated.
'Cheyenne':   One of the best, bred by Peter Ward.
'Fanny Meerbeck':   A good strong growing plant raised by Ben Simonite of Sheffield in 1898. Micropropagated, and so fairly readily available.
'Geronimo':   Peter Ward bred this fine variety.
'Grizedale':   A rich bright red with messy leaves, and somewhat similar to 'The Mikado'.

'Lechistan':   A fairly old variety. Micropropagated, and so fairly readily available.

'Lisa's Red':   A reliable red bred by Derek Telford.

'Mojave':   A lovely light red variety, the colour is very distinct.

'Neville Telford':   Raised by Derek Telford and named after his brother. It often wins prizes.

'Old Red Elvet':   Another of the old reds.

'Pat':   This classic standard was bred in 1966 by J. Ballard and is classed as one of the best reds, with attractive well mealed foliage. It is said to be prone to root rot, and so it is probably safer to keep it slightly drier than other varieties. A good parent in breeding.

'Red Beret':   Derek Telford's best red, it is consistently good for showing.

'Red Gauntlet':   Bright red, and raised in 1970 by Dr D.A. Duthie.

'Red Rum':   Bred by Derek Telford and named for the famous Grand National winner.

'Shere':   A lovely lightish red and flowers early. Bred by K.J. Gould.

'Trudy':   Bred by Derek Telford and named for his late cousin.

BLUE SELFS

'Blue Jean':   Named after Derek Telford's wife. Very neat foliage, but tends to be a much smaller plant than other auriculas. Micropropagated, and so fairly readily available.

'Blue Nile':   An attractive plant with neat leaves, bred by Robert Newton in 1962.

'Esso Blue':   Bred by Derek Telford, but has now been superseded by better varieties.

'Everest Blue':   A good parent if breeding is being considered.

'Margaret Thatcher':   Bred by Jack Wemyss-Cooke – an excellent new variety. Not expected to be generally available for a few years.

'Midnight':   A beautiful rich dark blue, which could almost be classed as navy blue. Another distinct plant from Derek Telford.

'Oakes Blue':   The best most reliable blue about, bred by Derek Telford.

'Remus':   An old variety that is a good parent for breeding.
'Renata':   A reliable variety, and bred by W.R. Hecker in 1970.
'Stant's Blue':   Somewhat temperamental, and bred by Jack Stant.
'Stella':   A very attractive blue, and bred by Robert Newton in 1966.

Derek Telford has recently raised some excellent new blue selfs selected from a batch of seed produced by John Gibson from crossing 'Everest Blue' with 'Remus'. Amongst these are 'Trumpet Blue', 'Martin Luther King', 'Faro', 'Atlantian' and 'Eventide'. All are well worth growing and showing.

YELLOW SELFS

'Beeches Yellow':   Bred by Lawrence Wigley of Carshalton Beeches. 'Melody' x 'Sunflower'.
'Bilton':   Bred by Derek Telford, and is a good showable variety. Micropropagated, and so fairly readily available.
'Brazil':   Another yellow bred by Derek Telford.
'Brompton':   The best yellow self in circulation, and bred by David Hadfield.
'Gleam':   An easy, reliable plant, but not the best for showing.
'Golden Fleece':   Les Kaye's best yellow.
'Guinea':   A lovely yellow, and bred by Derek Telford. He classes this as his best yellow.
'Leeside Yellow':   Tends to be a small plant.
'Lemon Sherbet':   A relatively new yellow, bred by Tim Coop, and already winning prizes.
'Lisa's Smile':   Bred by Derek Telford in 1982 and still winning prizes.
'Melody':   Bred by C.G. Haysom, and introduced in 1936. Pale yellow flowers with dense clear white paste. Good for showing.
'Moneymoon':   Bred by Tim Coop. A lovely yellow.
'Pot of Gold':   An attractive good yellow bred by Gwen Baker.
'Prince Charming':   An old variety, but rarely seen today.
'Queen of Sheba':   Also old, not very vigorous, but probably could be of use in breeding.

'**Sheila**': An attractive light yellow, vigorous and easy, which is good for showing, and was bred by Allan Hawkes in 1961.

'**Sunstar**': A fine true yellow self bred by Les Kaye.

'**The Baron**': An old variety, which still holds its own on the show bench.

'**Tracy Ward**': Bred by Peter Ward, an excellent yellow with deep coloured thick petals, with the widest and smoothest paste of all the yellows.

'**Tomboy**': An excellent new variety raised again by Tim Coop.

DARK SELFS

'**Barbarella**': A lovely plant, and one of the top prize winners, bred by Peter Ward.

'**Blackhill**': This can be very good.

'**Consett**': Tends to flower too early for the shows, this variety has lovely foliage, and it was raised by Derek Telford from seed obtained from Robert Newton.

'**Dakota**': A fine dark red bred by Derek Telford.

'**Gizabroon**': This early flowering plant has glorious foliage, but not one of the darkest in this group. Bred by Derek Telford.

'**Neat and Tidy**': Raised by Dr Newton in 1955, and is vigorous and rewarding. The flowers are so dark a red as to appear almost black. An excellent plant for the novice. Micro-propagated, and so fairly readily available.

'**Night and Day**': A reliable good grower, which does reasonably well on the show bench.

'**Nocturne**': A refined 'Neat and Tidy', also bred by Dr Newton. Excellent for the show bench. Micropropagated, and so fairly readily available.

'**Satchmo**': Another of Derek Telford's excellent dark selfs.

'**Super Para**': An excellent dark red, bred by Derek Telford, and worthy of any show.

'**The Mikado**': An old variety, going back to 1906, and raised by a southern grower, William Smith. The leaves are an unhealthy greenish yellow, and coarse in appearance. One of the darkest.

'**The Snods**': A reasonable dark self for showing.

OTHER SELFS

'Chorister':   A vigorous variety that needs skill to make it flower. Off-yellow colour. Micropropagated, and so fairly readily available.

'Eventide':   A dark purple blue self bred by Derek Telford.

'Flamingo':   Bred by Derek Telford from seed provided by David Hadfield from crossing 'Pat' and 'Moonglow'. Pink flowers, as are its sisters 'Sugar Plum Fairy' and 'Pink Panther'.

'Moonglow':   A very pale yellow self, the best of the other selfs. Micropropagated and so fairly readily available.

'Purple Sage':   Purple self.

'Rocksand':   An unusual light slightly off-yellow self. It is well named, and of the quality one expects from Les Kaye, a dedicated south Yorkshire grower, better known for his work on the gold-laced polyanthus.

'Tan':   Bred, flowered, was photographed then died. It does not exist.

'Fanny Meerbeck', 'Blue Jean', 'Bilton', 'Neat and Tidy' and 'Moonglow' would provide a good basis of show selfs for the novice.

BORDER AURICULAS

As the name implies, these are robust plants for the garden, but they can be grown and enjoyed in pots in the cold greenhouse, and there are classes for them at the auricula shows. Unfortunately they are not often offered by nurseries.

'Blue Velvet':   Bluish purple, with a white eye and fragrant.

'Broadwell Gold':   Large heads of bright yellow flowers and heavily mealed leaves.

'Chamois':   A lovely and distinct variety – the lightly frilled flowers are the colour of a clean wash leather.

'Dr Lennon's White':   White flowers, but rarely obtainable.

'Linnet':   Rare, green, mustard and brown. Dainty.

'McWatt's Blue':   A lovely variety with rich, purple blue flowers with a large well-farinaed white eye and heavily mealed leaves.

'Old Irish Blue':   Dark to light blue shaded and frilly. The most readily obtainable of the border auriculas, a lovely delicate plant that cannot be too highly recommended.

'Old Yellow Dusty Miller':   Heads of yellow flowers over heavily mealed foliage. The 'Old Yellow Dusty Millers' are very close to the wild yellow primula auricula.

There are other 'Dusty Millers' about, with self explanatory names: 'Old Gold Dusty Miller', 'Old Pink Dusty Miller', 'Old Red Dusty Miller': this is the best known, apart from yellow, but unfortunately many of the plants available under this name are not true, in fact the little pubescens 'Gnome' is sometimes christened 'Old Red Dusty Miller'.

'Old White Dusty Miller':   White flowers and mealed leaves.

'Paradise Yellow':   A very worthwhile vigorous plant, the bright yellow flowers often form a completely round head of colour similar to a drumstick primula. Micropropagated, and so fairly readily available.

'Queen Alexandra':   An old Irish variety with heads of large pale biscuit yellow flowers and sweetly fragrant. If grown in a pot for showing it is advisable to keep it well shaded, as it fades easily.

'Royal Velvet':   Bright purple with a cream centre.

'Southport':   Rich brick-red with a yellow eye – an old variety that is now very rare.

'Winifred':   Gold, brown and frilly flowers, not to be confused with the alpine auricula of the same or similar name.

DOUBLE AURICULAS

Although the double auriculas were widely grown in the past, for many years they were neglected, being classed as not worthy of the attention of the florists. However in America, Ralph Balcom of Seattle and Denna Snuffer of Oregon have been successfully breeding new strains of these lovely plants for many years, and their work has led to a reawakening of interest both in America and in England. Most of the doubles in cultivation today can trace their ancestry back to Balcom and Denna Snuffer seed. Certain auriculas contain a 'doubling' gene, for instance 'Gordon Douglas' and 'Remus', and this recessive gene could be of use in breeding new varieties.

The double auriculas can be grown in the garden or in pots, and the fully double flowers are very attractive.

'Camelot':   An old variety with heavy heads of purple flowers. Micropropagated, and so fairly readily available.

'**Catherine**':   Bred by Ken Gould, with lime-yellow flowers, and slightly frilled. Micropropagated, and so fairly readily available.

'**Doublet**':   A reliable purple double bred by Allan Hawkes.

'**Denna Snuffer**':   First introduced by Mr Smith from the American doubles, pale cream open centred flowers.

'**Diamond**':   Bred by Gwen Baker, with white flowers with a green to cream centre.

'**Ivory**':   An attractive double bred by Gwen Baker.

'**Jane Myers No.1**':   A primrose yellow double bred by Len Bailey.

'**Jane Myers No. 2**':   Similar to the preceding plant but more vigorous.

'**Marigold**':   Incredibly double, frilled flowers, of an unusual shade of dark marigold orange. Needs careful dressing and thinning to show well. Micropagated, and so fairly readily available.

'**Mary**':   A lovely shape, with lemon yellow flowers, and introduced by Ken Gould about 1960.

'**Moonstone**':   A primrose yellow double from Gwen Baker.

'**Sarah Lodge**':   A purplish double named after Ron Cole's mother's maiden name.

'**Shalford**':   This purple double was bred by Mr Hecker.

'**Sir Robert**':   Sometimes labelled 'Sir Robert Ewbank', this was introduced by Lester Smith about 1960 from the American Balcom doubles.

'**Standish**':   Cream double. Micropropagated, and so fairly readily available.

'**Vicky**':   A good yellow bred by Derek Salt of Donington.

'**Walton Heath**':   Purple double.

'**Zambia**':   An old variety with dark red flowers.

There are also a host of very beautiful Barnhaven doubles. Both the border and the double auriculas are exhibited at the auricula shows.

STRIPED AURICULAS: These are becoming more popular, especially in the south, where several growers are breeding new varieties.

AURICULA ALPINA (ALPINE AURICULA): Seed is available from the seed companies, and this produces very good plants for the garden, but the possibility of raising a good new variety worthy of a name is very slight. Over the years confusion has crept in, Alpine auriculas can either mean mixed garden auricula hybrids or the florists' alpine auriculas. Some seed offered is collected from named varieties, but usually it is a good general garden mixture.

AURICULA SEED: some of the specialist auricula nurseries sell seed from show and alpine auriculas, and it is an interesting exercise raising plants from this seed, which can occasionally yield a worthwhile plant.

11
The Vernales Section

This relatively small section is only to be found in Europe, where it is fairly widespread. Its habitat spreads from Britain, through much of Europe, and as far as the Caucasus mountains. The Vernales species are generally to be found in meadows and woods, and they are not high alpines like many of the members of the Auriculastrum. Although the primroses and cowslips have been known and loved for years, the pure wild species are rarely grown, but they possess a quiet charm, and the sweet fragrance of the wild primrose is so evocative of spring, that gardeners should spare a corner for them. The pretty *Primula juliae* deserves to be more widely acknowledged, and is ideal for a shady pocket on the rock garden.

Primula vulgaris (previously *Primula acaulis*) is a native plant of Britain, as too are *Primula veris* and *Primula elatior,* but they are now becoming rare because of indiscriminate plundering.

The cultivation requirements of the Vernales species vary, but they are all moisture lovers and hate dryness at the roots in summer. Details will be included with each species.

The Vernales section of primulas are characterised by their complete lack of farina.

DESCRIPTIVE LIST OF SPECIES

Primula amoena (altaica)
From the Caucasus and north-eastern Turkey where it grows in earthy banks and among boulders. It is closely related to *Primula elatior,* the main difference being colour, *Primula amoena* having violet blue through to purple flowers in a loose umbel on a 6in(15cm) stem, whereas *Primula elatior* has cream to yellow flowers. It is rare in cultivation but plants are often offered as *Primula amoena* or *Primula altaica,* which are in fact *Primula vulgaris subsp. sibthorpii.*
CULTIVATION: The true plant is reputedly easy to grow, though reports by current growers of this plant indicate the opposite. Certainly a single rare specimen would be safest grown in the alpine house, in a peaty, gritty compost.

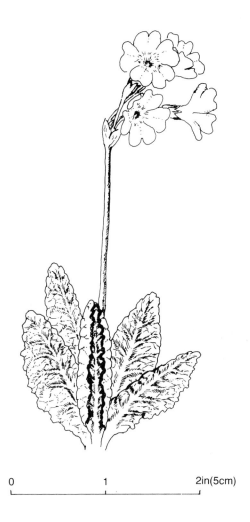

0   1   2in(5cm)

Primula amoena.

PROPAGATION: Seed, if obtainable, but beware of hybridisation of plants in cultivation.

AVAILABILITY: Try the seed lists.

Primula elatior:

The oxlip which is to be found throughout central and southern Europe, from East Anglia, and other isolated pockets in England, through to the Urals and probably further, where it is found growing in moist meadows, especially near water, in woodland and the northern slopes of mountain ranges. Generally it prefers some shade. There are many named geographical variants, which have given rise to a host of subspecies, the most important of which will be briefly described. The primrose-type leaves form loose rosettes, upright at flowering, but later forming an open flat rosette. The sulphur yellow flowers are carried in elegant one sided heads on 6in(15cm) stems. There is considerable confusion between *Primula elatior,* the oxlip, and the naturally occurring hybrid between *Primula veris* and *Primula vulgaris,* known as the False Oxlip.

Primula elatior subsp. elatior: is the commonest form as described above.

Primula elatior subsp. leucophylla: has leaves which narrow more at the base.

Primula elatior subsp. cordifolia: is a smaller plant with heart-shaped leaves.

CULTIVATION: It is an easy plant to grow in the garden, preferring some shade and a good rich moist soil.

PROPAGATION: By splitting established lumps, or from seed. Do try to get wild collected seed, as often that collected in gardens will not be pure. It is so disappointing to raise a batch of seedlings to flowering size only to find they consist of a selection of rather poor polyanthus types.

AVAILABILITY: Sometimes available from the specialist nurseries, or from the seed lists.

Primula juliae:

Discovered in the south-eastern Caucasus in 1900/1901 by Madame Julia Ludovikovna Mlokossjewicz, and plants were sent to the Oxford Botanic Garden by Professor Kusnetzof of the Dorpat Botanic Garden. It first flowered in 1911. In the wild it is to be found growing between rocks dripping with water and even under waterfalls in mountainous forests.

It is a small plant that dies back to little resting buds in winter, from which in early spring the small reddish green shiny leaves unfurl. These leaves are heart-shaped with narrow stems, and act as a good foil to the succession of bright purple flowers, with a yellowish eye and well separated petals.

The importance of this little primula to the gardens of today cannot be too highly stressed. It introduced a good rich purple into the breeding of primroses, and the many lovely hybrids that it fathered or mothered enhance our modern gardens.

CULTIVATION: It is a relatively easy plant to grow, only requiring a moist soil and a little shade, but, because of its small size a select peaty, shady pocket in the rock garden, or even at the front of the peat bed would be advisable. *Primula juliae* makes a lovely pan for the alpine house, and a fairly peaty compost is suitable. Do not overfeed with high nitrogen feeds or leaves will be produced to the exclusion of flowers.

PROPAGATION: As it spreads by means of underground runners it is easily divided, and the divisions are best established in pots before planting out.

AVAILABILITY: Occasionally available from specialist nurseries, though not as often as desired.

Primula megaseaefolia:

To be found in north-east Turkey near the Black Sea in moist shady gullies amongst thick shrubs. Small heads of pink flowers above rounded stalked leaves.

CULTIVATION: Careful treatment in the alpine house, using the standard Auriculastrum compost. Shading recommended in summer.

AVAILABILITY: Very rare in cultivation, seed lists are the best chance.

Primula renifolia:

Only discovered in the late 1970s and comes from the western end of the Caucasus. It grows in rocky cracks near the tree line, and is similar to a smaller version of *Primula megaseaefolia.* Each stem carries six to ten relatively large, 1in (2.5cm) diameter, pale blue flowers above a neat rosette of leaves.

CULTIVATION: Alpine house, Auriculastrum compost, moist in winter and increase watering when growth starts in March.

AVAILABILITY: Very rare in cultivation. Try the seed lists.

Primula veris:

The endearing cowslip is one of the most widespread of all the primulas. It prefers drier conditions than the primrose, and is to be found throughout most of Europe and into Asia. The flowers are usually bright yellow, but orange and even reddish forms are sometimes found.

Four sub-species are recognised:

Primula veris subsp. canescens: Distinguished by the underside of the leaves being greyish with very fine hairs and the flower being open bell-shaped. It is found in the lowland of southern Europe.

Primula veris subsp. columnae: This mountain form from southern Europe and Turkey has white undersides to the leaves, and an almost flat flower.

Primula veris subsp. macrocalyx: This has the largest flowers, which are usually orange, and comes from south-eastern Russia through to Asia.

Primula veris subsp. veris: This is the main form and is to be found in Britain and the rest of northern Europe. The flowers are bright deep yellow with a small orange mark near the base of each petal and they vary in shape from almost flat to bell like.

CULTIVATION: An easy vigorous plant, requiring only a soil that does not become too dry. It is rather large for the rockery, but could be incorporated near the base. A lovely plant for the mixed border, under shrubs or trees. The coloured forms today lack the delicacy of the pure wild species, but they are thoroughly recommended. The range of colours, from yellow through orange to bright red and russets is eyecatching, and they are even more attractive planted in drifts of mixed colours where space allows.

PROPAGATION: Seed is available from the commercial seed companies, though it does tend to need the action of frost and rain before it will germinate, and often germination does not occur until the second spring after sowing. Good colour forms can be easily split in spring after flowering.

AVAILABILITY: Fairly readily available as plants or seed, sometimes stocked by garden centres, or specialist nurseries.

Primula vulgaris (acaulis):

Our well loved native wild primrose, preferring open woodland and shady banks, especially if moist. It occurs over the whole of Britain and Ireland, and most of southern Europe, except Spain. It is only slightly variable in nature, considering the wide area over which it occurs, but there appears to be a larger, more vigorous form to be found in the Devon/Cornwall region. The flowers are usually of the light creamy yellow that is so well known, but there are reports of a purple form from Wales and Northumberland and Durham. There is also a pink form still in existence in the remoter parts of north Yorkshire that strongly resembles *Primula vulgaris sibthorpii*. The most important subspecies are:

Primula vulgaris subsp. balearica: A white fragrant form from the mountains of Majorca.

Primula vulgaris subsp. heterochroma: A rare subspecies from around the Caspian sea in northern Iran, which can have rose, purple, violet, azure blue or yellow flowers.

Primula vulgaris subsp. sibthorpii: Occurs in eastern Europe, this subspecies is usually mauve pink, but there are white, rose, purple and crimson forms. It has been known for nearly three hundred years and is the parent of many of the coloured primroses.

Primula vulgaris subsp. vulgaris: The common form as described previously.

The subspecies have been of great importance in the development of modern primroses, especially *Primula vulgaris sibthorpii* as it introduced colours other than yellow.

CULTIVATION: All primroses need a good rich, moisture retentive soil, and they revel in the light shade cast by deciduous trees. In very hot dry summers they can become almost completely dormant, the large leaves of spring dying away almost completely to tight resting buds, which after the autumn rains will start to sprout new leaves, and even the odd flower, and so carry on until spring when there will be a great amount of growth. The flowers can carry on coming for weeks, especially if dead headed regularly.

PROPAGATION: By splitting, usually after flowering in May, or in September. It is not worth collecting the seed as they will probably have crossed with other primrose/polyanthus cultivars/hybrids.

AVAILABILITY: The wild primrose is usually only available from a few specialist nurseries.

12
The Vernales Section: Its Cultivars and Hybrids

Primroses and cowslips had been grown for many years for their medicinal properties rather than garden decoration, and it was not until 1665 that John Rea first mentioned the coloured forms. They were obviously of foreign origin, and mainly of assorted red shades. It is thought that these were derived from *Primula vulgaris sibthorpii* (which was then called *Primula vulgaris rubra*). The introduction of the blue colours seems likely to have come from a blue *Primula vulgaris subsp. heterochroma*.

During the reign of Elizabeth I the curious sports of the primrose and cowslip were avidly collected, 'Jack in the Green', 'Hose in Hose' and various other curiosities were described in the literature of the period, and many are still grown today in some private collections, and at least one nursery stocks an interesting selection.

In areas where both primroses (*Primula vulgaris*) and cowslips (*Primula veris*) grow in close proximity they will hybridise to give the False Oxlip, which is believed to be the parent of the polyanthus of today, rather than the true oxlip (*Primula elatior*). The origins of the coloured polyanthus are rather more obscure but it seems to be generally accepted that they are the result of crossing red cowslips with the primrose, or red primroses with the cowslip.

Primula vulgaris was one of the earliest recorded plants in gardens, and was grown and loved for hundreds of years, though it unfortunately fell by the wayside in the wars, when the population of Britain grew food instead of plants. The advent of houses with smaller gardens and the decrease in availability of farmyard manure also led to the decline of the primrose – the dry impoverished soil of many modern gardens is not a suitable environment for the cultivars and hybrids of the primrose. Nowadays these lovely plants are becoming more widely grown as gardeners are becoming more willing to take the extra care needed for these heralds of spring.

The discovery and introduction of *Primula juliae* attracted little attention at first, and then it was discovered that this little charmer hybridised very readily with the other members of the Vernales section. German and Austrian growers were producing many interesting hybrids by 1920, and many of these were named. *Primula* 'Wanda' was the first hybrid of major significance, and the majority of the named primrose-type cultivars and hybrids bear some *Primula juliae* blood.

Many of these old primroses were grown in Ireland, and because of the cooler and moister climate they could flourish with less care than is needed in English gardens. Hence several of the old varieties have been found in old Irish gardens and re-introduced to England, and there are probably many more waiting to be rediscovered.

The advent of the primrose as a pot plant, with its huge flowers, has meant that many gardeners desire equally large flowered cultivars for the garden. It should be realised that the breeding of these large flowered forms has led to a decrease in both hardiness and longevity. The varieties listed in this chapter are good garden plants, and the use of primulas and polyanthus as pot plants for the house will be discussed in chapter 17.

The majority of the following varieties are reasonably easy to grow. Like their parents they prefer some shade and a rich moist soil that is not waterlogged. Some varieties are considerably more amenable than others, and this will be mentioned in the descriptions. It should be realised that most of the primroses and allied plants are less hardy in pots than they are in the ground. This is believed to be due to frozen compost expanding as the temperature drops, and, because the pots are not flexible and do not allow the frozen compost to expand outwards, it is the fleshy roots that are smashed to a pulp.

As the diagram shows, the primrose has a very short main stem buried deep in the leaves so it is not normally seen. In hot weather this main stem can become longer, so that the primrose can look very like a polyanthus. This characteristic is possessed by all the primrose cultivars and hybrids, including the doubles.

SEASONAL CULTIVATION

SPRING: Is the time to enjoy the plants, and removing the dead heads will encourage more flowers. Occasionally mar-

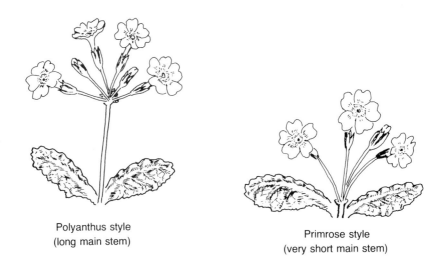

Polyanthus style
(long main stem)

Primrose style
(very short main stem)

Diagram showing difference between primrose-type and polyanthus-type.

auding slugs will decide that primrose flowers are a delicacy, and will happily eat every bloom in sight during the night– usually those on the plant that has been earmarked to grace the show bench. Slug pellets are helpful, or even the preparations that are watered in. Many growers have problems with birds, who especially love the yellow flowers. The best solution is a cat! Failing that there are many bird scarers on the market, or black cotton stretched over small twigs is very effective, the very weak cotton used for tacking is the safest, there is less danger of the birds becoming tangled. After flowering is the best time to split established clumps.

SUMMER: In times of severe drought and high temperatures keep a careful watch. A good soaking once a week will help, as will shading–the green shade netting loosely draped over the plants, though unsightly, is very effective. In a cool wet summer the plants can be left to their own devices, and will prosper. Watch out for caterpillars, and a good systemic insecticide is very effective.

AUTUMN: Any dry or dead leaves can be removed, as can any excessive build up of dead leaves from nearby trees. A few leaves will do no harm, but too many can cause rot.

WINTER: Look forward to spring, and enjoy the occasional early flowers that appear in mild spells.

PROPAGATION

SPLITTING: It is safest to split plants in May, after they have
finished flowering, the exact time will vary with the season,
and the variety. Established clumps are usually easy to split
but occasionally one will have very thick underground stems
that defy all efforts to tease them apart – a strong knife, such as
a carving knife, and a sawing action will soon remedy the
problem. Often the newly split plants are replanted directly
into the garden, in which case it is advisable to shade them and
keep them well watered until they are re-established. Sometimes it is easier for the gardener to pot them and they can then
be kept in a cool, shady place and inspected regularly. The size
of the pot depends on the size of the plant. It is sensible to
prune the roots to about 3in (7cm) long, using a sharp pair of
scissors, secateurs or a knife – this helps promote new,
healthy root growth. Sometimes the roots are found to be
brown and rotten in places, and any roots like this must be cut
right back to white healthy roots.

DESCRIPTIVE LIST OF PRIMROSES, POLYANTHUS, CULTIVARS AND HYBRIDS

(Excluding double primroses)

Primula x pruhociniana covers all the hybrids between *Primula
juliae* and other members of the Vernales section.

Primrose habit describes plants where the stem actually
holding the individual flower apparently comes from within
the leaf rosette; Polyanthus habit describes plants that have a
main stem carrying a head of flowers on individual stems;
Hose in hose describes plants where there are two flowers
one within the other, likened to two pairs of stockings, hence
the name; and Jack in the green describes a flower that is
surrounded by a ruff of green leaves, one to each petal
generally.

The distinction between hybrids and cultivars is somewhat
confused, and it is important to remember that hybrids and
selected forms do not breed true from seed.

All the hybrids and cultivars listed in this chapter flower
between March and May, often with the bonus of a smaller
flush of flowers in the autumn.

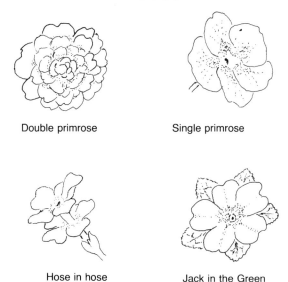

Double primrose   Single primrose

Hose in hose   Jack in the Green

Different primrose types.

'Barrowby Gem' (Polyanthus type):   Clear yellow flowers with a small greenish centre, very fragrant, and flowers from February to May.
AVAILABILITY: Rarely from specialist nurseries, but beware, as it does not breed true from seed and there have been several instances in recent years of other yellow polyanthus being sold under this name.
'Beamish Foam' (Polyanthus habit):   Pink flowers flushed with yellow, fairly early flowering and vigorous.
AVAILABILITY: Occasionally from specialist nurseries.
'Betty Green' (Primrose habit):   One of the early Dutch *P. pruhociniana* hybrids, crimson with a yellow eye. Some of the plants for sale under this name are not 'Betty Green'.
AVAILABILITY: Occasionally from the specialist nurseries.
'Blue Horizon' (Primrose habit):   Mid-blue with a yellow eye, and believed to be a sport from *Primula* 'Wanda'.
AVAILABILITY: Rare, but still present in private collections.
'Blue Riband' (Primrose habit):   A good blue primrose with a characteristic red tinge in the centre.
AVAILABILITY: Stocked by several specialist nurseries.
'Blutenkissen' ('Crimson Cushion') (*Primula* x *pruhociniana*): Large rich crimson flowers above characteristic rounded leaves, indicating the relationship to *Primula juliae*.
AVAILABILITY: Occasionally from specialist nurseries.

'Buckland Wine' (*Primula* x *pruhociniana*):   An old, very hardy variety of primrose habit with bronzed leaves and deep wine crimson flowers, each with a golden centre, and flowering in April.
AVAILABILITY: Occasionally from specialist nurseries.
'Cherry' (Polyanthus habit):   An old variety, and as the polyanthus stems are often so short as to be hidden by the leaves it is sometimes included with the primroses. The flowers are a bright cherry red, and the plant has a neat habit.
AVAILABILITY: From several specialist nurseries.
'Cowichan Polyanthus Duckyls Red':   A selected 'Cowichan'. The strong 10in (25cm) high stems carry good heads of rich scarlet red flowers with no yellow eye, and the slight stencilled lines near the centre enhance the effect. A lovely vigorous plant for the garden.
AVAILABILITY: From several specialist nurseries.
'Craven Gem' (Polyanthus habit):   A small delicate looking plant, very similar to 'Lady Greer' with heads of small cream flowers, and is equally vigorous. Appears to have some *Primula juliae* blood.
AVAILABILITY: Occasionally from the specialist nurseries.
'Crispii' (Primrose habit):   Described as being similar to *Primula vulgaris sibthorpii,* with mauve pink flowers, and slightly later flowering.
AVAILABILITY: Only in private collections.
'David Green' (Primrose habit):   Deep red eyeless flowers contrasting well with the bright green leaves.
AVAILABILITY: Occasionally from the specialist nurseries.
'Dorothy' (Polyanthus habit):   Similar to 'Lady Greer', but much smaller, and the petals have a delicately frilled edge.
AVAILABILITY: Occasionally from the specialist nurseries.
'Dr Mary' (Primrose habit):   Magenta pink with purple foliage.
AVAILABILITY: From at least one specialist nursery.
'Dr Molly' (Primrose habit):   Very similar to the above but the leaves are less green.
AVAILABILITY: From at least one specialist nursery.
'E.R. Janes' (Primrose habit):   The pink flushed orange (sometimes described as a tomato colour) flowers are freely produced over a long period, including a good autumn flush. It was bred by crossing *Primula* 'Wanda' with *Primula vulgaris*.
AVAILABILITY: Surprisingly only in private collections, but hopefully it will reappear in the lists of the specialist nurseries.

'Garryard Enchantress': Along with several other names under the 'Garryard' flag these are wonderful plants, and are virtually unavailable, but the occasional variety is to be found in private collections.

'Garryard Guinivere' (Polyanthus habit): A most beautiful plant of polyanthus habit, the large heads of soft pink flowers contrasting well with the bronze purple foliage. A vigorous and easy plant under the right conditions.
AVAILABILITY: Readily from the specialist nurseries.

'Garryard Lopen Red' See under 'Lopen Red'.

'Gloria' (*Primula* x *pruhociniana*): A 'Wanda' type, bright crimson with a clear yellow eye.
AVAILABILITY: From at least one specialist nursery.

'Gloriosa' (*Primula* x *pruhociniana*): This could be described as a larger, looser *Primula* 'Wanda'.
AVAILABILITY: Rarely from the specialist nurseries.

'Groeneken's Glory' (Primrose habit) (*Primula* x *pruhociniana*): A compact tolerant variety that originated in Holland, with soft mauve pink flowers, and a distinctive greenish yellow eye.
AVAILABILITY: Listed by several of the specialist nurseries.

'Iris Mainwaring' (Primrose habit): A compact and popular plant, the small mauve blue flowers are attractively flushed red and sit just above the bright green leaves.
AVAILABILITY: Occasionally available from the specialist nurseries.

'Kinlough Beauty' (Polyanthus habit) (*Primula* x *pruhociniana*): A very dwarf and free flowering plant of polyanthus habit, with rich salmon pink flowers, each petal carrying a lighter stripe down the centre.
AVAILABILITY: Reasonably easy from the specialist nurseries.

'Lady Greer' (Polyanthus habit) (*Primula* x *pruhociniana*): Neat green foliage, the leaves being more reminiscent of *Primula juliae* than the primrose, and short strong stems bearing large heads of small cream funnel-shaped flowers, that are lightly flushed pink on ageing. A lovely delicate plant that will thrive under varying conditions. One of the hardiest varieties, and very amenable to pot culture.
AVAILABILITY: From specialist nurseries, and occasionally from the better garden centres.

'Lambrook Pink' and **'Lambrook Peach':** The 'Lambrook' series were bred by Marjorie Fish, and are mainly of polyanthus habit.

AVAILABILITY: Both these varieties are sometimes offered by the specialist nurseries.

'Lingwood Beauty': Flowers of rich compact red of the small polyanthus-type like 'Lady Greer'.

AVAILABILITY: Occasionally from the specialist nurseries.

'Lizzie (or Lize) Green' (Primrose habit): The true plant should be bright red, but many of the plants available with this name are often 'Betty Green'.

AVAILABILITY: Sometimes listed by the specialist nurseries.

'McWatts Claret' (*Primula* x *pruhociniana*): Described as a dusky wine colour, sometimes said to be nearer the colour of the sediment of the claret than the actual wine. Small polyanthus type.

AVAILABILITY: Rarely offered by nurseries.

'McWatts Cream' (Polyanthus habit) (*Primula* x *pruhociniana*): Very similar to 'Lady Greer'.

AVAILABILITY: Rarely available.

'Mrs McGillvray': Violet coloured Primrose.

AVAILABILITY: Occasionally from the specialist nurseries.

'Perle von Bottrop' (Primrose habit): This plant of German origin has dark purple flowers.

AVAILABILITY: Rarely from the specialist nurseries.

'Old Port' (*Primula* x *pruhociniana*): The plants in cultivation under this name appear indistinguishable from 'Tawny Port' and 'Garryard Crimson'. A lovely plant with incredibly dark leaves and very rich dark purple flowers. Well worth growing.

AVAILABILITY: Occasionally from the specialist nurseries.

'Queen of Whites' *(Primula* x *pruhociniana):* Very similar to 'Snow White' and 'Snow Cushion', but this is the largest of the three white flowered varieties and is very attractive.

AVAILABILITY: Occasionally from the specialist nurseries.

'Snow Cushion' (*schneekissen*): A very neat plant with light green rounded leaves and masses of tiny white flowers on short stems. This is the smallest of the three listed white forms, and spreads by means of underground stems.

AVAILABILITY: Occasionally from the specialist nurseries.

'Snow White' (*Primula* x *pruhociniana*): A charming plant of primrose habit, very dwarf and free flowering with pure white flowers.

AVAILABILITY: Occasionally from the specialist nurseries.

'Tawny Port' (*Primula* x *pruhociniana*): Most of the plants in circulation with this name are identical to 'Old Port', but Jack Wemyss-Cooke in his book *Primulas Old and New* describes it as a polyanthus-type, with dusky port wine coloured flowers and dainty bronze leaves.

AVAILABILITY: Occasionally from specialist nurseries.

'Tipperary Purple' (Primrose habit):   An old Irish Jack in the Green, that became rare here but was re-introduced by John Main in the 1970s. It is a reasonably vigorous variety, with soft mauve pink flowers, each surrounded by the characteristic leafy ruff.

AVAILABILITY: Not common, but is in cultivation; try the specialist growers or the private collectors.

'Wanda' (*Primula* x *pruhociniana*):   The best known, and also the easiest. Rich dark purple red flowers on slender stems, with a little yellow eye. In a mild winter it is seldom without a flower from late February through to May. In winter it goes back to tight resting buds. After the introduction of *Primula juliae* at the beginning of this century many charming hybrids were raised, the good tempered *Primula* 'Wanda' being the most famous. It will stand a remarkable amount of neglect and is often to be seen giving vivid purple sheets of flowers in early spring. Unlike many of the other primrose types, this variety always flowers more freely and longer when grown in full sun. In the shade there is a tendency to produce large leaves rather than flowers. Beware of imitations, there is now a seed strain, *Primula* 'Wanda' *F1 hybrids,* which is in general commerce. Nurserymen being amongst the busiest of people tend to label the plants *P.* 'Wanda'.

AVAILABILITY: Often from the specialist nurseries.

'Wanda Hose in Hose' (*Primula* x *pruhociniana*):   A pretty little curiosity of identical colour and form as *Primula*'Wanda', but with one flower fitted inside another.

AVAILABILITY: Rarely from the specialist nurseries.

'Wanda Improved' (*Primula* x *pruhociniana*):   Reputedly has slightly larger flowers. There are many plants in cultivation as 'Wanda' that are slightly different, and this could be due to seed dropping between the plants, and the seedlings that germinated being very similar and thus getting mixed up with the *Primula* 'Wanda' stocks.

AVAILABILITY: Only in private collections.

'Wisley Red' (*Primula* x *pruhociniana*):   A very fine variety, with intense red flowers and dark foliage. A plant that is probably more suited to drier areas, as it seems to take exception to too much rain in winter.

AVAILABILITY: Occasionally available.

'Viridis':   The old green primrose was mentioned in Eliza-

bethan times, and is still in cultivation, but is not a strong grower.
AVAILABILITY: Only in private collections.

THE GOLD LACE POLYANTHUS

'Gold Lace Polyanthus': The first proper description of the gold lace polyanthus was in Thomas Hogg's book on the Florists' flowers in 1823, and by the middle of the century was accepted as a Florists' flower, and was being bred to perfect the symmetry of its blooms. The gold lace then fell out of favour, probably because of the decline of home industries and the advent of the Industrial Revolution. The natural style of gardening as advocated by William Robinson and Gertrude Jekyll in mid-Victorian times also caused Florists' flowers to become less popular. It was not until the last thirty years that the gold lace began to regain its popularity. This was primarily due to the work of the northern Florists, especially Mr H. V. Calvert of Wakefield and Mr J. Ollerenshaw of Hyde who have developed the strains in recent years. At present Mr L. Kaye of Stocksbride is producing a very fine strain, that adheres closely to the standards laid down by the Florists, and plants from this strain are available from a few of the specialist nurseries. There are classes for the gold lace polyanthus at the primula shows in the spring.
CULTIVATION: In the garden a good rich soil in light shade is to be preferred, and a north-facing position with a little early morning sun is ideal. Some Florists grow their gold lace in pots all year, giving them cool shade in the summer, and bringing them into the greenhouse in autumn where they will remain until after flowering in April and May.
PROPAGATION: Outside the plants need splitting annually, this can be done after flowering in spring, or in September. The newly split plants can be either replanted *in situ*, or established in pots before planting out. It is not advisable to leave the young plants in pots over the winter unless they can be protected.
    Many growers replace their plants every year. The plants need to be hand pollinated, taking care only to breed from the best forms. The seed should be ripe by June–July, and can be sown immediately on a peat based compost and kept in shade at about 60°F (15°C) until it germinates. Then the seedlings should be grown on in light shade until they are large enough

171

0   1   2in(5cm)

The classical gold lace polyanthus.

to handle comfortably. If there are problems finding anywhere cool enough to germinate the seed, don't forget that it can be germinated in the dark – a cellar or pantry is ideal.

AVAILABILITY: Seed is often available, but it is better to start with plants from a recognised strain, such as Kaye's Strain, which is available from a few of the specialist nurseries.

'Silver Lace Polyanthus':   Held in very low regard by the growers of the Florists flowers, fit only for the rubbish heap. They do not conform to the standards, so very few are grown. However, if ever obtainable, they are attractive and unique plants for the garden.

MODERN SEED STRAINS

Barnhaven Seeds have been the suppliers of an excellent range of completely hardy primroses and polyanthus for many years, but, at the time of writing this book the owner of Barnhaven, Jared Sinclair, is retiring. Hopefully another dedicated grower will take over and the Barnhaven strains will continue. When buying primulas, either as plant or seed, the name Barnhaven has been synonymous with both quality and hardiness for years, and many of the beautiful double primroses that have been micropropagated are Barnhaven stock. The Cowichan strains of polyanthus have also been improved and distributed by Mr Sinclair.

The Barnhaven strains include:

Barnhaven Primroses: Lovely strains in many colours, bred for hardiness as well as quality of flower.

Cowichan Polyanthus: These beautiful and vigorous plants have been improved and distributed by Barnhaven of Brigsteer, and are distinguished by the lack of an eye. There are strains of yellow, blue, red and other rich shades, and they are thoroughly recommended.

Elizabethan Primroses: A strain that includes the curiosities that were collected in the reign of Elizabeth I. Jack in the Green, hose in hose and a range of other absurdities.

New Juliana Polyanthus: These miniature plants are a joy in spring.

Silver Dollar Polyanthus: Very hardy, striking colours in a wide range.

Victorian Polyanthus: Unusual shades, the large flowers are often ruffled.

CULTIVATION: They are all hardy vigorous plants, only needing a good rich, moisture retentive soil and a modicum of shade in the summer months.
PROPAGATION: As for any other of the Vernales section.
AVAILABILITY: A few of the specialist nurseries list these lovely strains.

Most of the seed catalogues also include a small selection of hardy primroses and polyanthus. The *Crescendo Strain* is exceptionally hardy, but the colour range is not exceptional; the new *Primula Wanda Hybrids* are very striking, with a colour range including reds, purples and blues, often with bronzed foliage.

The polyanthus and primroses that are sold by the millions as house plants can be used to brighten the greenhouse in the winter months, and it is always worth planting them in the garden when they have outgrown their usefulness as household decoration. A very severe winter may cause a few casualties, but normally they will grow and prosper for many years.

DOUBLE PRIMROSES

The beautiful double primroses have been grown in British gardens since the sixteenth century. They were much easier to grow in the cottage gardens of yesteryear, as they received ample supplies of organic manure, and plenty of shade afforded by the taller plants. Johnson's *Gardeners' Dictionary*, originally published in 1846, and updated in 1917 gives a fascinating insight into the cultivars of *Primula vulgaris* that were in cultivation around that time – mostly double primroses were included with only a few coloured primroses.

The doubles fell into disfavour in the war years, presumably because all the available land was used for growing food, and with the advent of the smaller suburban gardens they became less commonly grown. Although easy and vigorous when planted in a rich soil with some shade, and split regularly, if planted in a hot dry sunny border they gradually fade away. In recent years they have regained much of their popularity, due in no small part to the efforts of the micropropagation firms, who having managed to perfect the techniques whereby thousands of plants could be propagated identical to the original, were able to release sufficient plants into commerce to enable virtually everyone to grow a representative selection.

Further details on micropropagation, or tissue culture, is included in chapter 3.

In double primroses the reproductive parts of the plant have sported at some time in the past to produce extra petals, and degrees of doubleness vary considerably between varieties. It also depends on culture, and an under-fed plant will often produce single flowers, as will a young plant that has recently been split. The last flowers to open in some varieties will return to being single, which can be useful in breeding.

The varieties described will be restricted to those that are available commercially, though perhaps not every year.

CULTIVATION

To achieve the best results it is essential that every care is taken to give these beautiful and special plants the conditions necessary to thrive. They will quickly show their unhappiness in the wrong place by becoming stunted, with very little root to anchor them into the ground and will then fade and die. They require a good, humus-rich soil. If at all possible a thick layer of well rotted farmyard manure 9in(25cm) below ground level will work wonders. They like a certain amount of shade. The primroses all hate a dry soil in the summer months, and equally dislike a waterlogged soil in winter. A good rich soil, with plenty of humus, that will remain pleasantly moist all year, with shelter from the sun at the hottest part of the day, is ideal.

It is also very important that they are split every year, or at the most every two years. If the crowns are allowed to become congested they seem to starve themselves and fade away. They are gross feeders and they can often exhaust a soil. This is often referred to as Primrose Sickness, but whether it is due to a build up of disease in the soil, or the essential minerals becoming out of balance is undecided. It is sensible to move plants if they cease to thrive in a certain position. Some gardeners are fortunate to have ideal conditions to grow the double primroses, others have to struggle, but the plants are worth every effort, and with a little care and thought the majority of gardens will yield a suitable corner.

If the gardener wishes to enjoy these lovely plants in pots in the cold greenhouse, it must be remembered that they will stand very little frost when pot grown. It is better to dig the plants out of the garden in February, and pot into a large enough pot, keeping the root ball intact, and filling the pot up with peat and John Innes compost. After flowering they should only be split if they are large enough, and replanted in the garden. Primroses are vigorous plants that do not appreciate the confines of a pot, and should only be pot grown out of necessity.

Seasonal cultivation is the same as discussed for the single primroses earlier in this chapter.

PROPAGATION

SPLITTING: The division of established crowns after flowering is usual, but late August, when the weather is becoming cooler and wetter can often yield good results. Spring splitting can cause problems if May and June are very hot and dry. You can prevent this by laying some of the green netting shade material over the split plants which can protect them from the worst of the sun's heat, and a good watering in the evening until they have grown into proper established plants will also help.
LEAF CUTTINGS: Many of the primroses can be propagated from leaf cuttings. (See chapter 3 for full details of this method).
SEED: Barnhaven of Brigsteer produce double primrose seed, which would yield a reasonable percentage of double flowered plants.

DESCRIPTIVE LIST OF DOUBLE PRIMROSES

'Alan Robb':   Pale orange, and a good new variety from the Barnhaven stable, which is compact with slightly bronzed neat foliage.
AVAILABILITY: Micropropagated, and stocked by many specialist nurseries.
'Alba Plena':   The good very old double white.
AVAILABILITY: Occasionally available from specialist nurseries.
'April Rose':   A good rich dark pink, and one of the Barnhaven seedlings.
AVAILABILITY: Micropropagated and stocked by many specialist nurseries.

The 'Bon Accord' double primroses are a group of double primroses raised at the Cocker Brother's Nurseries near Aberdeen about 1900. Some varieties are still in cultivation, and are more likely to be found in the Scottish nurseries, but several appear to have been lost. Some exhibit the primrose habit of growth, whereas others have short polyanthus type stems. The flowers are all of a similar form, being fairly flat and symmetrical.

'Bon Accord Cerise':   A reasonably reliable variety having small, very symmetrical deep rose flowers.
AVAILABILITY: Occasionally from specialist nurseries.
'Bon Accord Elegance':   A reputedly difficult variety, with beautiful large rosy lilac flowers flecked with white.
AVAILABILITY: Occasionally from specialist nurseries.
'Bon Accord Gem':   A strong growing variety with rose flowers shaded with lilac. Unlike the other double primroses this variety does not need dividing every year, but flowers more freely the second year.
AVAILABILITY: Occasionally from specialist nurseries.
'Bon Accord Lavender':   An easy compact plant with large rosy lavender flowers.
AVAILABILITY: Occasionally from specialist nurseries.
'Bon Accord Lilac':   Short polyanthus stems bearing rosy lilac flowers.
AVAILABILITY: Occasionally from specialist nurseries.
'Bon Accord Purple':   Polyanthus stems bearing deep purple flowers, the underside of the petals being a rich crimson.
AVAILABILITY: Occasionally from specialist nurseries.
'Captain Blood':   Blood-red, good double flowers which are vigorous and easy.
AVAILABILITY: Micropropagated and stocked by many specialist nurseries.
'Chevithorne Pink':   Raised in the 1930s. It is of polyanthus habit, late flowering, with orchid pink flowers, that fade rapidly to mauve. It is very hardy and vigorous and needs dividing annually.
AVAILABILITY: Occasionally from specialist nurseries.
'Chocolate Soldier':   A strange chocolate purple colour, with a delicate gold edging. One of those plants that inspire either love or hate at first glance.
AVAILABILITY: Micropropagated and stocked by many specialist nurseries.

'Corporal Baxter':   Described as scarlet, shading to crimson. Many of the rich reds about at present are very similar to the untutored eye.
AVAILABILITY: Micropropagated and stocked by many specialist nurseries.
'Crimson Beauty':   This is one of the beautiful double primroses from New Zealand that have been introduced and distributed by the Barkers of Hopleys Plants. This low growing, compact variety has deep red flowers and dark foliage.
AVAILABILITY: From the specialist nurseries.
'Dawn Ansell':   The well formed delicate pure white flower is surrounded by a classical 'in the green' ruff of leaves. One of the loveliest.
AVAILABILITY: Micropropagated and stocked by many specialist nurseries.
'Double Lilac':   *See* 'Lilacina Plena' and Quaker's Bonnets.
'Double Sulphur':   *See* 'Sulphurea Plena'.
'Ethel M. Dell:'   Described as a dusty, rosy pink.
AVAILABILITY: Micropropagated and stocked by many specialist nurseries.
'Eugene':   A lovely variety with mid blue flowers.
AVAILABILITY: Micropropagated and stocked by many specialist nurseries.
'Fife Yellow':   Yellow flowers which age to almost ochre. Its origins have been traced back to Fife in Scotland, hence the name.
AVAILABILITY: Stocked by at least one of the specialist nurseries.
'Freckles':   Dark red and spotted white.
AVAILABILITY: Micropropagated and stocked by many specialist nurseries.
'Granny Graham':   Described as cerise aging to purple with a white edging to the petals. In fact the colour is very reminiscent of *Primula* 'Wanda', and often traces of the yellow centre can be seen between the petals. The leaves also show evidence of *Primula juliae* blood in their shape and slightly bronzed appearance.
AVAILABILITY: Micropropagated and stocked by many specialist nurseries.
'Jubilee':   Another of the Hopley's introductions and very free flowering. The flowers varying in shade between pinks, purples and mauves.
AVAILABILITY: From the specialist nurseries.
'Ken Dearman':   The flowers are splashed irregularly in

shades of orange, yellow and copper, often with a trace of red. A lovely vigorous variety.

AVAILABILITY: Micropropagated and stocked by many specialist nurseries.

'Lilacina Plena' (Double lilac or Quaker's Bonnet): Dates back to the eighteenth century, and is thought by some authorities to be a double sport of *Primula vulgaris subsp. sibthorpii.* The soft lilac flowers are well formed. It is, in the right conditions, a vigorous, easy and free flowering variety.

AVAILABILITY: Micropropagated and stocked by many specialist nurseries.

'Lilian Harvey': Described as being pale pink edged ivory, but every plant seen with this name has been a rich bright cerise pink.

AVAILABILITY: Micropropagated and stocked by many specialist nurseries.

'Madame Pompadour': Believed to have originated in France early in the nineteenth century. It is a beautiful variety with rich, velvety, deep crimson flowers but is regarded as being temperamental, having a poor root system. Plenty of leaf mould and careful attention to watering at the end of the flowering season should yield the best results.

AVAILABILITY: From at least one of the specialist nurseries.

'Marianne Davy': Well formed cream flowers.

AVAILABILITY: Micropropagated and stocked by many specialist nurseries.

'Marie Crousse': An old variety, believed to be of French origin, which gained an Award of Merit from the Royal Horticultural Society in 1882. It is a good vigorous variety, with mauve flowers splashed with white, though it is said that the original was violet splashed with ivory, and that the mauve form is a variant.

AVAILABILITY: Micropropagated and stocked by many specialist nurseries.

'Miss Indigo': A beautiful and distinct form, being a really dark blueish purple, with a fine silvery white lacing to the petals. One of the Barnhaven Stable.

AVAILABILITY: Micropropagated, and stocked by many specialist nurseries.

'Olive Wyatt': Rich dark cerise pink.

AVAILABILITY: Micropropagated and stocked by many specialist nurseries.

'Our Pat': A seedling found amongst some *P. juliae* hybrids in Newry, Northern Ireland in 1935. It has small neat amethyst

violet flowers, with bronzy green foliage. A good, relatively easy variety. Sometimes described as a double *Primula* 'Wanda'.
AVAILABILITY: Stocked by a few specialist nurseries.
'Peach':   This Hopleys variety has distinctive rich peachy apricot flowers.
AVAILABILITY: From at least one of the specialist nurseries.
'Penlan Cream':   Raised by Dr Cecil Jones in 1959.
AVAILABILITY: Rarely from specialist nurseries.
'Prince Silverwings':   A very old and famous double of polyanthus habit, thought to have originated in Ireland. The semi-double crimson violet flowers are lightly flecked with white and edged with silver, a golden centre can be seen at the base of the petals, and the occasional single flower bears pollen and can be used in breeding.
AVAILABILITY: From at least one specialist nursery.
'Quaker's Bonnet':   The popular name for 'Lilacina Plena'.
'Red Paddy':   Otherwise known as 'Sanguinea plena', it has small rose red flowers edged with silver of almost perfect form. Another of Irish origin.
AVAILABILITY: Occasionally from the specialist nurseries.
'Red Velvet':   Red flowers and bright green leaves with a red margin. An easy vigorous variety introduced by Hopleys.
AVAILABILITY: From at least one of the specialist nurseries.
'Rhapsody':   A good free flowering mid–blue, the flowers are of similar form to 'Miss Indigo'. A Hopleys introduction.
AVAILABILITY: From at least one of the specialist nurseries.
'Rose O'Day':   Light rose red.
AVAILABILITY: Micropropagated and stocked by many specialist nurseries.
'Roy Cope':   A good vigorous red.
AVAILABILITY: Micropropagated and stocked by many specialist nurseries.
'Sue Jervis':   A strange shade of flesh pink, not a bright colour but has a certain charm.
AVAILABILITY: Occasionally from the specialist nurseries.
'Sulphurea Plena':   Possibly the oldest of the doubles, and a sport from *Primula vulgaris*. Thought to have been in cultivation since 1500.
AVAILABILITY: Rarely from the specialist nurseries.
'Sunshine Susie':   Rich bright golden yellow, thought by some to be too bright, and certainly needs careful placing or the vivid colour will detract from any other flowers in the vicinity. Vigorous and easy.

AVAILABILITY: Micropropagated and stocked by many specialist nurseries.

'Torchlight': Pale lemon flowers, compact and late flowering. Another Hopleys introduction.

AVAILABILITY: From at least one of the specialist nurseries.

'Val Horncastle': A lovely delicate pale primrose yellow with most attractive flowers.

AVAILABILITY: Micropropagated and stocked by many specialist nurseries.

Often double primroses are offered by colour alone, possibly Barnhaven seedlings. If the colour is attractive, do not hesitate: there are many beautiful plants in circulation that have never been named, but they are still extremely worthwhile.

13
The Primulas of America

The primulas from the New World show overlaps and similarities with both the Asiatics and the European Primulas. With the exception of *Primula parryi* they are fairly rare in cultivation as yet, but there are some very distinct and beautiful species for the cold greenhouse and several of the specialist nurseries are now listing a small selection of these demanding plants. A thorough search of the society seed lists should yield a few species. Ardent collectors should seriously consider joining the American Primrose Society, who boast a very fine seed distribution scheme.

DESCRIPTIVE PLANT LIST

Primula angustifolia (Section 26 Parryi):
Mainly to be found in Colorado and northern New Mexico, where it grows in dryish conditions in meadows and rocky slopes. The 2–4 flat lilac pink to purple red flowers have a bright yellow eye and are on stems of up to 4in (10cm). The narrow leaves curve inwards and are in loose upright rosettes. There is also a rare white form from New Mexico called *Primula angustifolia helenae*.
CULTIVATION: A pretty plant for careful culture in the alpine house, and an Auriculastrum compost is recommended.
PROPAGATION: Seed.
AVAILABILITY: Available from at least one specialist nursery, or try the seed lists.
Primula borealis (Section 19 Farinosae, subsection Eu-farinoasae):
A typical farinose primula. An attractive little plant found mainly on the shores of the Bering Straits, both in Asia and in North America. The heads of relatively large flowers are in shades from pink to lilac on stems 1–3in (2–7cm) in height. It is relatively short lived in cultivation, as are many of its close relatives.
CULTIVATION: Alpine house treatment in an Auriculastrum compost.

PROPAGATION: Seed.
AVAILABILITY: Try the seed lists.
Primula broadheadae:
Thought to be either a robust form of *Primula angustifolia* or a variant of *Primula cusickiana.*
Primula capillaris:
A close relative of *Primula angustifolia* from the mountains of Central Nevada, probably not in cultivation.
Primula comberi:
Probably a lilac flowered form of *Primula magellanica.*
Primula cuneifolia (Section 11 Cuneifolia):
A small plant which comes from the coasts of north-western America, north-eastern Asia, and northern Japan where it grows in wet meadows and rocky areas. The bright green leaves are a very distinctive wedge shape with the broad end of the wedge being toothed. The small loose heads of large dark rose to magenta flowers are on very short stems in the subspecies *Primula cuneifolia subsp. saxifragifolia,* but in the subspecies *Primula cuneifolia subsp. cuneifolia* the flower stems are taller, up to 12in(30cm) in height.
CULTIVATION: A distinctive and interesting plant for the alpine house. Requires the same treatment as the smaller members of the Auriculastrum section.
PROPAGATION: Careful splitting after flowering in spring; or by seed.
AVAILABILITY: Rarely offered by specialist nurseries. Seed often available in the seed lists.
Primula cusickiana (Section 26 Parryi):
A lovely plant from north-east Oregon and Idaho, where it grows in a variety of locations, from open woodland or wet meadows to stony slopes. From the loose upright rosette of leaves appears the 4in (10cm) stem which bears a loose head of up to four deep violet open bell-shaped flowers with a yellow, sometimes powdery eye. Earlier flowering than other American species.
CULTIVATION: Careful cultivation in the alpine house, using Auriculastrum compost, and plenty of water in the growing season. It is said to be a difficult plant in cultivation.
PROPAGATION: Seed.
AVAILABILITY: Try the seed lists.
Primula decipens (Section 19 Farinosae, subsection Eufarinosae):
Sometimes thought to be the same as *Primula magellanica.* This plant from southern South America forms compact rosettes

of silver farinose leaves, above which rise the sturdy 2–6in (5–15cm) stems with heads of pale pink yellow-eyed flowers.
CULTIVATION: Careful cultivation in the alpine house in a peaty, gritty compost. Similar treatment to *Primula scotica* is probably wisest, but it is not the easiest plant to keep in good health.
PROPAGATION: Seed if set; it is sensible to save some to ensure a continuity.
AVAILABILITY: Occasionally available from specialist nurseries, and has been labelled the 'Falkland Island Primrose'. Try the society seed lists.
Primula egaliksensis (Section 19 Farinosae, subsection Eufarinosae):
A fairly widespread species from the northern coasts of North America, with long stems and small flowers, likened to an unattractive relative of *Primula scandinavica*.
CULTIVATION: As for other small members of the Farinosae section, *see* chapter 5.
PROPAGATION: Seed.
AVAILABILITY: Try the society seed lists.
Primula ellisiae (Section 26 Parryi):
From moist crevices and cliffs in central New Mexico. It is a truly beautiful plant,that is often seen gracing the show benches. The tidy rosettes of long upright narrow leaves enhance the graceful stem bearing a loose head of bright violet to magenta flowers with a yellow eye. The petal colour often is shaded darker towards the eye giving a very distinctive appearance.
CULTIVATION: So far has settled well to cultivation in a cold greenhouse, using the Auriculastrum compost, with careful attention to watering in the spring and summer. It is a vigorous plant, so repot regularly. When it dies back for the winter it needs keeping almost dry.
PROPAGATION: Seed, or by very careful splitting after flowering.
AVAILABILITY: The society seed lists or sometimes the specialist nurseries.
Primula hunnewellii (Section 19 Farinosae, subsection Eufarinosae):
Found in an isolated location in the Grand Canyon, this species is closely related and very similar to *Primula specuicola*. Rarely if ever available.
Primula incana (Section 19 Farinosae, subsection Eufarinosae):

A small flowered relative of *Primula farinosa* with a wide distribution from eastern Alaska down to Colorado, and small pockets around Hudson Bay.

CULTIVATION: Safest in the alpine house, in a peaty, gritty compost.

PROPAGATION: Seed.

AVAILABILITY: Occasionally in the society seed lists.

Primula intercedens (Section 19 Farinosae, subsection Eu-farinosae):

Probably only a geographical variation of *Primula mistassinica* that is to be found on the shores of the Great Lakes in Canada and the United States. The main distinction being that the farina under the leaves is yellowish, as is the farina on the winter resting buds. For details of cultivation etc, follow *Primula mistassinica*.

Primula laurentiana (Section 19 Farinosae, subsection Eu-farinosae):

As would be expected from the name this species is to be found in the vicinity of the St Laurence River, around its estuary where it grows in marshy areas and on cliffs and stony hillsides. It is a variable species and in appearance is similar to *Primula farinosa*. The loose rosette of farinose leaves contrast with the heads of pinky lilac flowers on 6in (15cm) stems. One of the easiest of the American primulas to obtain and grow.

CULTIVATION: Safer in the alpine house, but will succeed in the open ground for a season or two.

PROPAGATION: It is advisable to save the seed, which it usually sets in quantity, for replacements.

AVAILABILITY: Occasionally to be found in the specialist nurseries' lists, or in the society seed lists.

Primula magellanica (Section 19 Farinosae, subsection Eu-farinosae):

From wet situations in southern South America and the Falkland Isles. One of the very few primulas to be found in the southern hemisphere. Another of the small relatives of *Primula farinosa,* with the flowers ranging from white through lilac to purple. It does reasonably well in cultivation, but do save any seed that is set for replacements. Probably synonymous with *Primula decipens* and *Primula comberi*.

CULTIVATION: For careful culture in the alpine house, in a peaty, gritty compost.

PROPAGATION: Seed.

AVAILABILITY: Try the specialist nurseries or the society seed lists.

185

Primula maguirei:
A close relative of *Primula cusickiana* and probably as lovely.
Primula mistassinica (Section 19 Farinosae, subsection Eu-farinosae):
Collected in 1792 near Lake Mistassini in Quebec, hence the name. It is to be found over a wide area of Canada and the north-eastern states of the United States, in moist areas in meadows, cliffs and lake shores. The slender 1–8in (2.5–20cm) stem carries a dense head of pink to lilac flowers that is often out of proportion to the tidy flat rosettes of leaves, which have a light coating of white farina on the undersides. A very small delicate plant that can make an attractive pan for the show bench. It requires careful treatment in the alpine house, remembering that it is probably short lived in cultivation and so it is essential to save any seed that is set. The true plant can be identified by the intense fragrance.
CULTIVATION: As for *Primula scotica,* careful treatment in the alpine house.
PROPAGATION: Seed.
AVAILABILITY: Search the society seed lists.
Primula nevadensis:
Another similar close relative of *Primula cusickiana.*
Primula nutans:
The new name for *Primula sibirica,* and is described in chapter 14. Note that the lovely Asiatic *Primula flaccida* was known as *Primula nutans* until quite recently.
Primula parryi (Section 26 Parryi):
A widespread species to be found locally in most of the mountainous areas of the western United States. It was introduced in 1856 and is reasonably established in cultivation. It is slightly reminiscent of a large loosely leaved *Primula rosea,* for although the flowers are a shade darker they are of a similar luminous pink. The leathery leaves are held in loose untidy rosettes, and the strong stems, up to 16in (40cm) high carry large loose heads of scented dark bright pink to reddish purple flowers with a yellowish eye.
CULTIVATION: As it is quite a large, vigorous plant it is better grown in the garden, ideally in the larger peat bed, and it will grow and flower well even in quite dense shade provided the root conditions are moist.
PROPAGATION: From seed, or carefully split large established clumps after flowering.
AVAILABILITY: Often available from specialist nurseries, or try the seed lists. It usually germinates well.

Primula rusbyi (Section 26 Parryi):
Mainly to be found in damp shady positions on rocky slopes high in the mountainous regions of south-east Arizona and south-west New Mexico. It is a lovely plant, closely allied to *Primula ellisiae,* though slightly smaller, and later flowering. The rose red through to purple flowers have a rich crimson ring surrounding the yellow eye, and are carried in a loose one sided head on a 2–8in (5–20cm) stem above a neat rosette of narrow leaves.
CULTIVATION: Same treatment as *Primula ellisiae,* remembering that it is a slower and smaller plant.
PROPAGATION: Seed.
AVAILABILITY: Try the seed lists, but be warned, it rarely sets seed in cultivation, and often *Primula ellisiae* is found masquerading under the name *Primula rusbyi.* It is also listed by at least one specialist nursery.

Primula specuicola (Section 19 Farinosae, subsection Eufarinosae):
To be found on cliffs in sun and shade in south-eastern Utah. Though related to *Primula farinosa* it is quite distinct. It is a small plant, up to 6in (15cm) high, with heads of violet, yellow-eyed flowers above rosettes of leaves that are thick with farina underneath. Rarely available, but try the seed lists.

Primula stricta:
Described in chapter 5.

Primula suffrutescens (Section 11 Cuneifolia):
Grows in rocky cracks in the Sierra Nevada in California. A very distinctive plant with almost shrubby rosettes of dull green, fleshy wedge-shaped leaves on branching stems, the flattish rose pink to purple red flowers can be up to 1in (2.5cm) across, and are carried in loose heads on 1–4in (2.5–10cm) stems. This lovely species was introduced in 1884, and has been found to be reasonably permanent, although it is not available commercially it is occasionally seen on the show benches. Well worth growing; try the seed lists.
CULTIVATION: Is said to be suitable for a select scree in the garden, but if only one plant is owned the alpine house would be safer, where an Auriculastrum compost is recommended.
PROPAGATION: By seed, or by cuttings; these are said to root well in summer.
AVAILABILITY: Rarely available from the specialist nurseries, but hopefully will be more readily available in the future.

Primula tschuktschorum (Section 25 Nivales):
From the areas bordering the Bering Straits, both in Asia and North America where it is found in wet meadows and on the banks of streams. There are two varieties described, *Primula tschuktschorum subsp. tschuktschorum* being the more delicate, and *Primula tschuktschorum subsp. arctica* the more common. A lovely little primula, up to 4in (10cm) high, with a small head of relatively large violet to purple red flowers, the typically nivalid leaves form neat upright rosettes. Well worth growing in either form, but unfortunately not available commercially, though it is to be found in private collections.
CULTIVATION: *Primula tschuktschorum* is as difficult to grow as it is to pronounce. Best in a peaty, gritty compost in the alpine house. Watch out for greenfly and beware of dryness at the roots in spring and summer.
PROPAGATION: Seed.
AVAILABILITY: Try the society seed lists.

14
Asiatics for the Garden

These beautiful primulas mainly come from the great mountains of central Asia, areas that are as yet largely unexplored and may yet yield further treasures of the plant world.

Many gardeners have been lead to believe that the growing of the Asiatic primulas is for the experts. Nothing is further from the truth – there are plants within this category for every gardener; easy, difficult and almost impossible, but it must be realised that suitable plants cannot be found for every garden. If the conditions are hot, dry and sunbaked, beware – it will be a struggle to keep the Asiatics alive and healthy. A small patch where the soil is, or can be kept moist can be found in most gardens so that the grower can enjoy at least one or two Asiatics.

Any gardener who wishes to obtain a representative collection of these intriguing plants is strongly urged to join the specialist societies in order to participate in their seed exchange schemes.

Certain Asiatic primulas can cause an allergic reaction in a small number of people, due to a chemical in the fine hairs. The worst offender is *Primula obconica,* but all the members of the Cortusoides, Soldanelloides, Muscarioides, Denticulata and other sections can cause problems. Care in handling and the use of rubber gloves is necessary.

CULTIVATION

Peat beds are the ideal environment for many of the Asiatic primulas and are described fully in chapter 3, but any moist soil in part shade mixed with peat will do equally well for the easier plants. More care is needed when dealing with the more delicate varieties, and this will be described in the individual descriptions of species.

The cultivation requirements of many of the Asiatic primulas are closely related to the section to which they belong, and cultural details are given below for the most important sections:

The Cortusoides (Section 1), being woodland plants, prefer part shade (such as that cast by deciduous trees) and a moist soil. Lovely clumps can be established under small trees and shrubs, delighting one with their delicate flowers. They also make lovely specimens for the alpine house, especially the cultivars of *Primula sieboldii,* which are available in a wide range of colours.

The Farinosae (Section 19) tend to be mixed in their requirements, and will be dealt with individually.

The Denticulata (Section 20) primulas are represented by one easy reliable species whose cultivation is discussed in the descriptive list.

The Capitata (Section 21) tend to be fairly small, short-lived plants, and are best grown under peat bed conditions. Although short-lived they are fairly easy to grow to flowering size.

The Muscarioides (Section 22) are small and fairly delicate. There is a tendency for them to be short-lived, but if conditions are ideal they will persist for several years in a peat bed. *Primula vialii,* planted in groups on the banks of a steam, will seed itself about and provide a continuous supply of young plants.

The Soldanelloides (Section 23) are amongst the most beautiful of the Asiatic primulas, both for the size and delicacy of the flowers, and also for the lovely perfume, which will fill the garden. They can be temperamental, but in the ideal conditions of a well made, well maintained peat bed they can produce good clumps.

The Nivalids (Section 25) are well worth growing, but more care must be taken to give them the correct conditions. They will very quickly show their dislike of unsuitable climates and soil by dying during the first winter. In cooler northern climates they are comparatively easy to grow, but it can be a real challenge to provide suitable conditions in hot dry areas like the south-east. When the plants become weakened by extremely hot conditions they can easily fall prey to garden pests like greenfly.

The Sikkimensis (Section 27) are rather more tolerant as a whole. Supplies of water are still essential and *Primula florindae* in particular will tolerate a much greater degree of water-logging than will the Candelabra section. They also exhibit a greater degree of winter hardiness, even in pots, but it is sheer cruelty to confine the huge thong-like roots within the confines of a pot – they will only be a shadow of their true selves. The effort taken in supplying them with a good rich soil will be amply repaid by a greater degree of health and quantity of flowers. They are magnificent grouped near water and the fragrance is lovely. The smaller members of this section, such as *Primula ioessa* will make a charming clump in the peat bed.

The Candelabra (Section 28) all have thick thong-like roots, and need copious supplies of water in the growing season, but they do not appreciate sitting in water in the winter. They are fairly tall plants and so need room, and look much better in a group. They will grow and flower well in sun or shade, but they need more water in a sunny position. They love a rich deep soil, with plenty of good compost, or even a layer of well rotted farmyard manure 12in (30cm) down. Periods of drought in the warmer counties will not immediately show any ill effects, but the plants most likely to succumb in a hard winter are those that have been subjected to drought. These plants do not succeed well in pots, and in fact they are difficult to overwinter in pots if there are any long periods of frost. This may be because water below freezing point expands, and as the pot is not elastic the roots are crushed by the ice. In a very severe winter, plants in the garden can be damaged in cold areas, but it is usually the oldest plants that are most affected. The Candelabra and Sikkimensis sections tend to be grouped together and be called 'Bog Primulas,' along with *Primula rosea* and any other that enjoy very wet conditions.

PROPAGATION

SEED: Seed can be obtained from the seed lists of the Alpine Garden Society, the Scottish Rock Garden Club, Harlow Car gardens and several other gardens that operate seed lists.

Like all primula seed excessive temperatures hinders and often prevents germination. This is variable, some seed being able to tolerate higher temperatures. To err on the side of caution it is sensible to keep all primula seed, both sown and in the packet, below 70°F (20°C). Many shops and garden centres keep seed racks in very warm areas – it is advisable to avoid these and obtain seed direct from the seed companies.

Everyone has different methods of seed sowing. The most foolproof method is to sow in January on a compost of two parts John Innes Seed compost, two parts moss peat and one part ¼in (6mm) grit. Cover with a merest sprinkling of grit (more to stop the seeds all being washed into a corner than for any other reason), and put outside, unprotected, preferably in full shade. Keep a check for slugs as they will soon eat a tray of seedlings. The seeds will germinate in March–May, and by May–June will have six or more leaves and can be potted into 3in (7cm) or 3½in (9cm) pots. The compost varies with the section. All the bog primulas, Denticulatas and Nivalids can be potted into a proprietary peat based compost, but the smaller more delicate species will benefit from a more open gritty compost of up to one part sphagnum moss peat, one part John Innes No.2 compost and one part grit. The larger species should be big enough to plant in the garden by July–August. With the smaller species that are not big enough to stand the rigours of the open, the pots need to be kept under cover and a cold frame or greenhouse is suitable in all but the coldest winters.

SPLITTING: Is a very useful method of increasing stocks of interesting primulas, and as there is always variation in any batch grown from seed it is often worthwhile to split and grow on the best forms. Most of the easier Asiatic primulas can be split at any time in the growing season, but hot weather in summer can be fatal to the young plants. It would be safest to do any splitting before three to four weeks of cool wet weather, but unfortunately most gardeners are not clairvoyant, and so the newly split plants need to be kept well watered in a shady position. The most suitable time is early spring, when the species that died back for the winter are just starting growth, and before the weather is very hot.

AVAILABILITY

There should be no problem in acquiring a collection of the plants described. Some are more obtainable than others, but most of the specialist alpine and herbaceous nurseries list a few of the Asiatics, as do many general nurseries and garden centres. Do check amongst the pond plants and alpines, where

Auricula 'Broadwell Gold'

Primula vulgaris subsp. sibthorpii

Primula vulgaris

Primula 'Kinlough Beauty'

Primula 'Appleblossom'

Primula 'Pat Barwick'

Primula 'Rufus'

Auricula 'Old Irish Blue'

Primula 'Hemswell Ember'

Primula 'Harlow Car'

Primula 'Christine'

Primula 'Mrs J.H. Wilson'

Cowichan Polyanthus 'Duckyl's Red'

Gold Lace Polyanthus 'Kaye's Strain'

Double Primrose 'Miss Indigo'

Double Primrose 'Sunshine Susie'

Primula ellisiae

Primula secundiflora

Primula melanops

Primula ioessa alba

Primula frondosa

Primula seiboldii

Primula 'Hyacinthia'

Primula marginata 'Pritchard's Variety'

Primula allionii 'Crowsley's Variety'

Primula 'Beatrice Wooster'

Primula scandinavica

Primula x *berninae* 'Peggy Fell'

Primula x *bileckii*

Primula marginata 'Holden Clough'

Primula bulleyana

Primula pulverulenta

Primula denticulata alba

Primula modesta (double form)

Primula 'Linnet'

quite interesting primulas may often be found. Again, the society seed lists, and the more comprehensive seed catalogues will yield some interesting plants.

REPRESENTATIVE STARTING COLLECTION:

Primula rosea
Primula sieboldii
Any *Candelabra primula*
Primula sikkimensis or *alpicola*
Primula vialii
Primula capitata

All these need a soil that does not dry out but is not waterlogged in winter. It should have some moss peat mixed in, (light shade helps, but is not essential).

RECOMMENDATIONS FOR THE MORE ADVENTUROUS:

Primula involucrata
Primula warshenewskiana
Primula nutans (flaccida)
Primula ioessa

DESCRIPTIVE LIST OF THE ASIATIC PRIMULAS FOR THE GARDEN

Primula algida (Section 19 Farinosae):
A short lived, very variable species that is found mainly in moist alpine meadows in the Caucasus region. It is very similar to *Primula farinosa*, with heads of mauve flowers, and the leaves can be with or without farina, giving rise to several subspecies. Farrer likened it to a rather large dingy *Primula farinosa,* perhaps not really worth the effort of finding unless the reader is a collector of names.
CULTIVATION: Lightly shaded rockery, or alpine house.
PROPAGATION: Seed, and stratification is probably not needed.
AVAILABILITY: Seed is occasionally offered by the specialist societies.
Primula alpicola (Section 27 Sikkimensis):
Named 'Joseph's Sikkimensis' by Kingdom Ward when he collected it, because of the wide variation in colour. It is often

offered as *Primula alpicola violacea, Primula alpicola luna* and *Primula alpicola alba*: these different colour forms readily hybridise to give a complete range of colour from violet through yellow to white. This species is confined to the basin of the Tsangpo river in south-eastern Tibet, where it grows in marshy ground and moist alpine pastures. From a rosette of matt bright green leaves, somewhat reminiscent of a primrose leaf, rise the 18in (45cm) high stems bearing a loose head of large fragrant bells in June and July.

CULTIVATION: All variants are lovely plants for the bog garden, peat bed or any position where the soil does not dry out in summer.

PROPAGATION: Usually by seed which should germinate fairly easily, but unless only one colour is grown the resultant seedlings will vary in colour. This species will cross with other members of the Sikkimensis section. A particularly fine colour form may be carefully split in early spring, taking care to keep the split plants shaded and moist.

AVAILABILITY: Occasionally from the specialist nurseries, or from the seed lists.

Primula anisodora (Section 28 Candelabra):
From moist alpine pastures in western China. It is a distinctive species having small dark crimson to purple flowers in the characteristic candelabra whorls, about 24in(60cm) high. The leaves are long, narrow and shiny, edged with small teeth, and are reputed to smell of aniseed – hence the name.

CULTIVATION: Not one of the hardiest varieties in very cold areas. An interesting plant for the peat bed.

PROPAGATION: Seed, which should germinate easily.

AVAILABILITY: Occasionally from the specialist nurseries or seed lists.

Primula aurantiaca (Section 28 Candelabra):
Discovered by George Forrest in 1922 in moist alpine meadows in western Yunnan in China. About 12in(30cm) high, it is reminiscent of a diminutive *Primula bulleyana,* having soft yellow to rich orange flowers in candelabra whorls, opening from deep red buds. The leaves are raggedly toothed, and often have a fine dusting of farina on the underside. A fine species, especially suited to the smaller gardens where there is insufficient room for the larger candelabra species.

CULTIVATION: Easy in moist peat bed conditions.

PROPAGATION: Seed which should germinate easily.

AVAILABILITY: Specialist nurseries, or from the seed lists.

Primula auriculata (Section 19 Farinosae):

Closely related to *Primula rosea,* though it can vary in size from 6–24in (15–60cm). It is found in Iran, Turkey and the Caucasus.
CULTIVATION: Peat bed.
PROPAGATION: Seed or careful splitting.
AVAILABILITY: Occasionally available through seed lists; has been listed by specialist nurseries, but not very often.
Primula beesiana (Section 28 Candelabra):
Discovered by George Forrest in the Likiang range of Yunnan in China, growing with *Primula bulleyana,* and was first distributed by Bees of Chester (the seed company) who financed the expedition, in 1908. Rose carmine to deep reddish purple flowers with a yellow eye, a smattering of farina on the pedicels and calyces, Lilac to flesh coloured midribs to the leaves, vigorous, up to 36in (90cm) high.
CULTIVATION: Easy in any moist to wet soil, sun or shade. The easier candelabra primulas love sun as long as the soil is moist at all times–the moister the soil the more sun they will tolerate. Also lovely for lightening a shady corner.
PROPAGATION: Easy from seed, but remember that all members of the Candelabra section interbreed very easily, though the resultant seedlings are usually very attractive and well worth growing. Large plants can be split in early spring when they start growth, but keep the split plants well shaded and moist.
AVAILABILITY: Fairly general, the better garden centres, specialist nurseries, or the seed lists.
Primula bulleyana (Section 28 Candelabra):
Another introduction by George Forrest, and comes from a slightly higher altitude than *Primula beesiana* but from the same area of China. The large rounded flowers are variously described as rich pure yellow through to deep orange, opening from crimson buds. This is a large, vigorous plant 30in (80cm) high, with five to seven whorls of flowers. There is a small smattering of farina on the pedicels, and the midribs of the leaves are red. As the members of the Candelabra section tend to hybridise readily with each other there is always the chance that any of the Candelabras you obtain may be hybrids, with intermediate characteristics, but they are all well worth growing and an asset to any garden that can provide the cool, moist soil so essential to their health.
CULTIVATION and PROPAGATION: See *Primula beesiana*
AVAILABILITY: Fairly general.

Primula x bulleesiana (Section 28 Candelabra):
A range of hybrids between *Primula bulleyana* and *Primula beesiana,* that are also sometimes listed as 'Asthore Hybrids', which were first raised in Edinburgh, soon after the introduction of the two species. They should bear tiers of flowers in shades of apricot salmon, but there is a wide variation in colour.
CULTIVATION: The same as its parents.
PROPAGATION: Careful splitting of very fine colour forms, or by seed which will probably yield a wide range of different colours.
AVAILABILITY: Sometimes from specialist nurseries, or the seed lists.
Primula burmanica (Section 28 Candelabra):
Found in Yunnan and upper Burma, where it grows at a slightly lower altitude than *Primula beesiana,* which it closely resembles. It is, however, without farina, except for inside the calyx. Whorls of rich red-purple flowers on 36in (90cm) stems. It is geographically separated from *Primula beesiana* in the wild, but in cultivation they readily hybridise with each other and other closely related species.
CULTIVATION: As *Primula beesiana.*
PROPAGATION: Seed, which should germinate well.
AVAILABILITY: Often listed by the specialist nurseries, or from the seed lists.
Primula capitata (Section 21 Capitatae):
Originally discovered by Hooker from Sikkim in 1849, but other forms have since been introduced, e.g. *Primula capitata LS17507* by Ludlow and Sherriff in the 1930s. It is a relatively small plant, up to 12in (30cm) high, with a flattened head of deep rich purple flowers in July–August, opening from exceedingly farinose buds above a neat rosette of light green leaves with a silvery reverse caused by an abundance of farina.
CULTIVATION: A pretty plant for the peat bed, short lived but, as it sets plenty of seed, a succession of plants can be reared.
PROPAGATION: By seed, which germinates well, but not really worth splitting as the results are difficult to rear.
AVAILABILITY: Fairly easily available, or from the seed lists. The lists usually have the subspecies *Primula capitata Mooreana* which has slightly larger flower heads of a richer colour, and *Primula capitata LS17507,* which is rich violet and has a relatively long flowering season.
Primula chionantha (Section 25 Nivales):
Found by Forrest in Yunnan, China. The easiest of the

Nivalids, a robust plant when happy, with one to four umbels of nodding creamy white flowers with a yellow eye, in tiers in April–May. The strap-shaped leaves are strongly farinose when they first emerge in spring. 12in(30cm) high.

CULTIVATION: It requires a permanently moist but not wet soil, and its long thong-like roots are far too big to be confined in a pot. Much easier to grow in the cooler northern areas, but with some care it can be grown in shade in the south. If it is grown in a position that is too warm and dry the plant will become weakened so that it will succumb to pests and diseases. Greenfly can be a menace, as can botrytis.

PROPAGATION: Easy from seed, but remember it crosses readily with the other members of the Nivalid section.

AVAILABILITY: Often from the specialist nurseries, or seed from the seed lists, which often yields plants of white or mauve purple shades.

Primula chumbiensis (Section 27 Sikkimensis):
A rare and attractive plant from the south Tibetan valley of Chumbi, with heads of yellow hanging bells, similar to *Primula sikkimensis.*

CULTIVATION: Peat bed.

PROPAGATION: Seed.

AVAILABILITY: Rare, try the seed lists, but it has occasionally occurred in the specialist nurseries lists.

Primula chungensis (Section 28 Candelabra):
Introduced by Kingdom Ward, and found near the Chung river in north-west Yunnan, after which it was named. It is also found in Assam, Szechuan and Bhutan. Bright yellow to pale orange flowers opening from orange buds on 24–36in (60–90cm) stems.

CULTIVATION: Bog garden or peat bed. Any permanently moist, but not waterlogged position.

PROPAGATION: Seed usually germinates freely.

AVAILABILITY: Plants from the specialist nurseries, or seed from the seed distribution lists.

Primula* x *chunglenta   (Section 28 Candelabra):
A fairly rare hybrid between *Primula chungensis* and *Primula pulverulenta,* that is occasionally offered by Specialist Nurserymen. Intermediate characteristics between the two parents, and variable colour.

Primula clarkei   (Section 19 Farinosae):
From Kashmir in the north-western Himalayas. The 2in (5cm) high stems carrying good rose pink flowers which emerge in early spring from the close tufts of crimson brown

leaves, somewhat reminiscent of a diminutive *Primula rosea* to which it is related. The leaves, when they expand are rounded and light green and shiny. A lovely plant for the peat bed or alpine house. One of the few primulas that spreads by means of underground runners.

CULTIVATION: Best in a select peat bed where it will not be overgrown by more vigorous neighbours, or it makes a lovely pan for the alpine house, grown in a peaty compost and kept well shaded and watered in the summer months. In a greenhouse that is glazed to the floor it can be kept under the staging – this provides excellent conditions, as long as watering is not neglected.

PROPAGATION: Careful splitting. It does occasionally set seed and a few hybrids have been raised from crossing it with its near relatives, *Primula rosea* and *Primula warshenewskiana.*

AVAILABILITY: Unfortunately not as available as it used to be, but try the specialist nurseries.

Primula cockburniana   (Section 28 Candelabra):
Fiery coppery-orange flowers, close relative of *Primula chungensis,* and a relatively small delicate looking plant, 12–18in (30–40cm) high. Short lived.

CULTIVATION: Peat bed, but treat as a biennial, and collect the seed to ensure continuity.

PROPAGATION: Easy from seed, which it sets in plenty.

AVAILABILITY: Fairly readily available from the specialist nurseries, and occasionally from good garden centres. Also the seed lists.

Primula concholoba   (Section 22 Muscarioides):
A somewhat rare plant from south-east Tibet, where it grows on steep grassy slopes. The 6in(15cm) high stems carry small heads of farinaed violet flowers above neat furry rosettes of leaves.

CULTIVATION: A tricky plant for the peat bed, or grow it in the alpine house. Use a fairly gritty compost under glass, but never let it dry out in the spring and summer months, and collect the seed as an insurance. In winter it goes back to small tight rosettes.

PROPAGATION: The seed germinates well, but the tiny seedlings are sometimes tricky to grow on. It is safest to leave them in the seed tray or pot until they are large enough to handle, then pot carefully into a fairly gritty compost, and keep lightly shaded and just moist.

AVAILABILITY: Sometimes from the specialist nurseries, or try the seed lists.

Primula cortusoides (Section 1 Cortusoides):
First brought into cultivation in 1797 from Siberia, and is to be found fairly widespread on the Asiatic mainland. An extremely attractive and hardy woodland plant, the 6in (15cm) high stems bear umbels of rich pink flowers in May to June above hairy foliage which dies back completely for the winter.
CULTIVATION: A lovely and easy plant for the peat bed, or a shady position under deciduous bushes where the soil is permanently moist.
PROPAGATION: Easy from seed, which is copiously set, but this species crosses easily with *Primula saxatilis* so be careful if you wish to keep it true. Mature clumps can be carefully split as they come into growth in spring.
AVAILABILITY: Occasionally from the specialist nurseries, and also from the seed lists.

Primula crispa (Section 21 Capitatae):
In commerce there is a plant under the name *Primula crispa,* which has much larger flowers than the usual *Primula capitata,* and is very attractive. There appears to be some argument as to its correct name, and it has been rumoured that it may even belong to the Denticulata section. This plant is said to be without farina, and the flowers are larger and more open than *Primula capitata,* although its habit, flower colour and leaf shape is very similar.
CULTIVATION and PROPAGATION: The same as for *Primula capitata.*
AVAILABILITY: From specialist nurseries or the society seed lists.

Primula denticulata (Section 20 Denticulata):
This carpets the hillsides of the north-western Himalayas in spring. Commonly known as the 'Drumstick Primula,' it is an easy rewarding plant which will grow successfully any-where but very hot, dry positions and will delight the grower with a display in April and May of round heads of flowers in shades of lilac, through to purple, red, pink, pale blue and a lovely pure white variant. The variety called *Primula cashmiriana* is a selected form, neither better nor worse that the original. The flowers emerge before the huge, somewhat coarse leaves, and the gardener needs to position it with care, as the leaves can swamp smaller plants. About 12in (30cm) high, when in full flower, but the flowers often open within the leaves.
Named cultivars include 'Bressingham Beauty', 'Cash-miriana Rubin', 'Glenroy Crimson', 'Inschriach Crimson', 'Rubinball' and 'Snowball'.

CULTIVATION: Easy in a border, or moist soil anywhere.
PROPAGATION: Seed, splitting of good coloured forms or even root cuttings.
AVAILABILITY: Almost everywhere in spring as plants, or as seed from most of the seed catalogues.
Primula farinosa (Section 19 Farinosae):
Occurs throughout northern Asia as well as Europe, and has been described with the European species in chapter 5.
Primula fauriae (Section 19 Farinosae):
A dry ground form of *Primula modesta,* and appears to be now accepted as a subspecies of *Primula modesta.* It was discovered in Japan in 1886. For further details see *Primula Modesta.*
Primula firmipes (Section 27 Sikkimensis):
A relatively new introduction, very similar to a smaller version of *Primula florindae,* with loose heads of rich yellow flowers.
CULTIVATION: Peat bed, or any moist position in the garden.
PROPAGATION: By seed, or by splitting large established clumps.
AVAILABILITY: Occasionally from the specialist nurseries.
Primula flaccida (Section 23 Soldanelloides):
Called *Primula nutans* but the botanists have decided it should be called *Primula flaccida.* Originally discovered by Delavay growing in open pine forests and rocky pastures, it was introduced by Forrest from the Yunnan in 1916. One of the most beautiful primulas, and although not often readily available it is worth every effort to obtain. Short spikes on 9–12in (22–30cm) stems, of enormous pale lavender blue bells, above rosettes of softly hairy leaves.
CULTIVATION: Careful treatment in the peat bed or makes a lovely specimen in the alpine house which it will fill with the glorious scent. A peaty, gritty compost is recommended, and careful attention to watering in the spring and summer months is required. It is advisable to keep the plant on the dry side in winter but not arid.
PROPAGATION: By seed, which is usually, but not always set. Like other primulas, if the plant is allowed to become too dry when in seed, the seed will abort in order to channel the plant's energies into keeping itself alive.
AVAILABILITY: Sometimes listed by specialist nurseries or seed exchange schemes.
Primula florindae (Section 27 Sikkimensis):
Introduced by Kingdom Ward from the Tsang-Po Gorge in

1924, it is commonly known as the 'Giant Himalayan Cow-slip,' and is a magnificent plant. The huge, heart-shaped shiny leaves make a magnificent contrast to the large mop heads of sweetly scented, hanging yellow bells on 36in (90cm) high stems. A glorious plant for any but the smallest garden, flowering freely over a long period in summer, even in dense shade. Also available are *Primula florindae* hybrids, whose colour ranges from yellow, through orange to rich copper or even crimson shades.

CULTIVATION: Easy, but remember it is a large vigorous plant. Soundly perennial and very hardy, it will tolerate anything from a moist soil to waterlogged conditions at the edge of a pond or stream.

PROPAGATION: Is easy from the copiously set seed, which germinates rapidly and well. Good colour forms can be split.

AVAILABILITY: Fairly general (often sold at garden centres as a pond plant), specialist nurseries, or seed lists.

Primula geraniifolia (Section 1 Cortusoides):
Like a coarse, hairy *Primula cortusoides* and is rarely offered.

CULTIVATION: An easy plant, but not one of the most interesting or beautiful. It likes moist shade under bushes, or a peat bed.

PROPAGATION: Seed or splitting.

AVAILABILITY: Seed lists or occasionally from specialist nurseries.

Primula glomerata (syn. crispa) (Section 21 Capitatae):
Compact heads of tiny rich purple flowers on 6in(15cm) stems in July–August, above neat rosettes of leaves. Originally introduced in about 1930 from wild seed, and is fairly widely distributed throughout Nepal, Sikkim and Tibet.

CULTIVATION: Careful treatment in a peat bed or alpine house, fairly similar to *Primula capitata*.

PROPAGATION: It tends to be short lived in cultivation, but can be easily replaced by growing a succession of plants from the ample seed that it produces.

AVAILABILITY: Occasionally available from the specialist nurseries. Also the seed lists, though not worth the effort of searching for as it is so similar to *Primula capitata,* which is more readily available.

Primula helodoxa (Section 28 Candelabra):
Originates from China. Soft rich yellow flowers, about 36in (90cm) high, and a typical candelabra appearance, not often available, apart from the seed distribution schemes, but well worth growing.

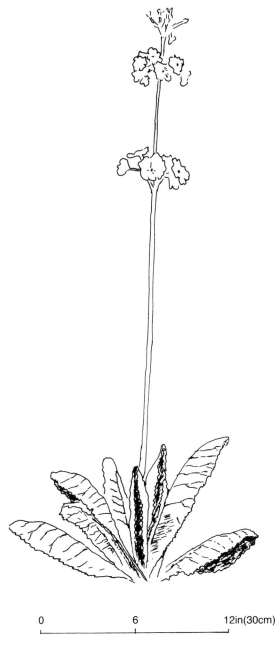

0   6   12in(30cm)

Primula helodoxa.

CULTIVATION: Moist to wet soil in bog garden or pond side.
PROPAGATION: Seed.
AVAILABILITY: Occasionally from specialist nurseries, or the seed lists.

Primula heucherifolia (Section 1 Cortusoides):
Pendant bell flowers of mauve pink to rich soft purple on 6in (15cm) stems. Very similar to other members of the Cortusoides primulas.
CULTIVATION: Peat bed or moist soil in shady border.
PROPAGATION: Seed or careful splitting in early spring.
AVAILABILITY: Specialist nurseries, occasionally garden centres, and seed lists.

Primula ianthina: (Section 28 Candelabra)
A rarely offered plant with violet flowers on 24in (60cm) high stems from Sikkim.
CULTIVATION: Peat bed is probably safest.
PROPAGATION: Seed.
AVAILABILITY: Seed lists are the only possibility.

Primula ioessa (Section 27 Sikkimensis):
First collected by Kingdom Ward in 1936 in south-east Tibet, where it frequents moist meadows, but was not properly introduced until Ludlow and Sherriff brought back seed in 1938. The heads of open mauve to violet bells are sweetly scented and hang from the 9–12in (20–39cm) stems, above neat rosettes of toothed leaves. A white form exists and is equally lovely. The plant dies back in winter to small resting buds below the soil, so it is a good idea to carefully mark its position.
CULTIVATION: A lovely plant to grace the peat bed, or the front of a moist (not wet) border.
PROPAGATION: Seed is freely set and germinates well, or an established clump may be split in early spring when it re-emerges.
AVAILABILITY: The seed exchanges often list it, or it may be occasionally found in specialist nurseries lists.

Primula involucrata (Section 19 Farinosae):
A lovely, moisture-loving plant that deserves to be more widely grown. The 8–12in (20–30cm) stems carry good heads of large creamy white flowers in May, above loose clumps of smooth light green leaves. It was first discovered in the early eighteenth century, and occurs throughout the Himalayas, usually growing in moist meadows and stream banks. In winter it dies back to small resting buds below the soil, and in

a dry summer can become dormant in August, but don't worry, it is very hardy and regularly re-emerges in the spring.
CULTIVATION: Easy in any soil that does not dry out.
PROPAGATION: The copious seed germinates easily and well, or established clumps may be split in early spring.
AVAILABILITY: Occasionally obtainable from specialist nurseries, and it is usually listed in the seed exchanges.
Primula japonica (Section 28 Candelabra):
This has been in cultivation since 1871, so was probably one of the first candelabras in cultivation. Originating from Japan, it is one of the easiest of this accommodating section, with tall stately 36in (90cm) high flower spikes in all shades from white through pink to red and almost purple. It is frequently and unfairly criticised as being a coarse plant, but for garden value it cannot be too highly praised.
CULTIVATION: Easy in any moist to wet soil.
PROPAGATION: Seed, but the resultant seedlings will probably vary in colour.
AVAILABILITY: Specialist nurseries, occasional garden centres, check the pond plant section, and the seed lists.
***Primula japonica* 'Miller's Crimson'** (Section 28 Candelabra):
A striking strain with velvety crimson flowers and a dark eye. If grown in isolation the seed will produce plants that are all almost completely true to type.
CULTIVATION, PROPAGATION and AVAILABILITY: As for *Primula japonica*.
***Primula japonica* 'Potsford White'** (Section 28 Candelabra):
A lovely contrast to the preceding plant, a seed strain which should yield pure white flowers with a yellow eye.
CULTIVATION, PROPAGATION and AVAILABILITY: As for *Primula japonica*.
Primula luteola (Section 19 Farinosae):
This attractive plant occurs in both Europe and Asia, and it has been fully described in chapter 5.
Primula macrophylla (Section 25 Nivales):
An attractive Himalayan plant, dwarfer than other members of this section, and so is often grown in the alpine house. Neat rosettes of leathery leaves and large purple flowers with a dark eye on 8–12in (20–30cm) stems covered in farina.
CULTIVATION: Well worth trying in the peat bed or alpine house in a peaty, gritty compost.
PROPAGATION: Seed if set.
AVAILABILITY: Quite rare, occasionally from specialist nurserymen or seed lists.

Primula melanops (Section 25 Nivales):
Theoretically this plant should have rich mauve flowers and an almost black eye on 18–24in (45–60cm) stems, but in practice the grower is very lucky if the plant obtained tallies with the description as regards colour. As previously discussed, most of the Nivalids have interbred to such an extent that it is difficult to separate them into distinct species. All are well worth growing if you can provide the right conditions.
CULTIVATION: A moist but not waterlogged soil, and cool moist air – all the Nivalids hate hot arid conditions.
PROPAGATION: Very easy from seed.
AVAILABILITY: Specialist nurseymen or seed lists.

Primula modesta (Section 19 Farinosae):
A most attractive and worthwhile plant from the mountains of Japan. Somewhat akin to a dwarf *Primula frondosa,* and nearly as amenable. The neat rosettes of heavily farinaed leaves reduce to a tight resting bud of leaves in the autumn, from whence emerge the 4–6in (10–15cm) flower stems in May – round heads of small flat flowers in shades of mauve, pink, pale blue through to the desirable white form, all with a distinct yellow eye. Occasionally some doubling of the flower may occur, and it is always worth saving the freely produced seed, as there will be variations amongst the seedlings.

At least two subspecies exist, and can be offered as *Primula fauriae* and *Primula yuparensis,* or as *Primula modesta fauriae* and *Primula modesta yuparensis.* Whatever the name *Primula modesta* in any form is a very worthwhile plant.
CULTIVATION: Lovely for the cold greenhouse in a gritty compost, or for a select position on a sunny rockery, making sure the soil never dries out completely.
PROPAGATION: Easy from the copiously set seed.
AVAILABILITY: Once quite rare, but becoming more readily available from nurseries, and usually on the seed exchange lists.

Primula muscarioides (Section 22 Muscarioides):
A small plant from wet meadows, found from south–eastern Tibet through to Szechuan and Yunnan. The small, deep purple, tubular flowers are in a close head on 4–15in (19–40cm) stems, above a neat rosettes of soft leaves, which die back in winter to a hard round resting bud. Though not spectacular this plant has a unique charm.
CULTIVATION: Careful treatment in the peat bed, where if conditions are to its liking, it may well achieve a height of 15in (40cm). It can also be grown in the alpine house in a gritty

peaty compost with careful attention to watering in the growing season, and nearly dry when dormant, pot culture does tend to dwarf it to about 6in(15cm). Not long lived but it sets plenty of seed.

PROPAGATION: Seed, which germinates fairly freely. Do let the seedlings grow to a manageable size before potting on.

AVAILABILITY: Occasionally from the specialist nurseries, or usually in the seed lists.

Primula nutans (Section 19 Farinosae):
Previously called *Primula sibirica*. It is widely distributed in Arctic and central Asia extending into Arctic Europe and Alaska, and has been in cultivation for 150 or more years. It is very variable and closely related to *Primula involucrata* and *Primula yargongensis,* but is rather more temperamental, and not as amenable to cultivation. It has heads of yellow-eyed lilac to pink flowers on stems up to 12in (30cm) in height. The lovely pale blue flowered species that used to be called *Primula nutans* has now been renamed *Primula flaccida*.

CULTIVATION: Peat bed.

PROPAGATION: Seed.

AVAILABILITY: Occasionally from the specialist nurseries, or the seed lists.

Primula polyneura (Section 1 Cortusoides):
First described in 1895 by Franchet and is fairly common in parts of western China. It is described as being a variable plant in the wild, but in cultivation it is fairly consistent. The typical Cortusoides leaves are densely felted on the undersides, and are unmistakable. The flowers are in loose heads on the 6in (15cm) stems in May, and are a particularly virulent pink – lovely to relieve the gloom under shrubs or a shady corner. It dies back completely for winter, but is reliable and hardy. A worthwhile plant, not offered as often as one would like.

CULTIVATION: Easy and permanent in the peat bed, or in a cool position in moist soil under dwarf shrubs.

PROPAGATION: Readily from seed or by dividing established clumps in early spring.

AVAILABILITY: Specialist nurseries or seed lists.

Primula poissonii (Section 28 Candelabra):
From western Szechuan and Yunnan and was first recorded by Delavay in Yunnan in 1882. It is said to tolerate more sun and drier conditions than other Candelabras, and the shiny green leaves do not die back in winter. It bears deep purplish flowers on 24in (60cm) stems in whorls. Similar to a scentless *Primula anisodora*.

CULTIVATION: Peat bed, but can be lost in very severe winters.
PROPAGATION: Seed.
AVAILABILITY: Occasionally from specialist nurseries or seed lists.
Primula prolifera (Section 28 Candelabra):
A yellow candelabra from Assam that is not often available.
CULTIVATION: Large peat bed or bog garden.
PROPAGATION: Seed.
AVAILABILITY: Occasionally from the specialist nurseries or seed lists.
Primula pulverulenta (Section 28 Candelabra):
Discovered by Ernest Wilson in 1905 in western Szechuan. It bears vivid crimson flowers, and the 24–36in (60–90cm) stems and buds are covered in farina. The colour of the flowers can vary, but it is an excellent plant, especially grouped near water. One of the more readily available Candelabras.
CULTIVATION: Easy and permanent in any moist to wet position.
PROPAGATION: By seed, or careful splitting of an established clump of a particularly fine colour, in early spring, being careful to keep the young plants shaded and moist until they are established.
AVAILABILITY: Good garden centres (Look for pond plants), specialist nurseries or the seed lists.
***Primula pulverulenta* 'Bartley's Strain'**
(Section 28 Candelabra)
A lovely seed strain fixed after many years of selection by G.H. Dalrymple of the Bartley Nurseries, Southampton in the 1920s, and should have flowers in lovely shell pink shades.
CULTIVATION and PROPAGATION: As for *Primula pulverulenta*.
AVAILABILITY: Occasionally from the specialist nurseries, or the seed lists.
Primula reidii (Section 23 Soldanelloides):
The star of this difficult section and comes from damp rocky areas near glaciers in the north-west Himalayas. Reputedly difficult, but in actual fact not nearly as taxing as many others. The huge open hanging bells are creamy white with a waxy bloom on 8in (20cm) stems, and the calyces are heavily mealed. The perfume is sweet and all pervading, filling the greenhouse or garden in May and June.
CULTIVATION: It can be grown successfully in a cool peat

bed, providing one accepts that it may be short lived and collects the seed to ensure a succession. It makes a lovely specimen in the alpine house, grown in a peaty gritty soil, moist in the growing season, and dry whilst dormant.

PROPAGATION: Seed, large plants can be split, but one is loath to run the risk of losing them all.

AVAILABILITY: Specialist nurseries, especially the northern ones, or seed lists.

Primula reidii williamsii (Section 23 Soldanelloides):
Introduced in 1952 and 1954 by two expeditions to western and central Nepal, led by L. H. J. Williams of the British Natural History Museum. It is a slightly more robust form with crystalline bells of pale blue to white, often shaded from one colour to the other and with the same delicious fragrance as *Primula reidii*.

CULTIVATION, PROPAGATION and AVAILABILITY: As for *Primula reidii*.

Primula reidii hybrids (Section 23 Soldanelloides):
This is the result of growing the preceding two plants in close proximity. It is often difficult to differentiate between the two species, and many beautiful plants are available under this heading. Highly recommended.

CULTIVATION, PROPAGATION and AVAILABILITY: As for *Primula reidii*.

Primula reticulata (Section 27 Sikkimensis):
A small relative of *Primula sikkimensis* with white to yellow flowers, and comes from the mountains of northern India and southern Tibet.

CULTIVATION: Peat bed is the safest bet.

PROPAGATION: Seed.

AVAILABILITY: Occasionally in the seed lists.

Primula rosea (Section 19 Farinosae):
One of the best known and loved of the primulas, being very tolerant of a wide range of conditions, so long as it never dries out. It originates in the north-western Himalaya, where it grows by, and even in streams, and in wet meadows, it has long been associated with *Caltha leptosepala,* the white Marsh Marigold, near which it often grows. From the tight rosette of dark glossy brown-red of the winter resting leaves, emerge the flowering stems in March and April, the flowers often opening before they have cleared the leaves. There are several variants grown, the best are *Primula rosea grandiflora* and *Primula rosea* 'Viseer de Greer', which both have large flat flowers. Other forms have smaller less striking flowers, but

they are still the rich bright pink which is so welcome in early spring. The flower stems are 4–6in (8–10cm) high, and carry several flowers to a stem. In seed the stems elongate, a habit shared with many primulas, and *Primula rosea* usually sets a good crop of fertile seed.

CULTIVATION: Easy in any moist to wet soil.

PROPAGATION: By seed or careful splitting in spring. This can be done after flowering, the young divisions need to be kept shaded and moist until they are established.

AVAILABILITY: Garden centres, specialist nurseries, seed catalogues and the seed lists.

Primula saxatilis (Section 1 Cortusoides):

A small woodland plant from northern Korea and China. It is very similar to *Primula cortusoides,* the main difference being the length of the pedicels at flowering time, 2/5in (1cm) or less the plant is probably *Primula cortusoides,* longer and it is probably *Primula saxatilis.* It is quite possible that the two species have interbred in cultivation, making it even more difficult to correctly identify. Whichever plant you have it is a lovely thing for a shady corner that doesn't dry out, the bright pink flowers held well above the leaves are very delicate and distinctive. Not at all difficult and reasonably perennial.

CULTIVATION: Easy in peat bed or shady moist soil. Reasonably tolerant as long as it does not have to suffer extreme drought.

PROPAGATION: Seed, or split established clumps in spring.

AVAILABILITY: Occasionally offered by specialist nurserymen, and usually included in the seed lists.

Primula secundiflora (Section 27 Sikkimensis):

First found by Delavay in 1884 in the glacial region of the Likiang range in Yunnan. It occurs in wet meadows in Selachian and Yunnan. Unlike other members of this group that are in cultivation the leaves do not die back in winter, and the neat rosettes of bright, shiny, finely toothed leaves will persist throughout the winter. The 12in (30cm) stems carry loose heads of pendant, rich purple-red, flaring bells which repay closer examination, for the inside of the flower is often attractively powdered with silvery white farina. One of the most beautiful of all the Asiatics.

CULTIVATION: An easy rewarding plant for the peat bed, or any moist, peaty position, and should be more widely grown.

PROPAGATION: Easy from seed, or by dividing established clumps, preferably in spring.

0   2   4in(10cm)

Primula secundiflora.

AVAILABILITY: Sometimes available from the specialist nurseries, and easily grown from the seed that is regularly included in the society seed lists.

Primula serratifolia (Section 28 Candelabra):
From upper Burma, the Yunnan and south-eastern Tibet. It is described as being a typical candelabra, with yellow flowers, and each petal being marked with an orange bar.
CULTIVATION: One assumes peat bed.
PROPAGATION: Seed if obtainable.
AVAILABILITY: Try the seed lists.

Primula sibirica:
Now correctly called *Primula nutans*.

Primula sieboldii (Section 1 Cortusoides):
A glorious plant from Japan, both easy to grow and spectacular when in flower. It was introduced in 1862 and named after the Chevalier P.F. von Siebold of Leyden in Germany, and was later distributed by the famous London firm of Veitch. The growing of this lovely plant in Japan can be likened to the cultivation of the Florists' auriculas in this country, and will be further described in chapter 19.

The slightly hairy, irregularly lobed leaves are held on stems, and the 9–12in (22–30cm) flower stems bear a loose head of very large flat flowers, in shades of pink, white, and even pale blue, the outer side of the petal often being a different shade to the face, and the colours often being feathered. The shape of the petal also varies, from lightly cut to so deeply cut it is almost fernlike. There exist a multitude of beautiful forms, some named, some not, and some excellent seed strains. All are highly recommended.
CULTIVATION: Very easy in the peat bed, or any shady, permanently moist position that does not dry out. This plant dies back to an unusual underground rhizome in late summer, and the time of going into dormancy varies from season to season. As soon as the ground starts to become dry in a hot summer, the plant retreats, often not emerging until May after a cold winter, and within a few weeks the flower stems will emerge. It makes a spectacular specimen in the alpine house, going from strength to strength every year. A fairly gritty, peaty compost and ample water is needed in the growing season, but it should be kept just moist in winter.
PROPAGATION: Seed, which is said to benefit from stratification, but it is not always necessary. Good forms may be split after flowering, the newly divided plants benefit from shading, and keeping the compost moist.

AVAILABILITY: Most specialist nurserymen list several forms, as do the seed catalogues with the larger ranges, also the seed lists.

Primula sikkimensis (Section 27 Sikkimensis):
Originally discovered in Sikkim by Sir Joseph Hooker in 1849, and then later introduced from the Yunnan by Forrest. This is the most widespread plant of the Sikkimensis section, and can be found clothing wet meadows all over the Himalayas and the mountainous regions of China and Burma. As it is so widespread various geographical variants have evolved. Generally the 12in (30cm) high stems carry elegant drooping heads of soft yellow bells over neat upright rosettes of narrow shiny lightly toothed leaves. The main subspecies are:

Primula sikkimensis subsp. hopeana: A more slender form from Bhutan and southern Tibet.

Primula sikkimensis subsp. pudibunda: Is the smaller, alpine form of fairly widespread distribution.

Sometimes offered are the seed strains *Primula sikkimensis* 'Crimson and Gold' which has flowers of rich crimson to dark yellow and *Primula sikkimensis* 'Tilman No.2', which is a selected strain with beautiful rich golden yellow flowers.

CULTIVATION: Peat bed or moist soil in sun.
PROPAGATION: Easy from seed.
AVAILABILITY: Sometimes to be found in the better garden centres, specialist nurseries, or seed lists.

Primula sinoplantaginea (Section 25 Nivales):
A mountain plant from Yunnan, Szechuan and adjacent areas of Tibet, it was first introduced by Forrest who brought back seed in 1914. It is a relatively small Nivalid, reputedly short lived in cultivation, with heads of deep purple, fragrant flowers and a grey eye. As with the other Nivalids it tends to hybridise in cultivation so it is difficult to tell if the true species is offered.

CULTIVATION: Careful culture in a peat bed offers the best chance of success.
PROPAGATION: Seed.
AVAILABILITY: Occasionally offered by specialist alpine nurseries, or try the seed lists, taking note that it is probably unlikely that any seedlings raised will be the true species.

Primula sinopurpurea (Section 25 Nivales):
A relatively common plant from the mountainous ranges of western Yunnan, north into Szechuan, and west towards Bhutan. Forrest sent back seed in 1911, and it is now in fairly general cultivation, albeit hybridised with *Primula chionantha*.

The loose heads of violet purple to mauve flowers, sometimes exhibiting the candelabra habit are on 12–24in (30–60cm) stems, above the neat rosettes of heavily farinaed leaves, that die back in winter to an untidy brown clump. It is not advisable to try and tidy the plant, as any wounds can allow access to disease, which is often fatal.

CULTIVATION: In the drier parts and the south of England, very careful treatment in a cool moist peat bed is advised, as is regular collection of the seed to ensure continuity. In the cooler, moister north, the only essential is a cool, moist soil, and the plants will be found to last several years without needing replacement.

PROPAGATION: Seed is easy and germinates well.

AVAILABILITY: Specialist nurserymen, also the seed lists.

Primula smithiana (Section 28 Candelabra):
From the Chumbi region of the eastern Himalayas. It is a neat species, very similar to *Primula prolifera* with heads of pale yellow flowers in June to July.

CULTIVATION: Needs a rich moist loam in an open sunny position.

PROPAGATION: By seed.

AVAILABILITY: Quite rare, but occasionally offered by specialist nurseries, or from the seed lists.

Primula vialii (Section 22 Muscarioides):
From north-western Yunnan and south-western Szechuan, and was introduced at the beginning of this century. A slightly more vigorous form may be found under the name *Primula littoniana,* named after George Forrest's fellow collector, G. L. Litton.

It is known as the 'Red Hot Poker Primula', and is unique in its appearance. The 18in (45cm) high tight spikes of red flower buds open to give lavender flowers, starting at the bottom, above loose rosettes of softly hairy, narrow leaves. Fairly late flowering, usually just after the Candelabras in June to July. Short lived.

CULTIVATION: Peat bed, or a rich moist soil, often used for waterside planting, where, when happy it will ensure a continuity by self seeding.

PROPAGATION: Easy from seed, but do let the seedlings get to a decent size before potting up, and keep shaded and moist until they are established.

AVAILABILITY: Fairly readily available, in garden centres, especially amongst pond plants, specialist nurseries, seed catalogues, and seed lists.

Primula waltonii (Section 27 Sikkimensis):
First discovered by Captain H. J. Walton in the hills above Lhasa in Tibet, and was later introduced into cultivation by Kingdom Ward from south-east Tibet. It was reputedly a very poor grower and plants now available offered under this name are probably hybrids between the true species and other members of the Sikkimensis section. The hybrids in cultivation are about 12in (20cm) high, and the pendant heads of flowers vary in colour from bright pink to rich violet and even maroon, and are very attractive.
CULTIVATION: Safest in the peat bed, though worth trying in a rich moist soil in sun.
PROPAGATION: Easy from seed.
AVAILABILITY: Occasionally offered by the specialist nurseries, or try the seed lists.

Primula warshenewskiana (Section 19 Farinosae):
A delightful, fairly recent introduction which arrived from Afghanistan via Germany. It is to be found from Turkestan to the north-west Himalayas where it grows alongside small streams and in moist ground. It is a very dwarf plant closely related to *Primula rosea* and *Primula clarkei,* forming compact mats of small, pale green leaves, rather more elongated than the little round leaves of *Primula clarkei,* and produces masses of brilliant rose pink flowers on 2in (5cm) stems in early spring. It dies back for the winter, and spreads by means of underground runners.
CULTIVATION: Careful culture in a peat bed. It is such a dwarf plant that it seems to dry out easily and can be lost if the surface of the peat bed dries out. Also makes a marvellous pan for the alpine house in a peaty compost, best kept well watered in light shade for the hot summer months.
PROPAGATION: Easy by splitting or by detaching runners that have roots attached. This species does not usually set viable seed.
AVAILABILITY: Stocked by several specialist nurseries, especially the more northern ones.

Primula wilsonii (Section 28 Candelabra):
From western Yunnan and western Szechuan, and is closely related to *Primula poissonii,* with purple flowers on 36in (90cm) high stems, and winter persistent leaves. Not one of the hardiest.
CULTIVATION: Peat bed, or moist soil.
PROPAGATION: Seed.
AVAILABILITY: Seed lists or occasionally specialist nurseries.

Primula yuparensis (Section 19 Farinosae):
See *Primula modesta.*
Primula yargongensis (Section 19 Farinosae):
This is the lovely lilac counterpart to *Primula involucrata,* that comes from wet meadows and streams in south-western Szechuan, north-west Yunnan and south-eastern Tibet. The elegant heads of fragrant lilac flowers in May–June are on 12in (30cm) stems above the loose, somewhat untidy rosettes of light green leaves. It dies back completely to small resting buds below the level of the soil in winter. A vigorous, easy plant that deserves to be more widely grown.
CULTIVATION: Easy in the peat bed, or in any rich moist soil that does not dry out in summer.
PROPAGATION: Seed, or by careful division of established clumps in early spring.
AVAILABILITY: Stocked by several specialist nurseries, or grown easily from seed from the seed lists.

ASIATIC HYBRIDS

Primula 'Johanna'
Reputedly *Primula warshenewskiana* x *Primula clarkei,* but its appearance indicates some *Primula rosea* blood. A lovely reliable plant, with loose heads of good pink flowers on 4–6in (10–15cm) stems.
CULTIVATION: Easy in the peat bed, or in any rich moist soil that does not dry out in summer. Also makes an attractive plant for the alpine house, best grown in a fairly peaty compost.
PROPAGATION: Is by careful division of established clumps in early spring.
AVAILABILITY: Stocked by several of the specialist nurseries.
Primula 'Peter Klein' (*Syn.* 'Rose Clarke'):
Accepted as being a true hybrid between *Primula rosea* and *Primula clarkei,* with intermediate features. The flowers are similar to those of *Primula clarkei,* a good clean pink, and are carried on loose heads on 4in (10cm) or more stems. The rounded leaves are somewhat tidier than *Primula rosea* and it can be classed as a good reliable garden plant. It sets fertile seed and the offspring are nearer to *Primula rosea.*
CULTIVATION: Easy in the peat bed , or in any rich, moist soil that does not dry out in summer. It is also very suitable as

a specimen for the cold greenhouse, provided it is given a peaty compost.

PROPAGATION: Division of established clumps in early spring.

AVAILABILITY: Stocked by several specialist nurseries.

15
The Petiolarids

The Petiolarids (Section 12) present a whole realm of beauty and frustration. Anyone seeing these exotic plants will long to grow them and no apologies are necessary for describing plants that are as difficult to acquire as they are to grow. Search amongst the specialist nurseries, especially those in the north of England and in Scotland, and your diligence will yield untold riches. Dedication is essential, they are not plants that will tolerate the open garden, and patience and love is needed to ensure any chance of success. In cooler, moister areas some species will succeed and flourish in the peat bed, but as one travels further south and east they become more temperamental.

The section Petiolares is the second largest in the primula genus, boasting at least sixty species, of which eighteen or more are in cultivation, as well as the hybrids and cultivars. Though not easy to grow these beautiful plants are much sought after, and the few nurseries distributing them have difficulty fulfilling demand, so be patient: careful searching will yield results.

They are fairly dwarf perennials with a fibrous root system, and they flower in the winter, sometimes as early as Christmas or as late as the end of April – a lot depends on the severity of the winter.

Many of the petiolarids have two leaf forms, one for winter and one for summer. During autumn the leaves of some species start to take a tighter form with the flower buds forming in the centre of the rosettes of tiny leaves, and other varieties form a huge egg-like bud. The contracted winter form is often farinose, and in the past there has been much confusion, as the seasonal variation in the leaves has led to at least one variety being given two names.

CULTIVATION

There are many different ways of cultivating these temperamental plants. An understanding of the climate and conditions under which they grow in the wild is the first step towards a full understanding of their needs.

They are plants from the high mountains, often growing in shade amongst rocks, in moist meadows and even at the snowline. They come from areas where there is high summer rainfall, and dryish winters, when they are often covered with snow.

The Petiolarids are gross feeders and the searching roots will soon exhaust the pot of nutrients. In dry and warm areas special arrangements need to be made to cater for their somewhat specific needs. A frame containing a good rich loam mixed with plenty of humus is ideal. It should be kept shaded in summer with green netting, and the moisture content carefully monitored. In winter the green shading can be replaced by glass frames, making sure there is plenty of fresh air circulating.

In Scotland and the north of England, where it is cooler, and the air is moister in summer, some varieties can be successfully grown in shady places in the garden. A suitable microclimate has to be created, for they love shade and moist, cool air, which is not stagnant but remains buoyant. *Primulas edgeworthii,* 'Linnet' and *sonchifolia* can all be grown successfully in peat block walls, provided the atmosphere is congenial, north facing, cool etc. A few minutes' sun in May and June can easily burn the new leaves. In a few gardens, where they have been grown in a suitable position, such as a shady stream side, they have become naturalised and the plants are self seeding in the vicinity.

PROPAGATION

SPLITTING: As soon as there are several crowns it is possible to split these lovely plants. In fact this is often beneficial, and *Primula aureata* especially does better when split regularly. If it were possible to forecast the weather accurately it would be a virtually foolproof method.

After splitting the young plants need either potting or lining out in a nursery bed, being kept cool and shaded, with ample water until they have established a good root system and are seen to be growing away strongly. Spring is the best time, after flowering, as in the autumn the Petiolarids start to assume their winter characteristics, and go into semi dormancy.

SEED: The Petiolarids do not always set seed. If seed is required it is sensible to artificially pollinate the plants by transferring pollen from the stamen on to the stigma with a very fine paintbrush. Although seed is sometimes set by using pollen from the same clone as the stigma, it is never as good or as plentiful.

The seed is almost ripe when the seed capsule turns transparent. On close observation the seed can actually be seen under this transparent cover, and it will be noticed that they are gradually turning brown. Be careful, this transparent cover is about to disintegrate, and when it does the seeds will be cast far and wide. Many books say 'sow the seed green' – this does not mean green in colour, it means to sow as soon as the seed is ripe. When the Petiolarids set seed there is often a reasonable amount of seed in a pod. One grower who is very successful in germinating and raising Petiolarid seedlings, divides all batches of seed in two. The first half is sown immediately, and kept cool and moist in the shade. The other half is cleaned, packeted and labelled, and kept in an airtight container in the salad compartment of the fridge, and then sown in December or January and the tray kept outside, so that the seed is stratified.

Many authorities state that if the seed does not germinate within a few weeks it never will. Personal experience does not bear this statement out. Seed collected from *Primula gracilipes minor* (now called 'Linnet') (which is said not to set seed), and sown straight off the plant in July did not germinate until the following spring. The seed of the Petiolarids is sometimes listed in the Society seed lists, and is well worth trying. Nothing is lost if it never germinates, but what a bonus if it does!

When (or is it if ?) the seed germinates it needs to be looked after carefully, in shade in the greenhouse, or a cold frame. Do make sure they are shaded and kept moist as one day's neglect can result in total loss due to scorching. Take precautions against slugs having a tasty snack. When the seedlings are growing well in spring, and are large enough to handle comfortably, they may be potted up as described previously in chapter 3.

LEAF CUTTINGS: Use the methods described in chapter 3. Note that not all the Petiolarids possess the incipient bud required for this method.

DESCRIPTIVE LIST OF PLANTS IN THE PETIOLARES SECTION

Subsection Petiolares-Sonchifolia

Group vera is characterised by the lack of a main stem, giving a primrose-style flowering habit.

Primula deuteronana:
Brought back from Sikkim in the 1980s, and is a lovely large Petiolarid, which will hopefully be available in the future. The large purple-tinted bright pink flowers have a white eye, and the light green leaves have reddish stalks.
AVAILABILITY: Rare in cultivation, as yet only in private collections.

Primula gracilipes:
A dwarf plant with loose rosettes of longish leaves, tinged slightly red in summer, and as with many of this section, the winter leaves are smaller and tighter. This species must not be confused with *Primula gracilipes minor* which has now been renamed *Primula* 'Linnet'.
AVAILABILITY: Occasionally from the specialist nurseries.

Primula 'Linnet':
A lovely plant, and the easiest of this section. It forms tight rosettes of neat, bright green leaves, neatly serrated, and in the autumn the flower buds form in the centre of each rosette. These buds sit all winter until April, and then they open up to a solid posy of rich, mauve pink flowers with a distinctive large green and yellow eye. After flowering the leaves elongate into the somewhat looser summer form.
AVAILABILITY: One of the most readily found, from several specialist nurseries.

Primula petiolaris:
The plant often available under this name is indistinguishable from *Primula gracilipes minor,* and has now been renamed 'Linnet'.

Primula petiolaris LS 19856:
This a very desirable very dwarf plant was introduced by Ludlow and Sherriff from the Bhutan-Sikkim border. It is similar to a smaller *Primula* 'Linnet' with slightly darker foliage, and a profusion of rich, satin purple flowers in April. It has been suggested in the past that this plant may in fact be a hybrid of *Primula petiolaris* with *Primula boothii.*
AVAILABILITY: Only in private collections.

Primula sessilis:
Again this is similar to *Primula petiolaris,* but the petals have only one tooth whereas the petals of *Primula petiolaris* have three.
AVAILABILITY: Rarely available.

Group scapigera is characterised by having a very short main stem 2in (4cm) or less at flowering time, but elongating later. The general appearance is still that of a rather exotic primrose.

Primula aureata:
One of the most beautiful of all the primulas. From the contracted foliage, almost silver with farina, emerge the beautiful rich cream flowers, shading into bright yellow with well serrated leaves in March and April.
AVAILABILITY: Readily available from the specialist nurseries.

Primula aureata fimbriata:
Very similar to the above, but the flowers are smaller and more deeply serrated. This is thought to be the same as *Primula aureata forma.*
AVAILABILITY: Occasionally from specialist nurseries.

Primula boothii:
A dwarf plant without farina, the darkish leaves have a distinct red midrib, and the flowers in spring are pink to purple. Several different forms are available. In winter the leaves form loose upright bunches, and the backs of the leaves are pinkish brown. The protection of a cold greenhouse is recommended as this plant does not seem as hardy as others in this section.
AVAILABILITY: Stocked by a few specialist nurseries.

Primula boothii alba:
Brought back from the Ghurka Himalayas of central Nepal by Cabot and Schilling in 1983, and should become available. It has brilliant white flowers with a yellow eye, over mid green foliage, marked with lighter veins.
AVAILABILITY: Listed by one specialist nursery at present.

Primula boothii 'Edrom':
Pale pink, fringed flowers with a white eye. The dark green leaves are finely toothed and have a reddish underside. Flowers in April.
AVAILABILITY: Occasionally by the specialist nurseries.

Primula bracteosa:
Bright pink, yellow-eyed flowers and light green, narrow

serrated leaves. A clump of leaves (bracts) develops at the top of the stem, which may be detached and rooted.
AVAILABILITY: Listed by several specialist nurseries.
Primula irregularis:
Although plants are in cultivation under this name there seems to be disagreement whether it is this species or a pink *Primula edgeworthii*.
AVAILABILITY: In private collections only.
Primula scapigera:
A dwarf plant forming clumps of leaves, with pink flowers with a yellow eye.
AVAILABILITY: Rarely from specialist nurseries.
Primula 'Sandy's Form':
Believed to be a seedling of *Primula boothii*. It has pink flowers in spring, and is somewhat similar to *Primula* x *scapeosa*.
AVAILABILITY: Rarely from specialist nurseries.
Primula x *scapeosa:*
The hybrid between *Primula scapigera* and *Primula bracteosa* and is intermediate in form. In very severe winters the roots can be frozen in the open ground for many weeks and when the weather improves it has been known for the leaves to suddenly turn dry, brown and die as if a flame thrower had been played over them, and the plants are found to be totally dead. This can also happen to *Primula bracteosa* and *Primula scapigera*.
AVAILABILITY: Occasionally from the specialist nurseries.

Group hookeri.

Primula hookeri:
Small white, almost stemless flowers. Not showy but possesses a quiet charm, and it flowers very early, even before *Primula edgeworthii*. Now thought to be the same plant as *Primula vernicosa*.
AVAILABILITY: Only in private collections.

Group edgeworthii have very different leaf forms in summer and winter. In winter they have tight resting rosettes of leaves.

Primula edgeworthii:
A lovely petiolarid, the flowers varying in colour from almost pale blue through to a strange mauve blue shade. The petals are solidly coloured, not the delicate sky blue of *Primula bhutanica*. In flower they tend to fold backwards on themselves. The flowers are grouped in the centre of the highly farinose leaves.

AVAILABILITY: From several specialist nurseries.
Primula edgeworthii 'Ghose Form':
Raised by R. Masterton from seed supplied by the seed company 'Ghose'. It was noticed that it was a larger flowered, more vigorous form than those previously in cultivation. This selected strain has pale, mauve blue flowers with yellow eyes and light green toothed foliage. The foliage is well covered in farina in winter, which gradually disappears as the leaves expand in spring. It usually flowers in February–March, but the odd flower may be seen as early as Christmas.
AVAILABILITY: Occasionally from specialist nurseries.
Primula edgeworthii alba:
The equally lovely white form, which is somewhat easier to please.
AVAILABILITY: Occasionally from the specialist nurseries.

Group sonchifolia members go back to large resting buds that sit on the soil surface in winter.

Primula sonchifolia:
From the contracted winter bud a large globose head of very distinctive mauve blue to blue flowers, with a large deep yellow eye outlined in green emerges in spring. The flowers start to open before the head has cleared the leaves, giving a 'posy' effect.
AVAILABILITY: Listed by several specialist nurseries.
Primula sonchifolia 'Soup-plate':
A really beautiful plant, similar to *Primula whitei,* but with some *Primula sonchifolia* in its makeup. It is believed to have appeared at Ascreavie, in Scotland, where both parents grow and self seed, and is undoubtedly a hybrid.
AVAILABILITY: Only in private collections.

To avoid the confusion regarding the names of *Primula whitei* and *bhutanica,* this book will use the classification proposed by J. Jermyn of Edrom Nurseries.

Primula whitei:
The subject of controversy for many years. There are several forms about, and at one time the form labelled *Primula whitei* was rather indistinct mauve blue, with smaller flowers and a less pronounced eye, whereas the plant labelled *Primula bhutanica* was the very beautiful form that is seen illustrating books.

The forms grown today are descended from those introduced by Ludlow and Sherriff about 1949. The resting buds are liberally coated with farina, and they unfold to reveal a glorious posy of delft blue flowers in early spring.
AVAILABILITY: From several specialist nurseries.

***Primula whitei* 'Arduaine':**
A selected sterile form with slightly darker flowers and a clearly defined, large pale yellow eye. The long narrow serrated leaves are covered with farina in the winter, and the plant, like *Primula sonchifolia,* overwinters in a highly contracted form as an egg-like bud. In March the leaves start to expand and the lovely flowers open. It is recommended that the large clumps are split every two or three years.
AVAILABILITY: From the occasional specialist nursery.

***Primula whitei* subsp. *bhutanica*:**
This name is used to describe a form that is very similar to *Primula whitei,* but slightly later flowering. The foliage is shorter, and it is not as vigorous – the petals are more noticeably fringed.
AVAILABILITY: From the occasional specialist nursery.

***Primula* 'Tantalon':** (*Primula bhutanica* x *Primula edgeworthii*)
Stunning blue flowers and is closer to *Primula edgeworthii* in appearance.
AVAILABILITY: Rarely from the specialist nurseries.

***Primula* 'Tinney's Appleblossom':**
A hybrid between *Primula boothii* and *Primula aureata*. It has cream flowers with orange eyes and dark green, toothed leaves, the undersides of which are reddish in colour.
AVAILABILITY: Only in private collections.

There are several other flamboyantly beautiful hybrids under the Tinney heading, bred by G.R. Mundey of Wiltshire, all of which are well worth growing, but are only in private collections at present.

Subsection Griffithii

Members of this subsection are completely herbaceous, and disappear below ground for the winter. This attractive, but not spectacular group of plants are less available now than they were ten years ago, and they seem to have been superseded by the more glamorous and exotic Petiolarids. At flowering time they superficially resemble the Denticulata primulas, with a much looser head of flowers on a strong stem. As the season progresses the leaves grow, and the plants become quite large, with big dark green leaves.

Primula calderiana:
A lovely plant with rich purple flowers, darkening near the centre, and a yellow five-sided eye. Height is very variable, from 6–12in (15–30cm). The leaves of this plant are strap-shaped, somewhat reminiscent of a Nivalid primula.
AVAILABILITY: Occasionally from the specialist nurseries.

Primula calderiana 'pink form':
A lovely new colour break, grown from seed from the Beer Expedition, with clear medium pink flowers.
AVAILABILITY: Only in private collections.

Primula griffithii:
Collected and introduced by Ludlow and Sherriff around 1949. It is a slow plant to increase, and gradually forms congested clumps of large swollen, winter resting buds which produce heads of bright purple flowers with a yellow eye, 8in (20cm) high at flowering.
AVAILABILITY: Occasionally from the specialist nurseries.

Primula griffithii hybrids:
Originally raised at Keillour Castle, with *Primula strumosa* as the pollen parent. They range in colour from yellow through to purple.
AVAILABILITY: Only in private collections.

The four following species are very similar, all having cabbage-like leaves for the summer, and resting buds in the winter – some above and some below soil level.

Primula nepalensis:
Heads of yellow flowers on 8–12in (20–30cm) stems in April, very similar to *Primula strumosa*.

Primila strumosa:
Yellow with an orange eye.

Primula tanneri:
Yellow flowers.

Primula tsariensis: Pinkish purple.
AVAILABILITY: Occasionally the odd specialist nursery will list one of the above plants.

16
Asiatics for the Dedicated

It is impossible to generalise about these plants, and this chapter will contain details of a good selection of the rarer Asiatic primulas in cultivation that cannot be classed as garden plants, even though some of the species described will flourish in the garden in areas where the climate is suitable.

Many of the plants listed in this chapter are rare, and it will need great perseverance to find a source.

The smaller Asiatic species are mainly plants for the alpine house or for very careful culture in the peat bed. The seed exchange schemes offer the best chance of obtaining these little treasures, but sometimes a nursery will list one or two.

The sections will be dealt with in order as they nearly all need very specific treatment. They are not plants for the inexperienced grower, though the difficulties in obtaining the plants are sufficient to deter all but the most determined of cultivators.

SECTION 1 CORTUSOIDES

SUBSECTION GERANIOIDES

Primula jesoana:
An attractive plant from the mountains of Japan, and carries loose heads of rose pink flowers above lobed, pale green, hairy leaves. Needs a moist position, sheltered from the midday sun. Also suitable for the alpine house, in a moisture retentive compost that never dries out.
AVAILABILITY: Occasionally from the specialist nurseries, or try the society seed lists.

Primula kisoana:
This has very hairy leaves, and 4in (10cm) stems carrying a loose head of up to six rosy mauve flowers with a dark pink eye. It comes from a small area in south-west Japan, and has been in cultivation in Japan for 300 years. If fortunate enough to obtain a plant it would be safest in the alpine house.
AVAILABILITY: Try the seed list.

Primula kisoana shikokiana alba:
Brought to this country by the Japanese visitors to the 1981 Conference of the Alpine Garden Society, and has found to be a thoroughly satisfactory plant for a cool peaty soil, quickly forming plants on near surface roots to form good clumps.
AVAILABILITY: Rarely from the specialist nurseries. Watch the society seed lists.

SUBSECTION EUCORTUSOIDES

Primula mollis:
An attractive perennial with heads of dark pink to crimson flowers, but the very hairy leaves are not lobed like the other members of the Cortusoides section. Not hardy, but excellent under glass.
AVAILABILITY: Often included on the Society seed lists.

SECTION 2 REINII

A small section from the mountains of Japan, not easy to acquire and far from easy to grow. They come from wet and shady rocky cliffs, where the swirling mists maintain a constantly high level of humidity in summer, and in winter the dormant resting buds are protected by snow.

All the species in this section require shade. Cool conditions and dappled sunshine is best; too much sun and the leaves turn yellow and growth ceases. Drainage must be perfect, a shady scree would be ideal, but overhead protection in winter is really needed.

In pots a free draining compost is essential, the conventional compost for the Auriculastrum section possibly with added grit, is recommended, but care must be taken so as not to allow drying out in the growing season.

Primula hidakana:
A distinct plant with small palmate leaves of shining bronze green, growing from a short creeping rhizome. The delicate rosy mauve flowers are enhanced by a raised yellow eye, and are up to 1in (2.5cm) across. They are held singly on the stems just above the foliage. The young leaves are tinged coppery red in spring.
PROPAGATION: By fresh seed or by careful separation of the tiny rhizomes in spring.

AVAILABILITY: Occasionally from the specialist nurseries, or seed from the Society seed lists.

Primula kamuiana:

A little treasure. A single rose coloured flower on a 3in (7cm) stem, and possibly only two small leaves.

AVAILABILITY: Only in private collections at present.

Primula reinii:

A rare plant from the mainland of Japan. In nature it is to be found on rocky shaded cliffs, and is very variable. The flowers can be up to 1in (2.5cm) across and are usually solitary, though there can be up to three rose, pink to mauve flowers, with a small yellow eye, outlined in white. The deeply notched petals give a delicate, fragile appearance to this plant.

AVAILABILITY: Only in private collections.

Primula takedena:

From sub-alpine meadows, especially wet, rocky areas. It is rare in the wild and intermediate between *Primula hidakana* and *Primula rienii*. The red stems bear rounded leaves with pronounced lobes, each one with two or three rounded teeth, and covered in fine hairs, which disappear as the plant matures. The two to three fragrant white bell-shaped flowers are about the size of a five pence piece. There may be two tiers of flowers in well grown specimens.

AVAILABILITY: Has been listed by at least one specialist nursery.

Primula tosaensis:

The most southerly member of this section, described as widespread but not abundant. It is very like *P.reinii*. The soft hairy leaves are finely toothed and carried on densely hairy pink stems. The 6in (15cm) high flower stems carry up to six mauve pink, long tubed flowers with yellow eye outlined in white. Two subspecies exist: *Primula tosaensis brachycarpa* and *Primula tosaensis rhodotricha*.

AVAILABILITY: Only in private collections at present, but as it sets seed in captivity there is a good chance it may become available.

SECTION 10 AMETHYSTINA

These beautiful species are sometimes reintroduced by seed collected on expeditions, but they never survive for long. If seed were to be obtained treatment as for the section Reinii would be most suitable.

Primula dickieana:
A short lived perennial that requires winter protection, and shade in summer.
AVAILABILITY: Only in a very few private collections.
Primula kingii:
Rich wine-coloured, pendulous flowers. Likes moist, very acid soil, and cool conditions.
AVAILABILITY: Private collections only.

SECTION 15 BULLATAE

Primula forrestii:
This attractive semi-shrubby species tends to have a long woody rootstock and was discovered by Forrest trailing down dry limestone crevices. In milder districts it can be grown outside, but otherwise it is safest in the alpine house. The rich yellow flowers with an orange eye are carried in good heads on 4–18in (10–45cm) stems above the leaves. An interesting plant for the alpine house, where a gritty compost is recommended, and as it is a relatively large plant repotting once a year would be sensible.
AVAILABILITY: Sometimes listed in the Society seed lists.
Primula redolens:
Very similar with white or lavender fragrant flowers.
AVAILABILITY: Rarely in the seed lists.

SECTION 17 MINUTISSIMAE

SUBSECTION EU-MINUTISSIMAE

Primula reptans:
Strongly rhizomatous, and forms compact cushions of bright green leaves above which appear the large purple flowers. When in active growth this plant is happy creeping through moist moss, but when dormant is apt to disappear forever.
AVAILABILITY: Occasionally from a specialist nursery.
Primula stirtoniana:
Seed of this tiny plant was collected by Ron McBeath of the Edinburgh Royal Botanic Garden in 1983 from moist ledges on the north face of Annapurna III. How well it will settle to cultivation is questionable.
AVAILABILITY: Only in private collections.

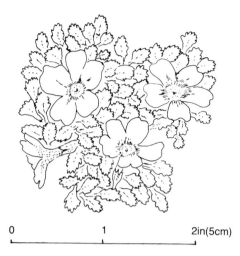

0   1   2in(5cm)

Primula reptans.

SUBSECTION BELLA

Primula primulina:

A tiny plant with heads of small deep purple flowers on a short stem, above small rosettes of deeply toothed spatulate leaves. It dies back to a small resting bud in winter. Although common in the Himalayas it is relatively rare in cultivation. Probably safest in a pot in the alpine house, using gritty compost which is never allowed to become dry.

AVAILABILITY: Occasionally from Society seed lists.

SECTION 19 FARINOSAE

SUBSECTION EU-FARINOSAE

Primula concinna:

A minute plant with a cluster of delicate amethyst flowers nestling in a rosette of blunt leaves.

AVAILABILITY: Private collections only.

Primula hazarica:

A rare species from Hazarica and Kashmir, related to *Primula farinosa*. The head of mauve purple flowers is carried above rosettes of leaves covered in white farina.

AVAILABILITY: Private collections only.

Primula jaffreyana:
From around the Bhutan–Tibet border. The 4in (10cm) high, stems carry heads of large deep lilac flowers above rosettes of narrow leaves, with thick white farina on the reverse.
AVAILABILITY: Only in private collections.

SUBSECTION INAYATII

Primula inayatii:
From north-west Nepal and Kashmir. The 2–4in (5–10cm) stem carries a head of pale lilac flowers with a white or yellow eye above a flat rosette of glossy, mid-green leaves, the undersides of which are heavily coated with cream coloured farina.
AVAILABILITY: Only in private collections.

SUBSECTION GLABRA

Primula glabra:
A small hairless Indian alpine, 3–4in (7–10cm) high, with six or more flowers like an exaggerated *Primula farinosa*. A pretty plant with its small globose heads in shades of mauve. Cold greenhouse protection is required.
AVAILABILITY: Rarely from the Society seed lists.

SUBSECTION SIBIRICA

Primula tibetica:
A smaller *Primula involucrata* with pink flowers.
AVAILABILITY: Only in private collections.

SUBSECTION AURICULATAE

Primula elliptica:
Introduced from the Kashmir Botanical Expedition in 1983. It has up to ten pinkish mauve flowers in a loose head, and the sharply toothed leaves are nearly upright. For scree or alpine house, and like its close relatives *Primula rosea* and *Primula clarkei* moisture is essential.
AVAILABILITY: Did not appear to settle to cultivation very well. Possibly still present in private collections.
Primula fedtschenkoi:
This requires a summer baking. The flowers are deep rose pink, every petal is marked with a magenta spot.

AVAILABILITY: Has been offered by one specialist nursery, but whether it will survive for long in cultivation is another question.

SECTION 20 DENTICULATA

Primula drummondiana:
Sets seed in cultivation, so hopefully will be available in the next few years. Described as a miffy little thing, like a miniature lavender *Primula denticulata* only 2–3in (5–7cm) high. Attractive grown in a pan.
AVAILABILITY: Only in private collection at present, but watch the Society seed lists.

SECTION 22 MUSCARIOIDES

Primula bellidifolia:
The 4–12in (10–30cm) high stem carries a tight head of purple flowers, well covered in farina, above a neat rosette of softly hairy leaves, shaped like the leaves of a daisy. Like the other members of this section it dies back to a resting bud for winter. Safest in the alpine house, but never allow it to become dry. If sufficient plants are available it is an attractive and unusual plant for the peat bed.
AVAILABILITY: Occasionally from the specialist nurserymen, or from the Society seed lists.

SECTION 23 SOLDANELLOIDES

The plants in this section have beautiful fragrant flowers, and soft hairy leaves, that die back completely for winter. Alpine house treatment is recommended. They require a gritty compost, but in the spring and summer they must never be allowed to become dry. Whilst dormant in the winter they are usually kept on the dry side.
Primula cawdoriana:
Similar to *Primula reidii* with a narrower flower and frilly petals. Conical mauve bells with notched edges hang above a flat rosette of sharply toothed leaves.
AVAILABILITY: Occasionally from northern specialist nurseries.

Primula eburnea:
A typical member of this section with ivory white flowers.
AVAILABILITY: Only in private collections.

Primula sapphirina:
The flowering stem is only 2in (5cm) high, and carries one to four semi pendant flowers which are funnel-shaped and violet purple. The little leaves are lobed and hairy.
AVAILABILITY: Seed of this little treasure is sometimes offered by the more extensive seed catalogues.

Primula sherriffiae:
Large, pale violet flowers edged with white, and flecked with farina outside and in the throat.
AVAILABILITY: Private collections only.

Primula uniflora:
Recently reintroduced from Nepal. Small hairy, deeply lobed leaves, 1in (2.5cm) long, with an upright 3in (7cm) stem, that carries nodding fragrant lavender bell-shaped flowers. The plants have a light dusting of farina early in the year that disappears in summer, and in winter the whole plant dies back to a tight cluster of winter leaves.
AVAILABILITY: Private collections only.

Primula wollastonii:
Originally found by Dr A.F.R. Wollaston during the 1921 Everest Expedition in southern Tibet, and was later found again in Nepal. It has recently been reintroduced. The nodding, open bell-shaped, violet blue flowers are lightly powdered inside with farina, and new plants grow from surface roots.
AVAILABILITY: Private collections only.

SECTION 24 ROTUNDIFOLIA

This section is characterised by the rounded, stalked leaves. They all die back for the winter, and it is recommended that they be grown in the alpine house in an Auriculastrum compost.

Primula barnardoana:
A rare Nepalese species that was reintroduced in the late 1970s, with yellow farina on the undersides of leaves and yellow flowers.
AVAILABILITY: Only in private collections.

Primula caveana:
First collected from Nepal in 1909, but has always been very

rare in cultivation. It is reputedly the highest growing primula. The flowers vary in colour, from pinky lilac through to almost purple, but they are all attractively perfumed. The small leaves are heavily mealed underneath.
AVAILABILITY: Only in private collections.
Primula gambeliana:
This small plant with large flowers has rounded leaves on long stalks, and violet purple to purplish pink flowers with a yellow eye. It can be distinguished from *Primula rotundifolia* by the absence of farina on the flower head. From the Nepal Sikkim border.
AVAILABILITY: Only in private collections.
Primula ramzanae:
Found in eastern Nepal and was first found by Polunin in 1952. It has small round, farinose leaves and the 1in (2.5cm) high stems carry large rosy purple flowers.
AVAILABILITY: Private collections only.
Primula rotundifolia:
Heads of purplish pink flowers with a distinct yellow eye, on 4–12in (10–30cm) stems, above neat rosettes of long stemmed, rounded shiny leaves. It dies back to a resting bud in winter, and normally flowers in April–May in cultivation. Requires a gritty, well drained compost, but do not allow to become too dry.
AVAILABILITY: Occasionally from the specialists' nurseries, or sometimes on Society seed lists.

SECTION 25 NIVALES

Careful treatment under glass in a gritty, peaty compost.

SUBSECTION EU-NIVALES

Primula duthieana:
Reintroduced from the Pakistan Himalayas where it flowers in wet snow-melt meadows. It is a typical Nivalid with farinose strap-shaped leaves and a pale midrib. The leaf surface is nearly shiny, and the flowers are pale yellow with a darker eye.
AVAILABILITY: Only in private collections.
Primula obliqua:
Recently reintroduced from Nepal in the mid 1970s with pale yellow to white flowers. Grown under the same conditions as

the Petiolarids, it sometimes flowers twice in the year, in spring and autumn. It strongly resents root disturbance, but it is possible to divide in early spring before the long strap-shaped leaves are properly developed.
AVAILABILITY: Only in private collections.

SECTION 29 CANDELABRA

Primula prenantha:
Probably the smallest Candelabra, and is not really considered a plant for the open garden. The dainty pendulous yellow flowers are carried in the typical whorls of that section.
AVAILABILITY: Occasionally from the specialist nurseries, or the Society seed lists.

SECTION 30 FLORIBUNDAE

This section of plants are not fully hardy, but if they are kept dryish, but not bone dry, they will succeed in a cold green-house in all but the severest winters. They all have yellow flowers in late winter, and certainly bring colour when there is little else.

Primula edelbergii:
A rare plant from eastern Afghanistan, with heads of golden yellow flowers over bright green, crinkled foliage.
AVAILABILITY: Only in private collections.
Primula floribunda:
Like the following but with bright yellow flowers.
AVAILABILITY: Occasionally in the Society seed lists.
Primula floribunda 'Isabellina':
Candelabra-style flower stems 4in(10cm) high, with up to ten cream flowers in each of the three whorls.
AVAILABILITY: Private collections only.
Primula gaubaeana:
From south-west Persia (Iran). It is a strong growing plant, in cultivation usually 12in (30cm) high. There is no farina on leaves, but slight speckling on stem, one or two whorls, each with 4–6 flowers, bright yellow with a small orange spot at the base of each petal. Prefers to be dry in winter.
AVAILABILITY: Private collections only.

Primula verticillata:

Although this group of plants are not hardy outside, they make excellent long lived plants in a cold greenhouse. A standard compost, light shading and ample water in summer, reducing the water in winter. It is divided into three subspecies:

Primula verticillata subsp. boveana:

Found on Mount St Catherine in the Sinai Peninsula.

Primula verticillata subsp. simensis:

From the mountains of Ethiopia and is probably the only African primula.

Primula verticillata subsp. verticillata:

From the Yemen.

AVAILABILITY: From the Society seed lists.

17
Primulas for the Warm Greenhouse
(and as house plants)

These may be divided into two groups: the non-hardy Asiatic primulas, and the cultivars and hybrids of the primrose and polyanthus that are used for decoration in the home.

NON HARDY ASIATICS

CULTIVATION: They are best grown in a compost of four parts John Innes No.2, one part moss peat and one part grit, and the final pot size will be about 5in(12cm). As soon as the flower stems start to lengthen it is advisable to liquid feed once a week with a balanced fertiliser. Always keep the compost moist, but not too wet.

PROPAGATION: The following Asiatic species are all grown from seed, which is sown between April and July on a proprietary peat based compost, the recommended germination temperature being 60°F (15°C). It is essential that the seed trays are kept moist, shady and cool. The seed should germinate within 3–5 weeks, and the young plants may be potted into 3in (7cm) pots as soon as they are big enough to handle, and plunged in a shady frame for the summer months. They will need repotting into larger pots about September–October, put into the greenhouse, and a minimum temperature of 45°F (7°C) should be maintained. Some of the plants from the earlier sowings should be starting to flower for Christmas.

AVAILABILITY: All the major seed companies list a few of these colourful plants, but do deal with them direct, and send for the seeds by post. Grown plants are for sale in garden centres and shops from late autumn onwards.

Primula x Kewensis (Section 30 Floribundae):
This hybrid occurred at Kew originally, as a result of crossing

237

Primula verticillata and *Primula floribunda*. It was at first sterile, but later gave rise to a fertile form, which breeds reasonably true from seed. This perennial is about 15in (40cm) high, with light green leaves that may or may not be covered in farina. Many bright yellow flowers are carried in whorls, from December to April, like the Candelabra primulas. It is very nearly hardy and can be used to decorate the alpine house in the winter months.

Primula malacoides (Section 13 Malacoides):
'Fairy Primula', this lovely and colourful plant is in fact perennial, but it is normally grown as an annual. It has toothed hairy, pale green leaves, and from the middle rise one or more 12–18in (30–45cm) slender stems bearing a large number of fragrant flowers on Candelabra-like whorls. They flower from December to April in a wide range of colours, from white, pale lilac, pink, through every shade to red. At one time there was a lovely double lilac pink strain in existence, but it seems to have disappeared from cultivation.

Primula obconica (Section 5 Obconica):
Light green slightly hairy leaves, and heads of large flat flowers on 9–15in (25–40cm) stems from December until May. There is a startling range of colours in white, mauve, pink through to red and even dark blue, sometimes the flowers are bi-coloured. This lovely primula has one great setback, the hairs on the leaves carry a chemical, which can set up quite a bad allergic reaction in some people. After flowering it may be grown on for another year to flower again, but it will never be as good – so throw it away and grow new stock every year.

Primula sinensis (Section 6 Sinensis):
'The Chinese Star Primula', this lovely plant is not as popular as it used to be. The mid-green, hairy leaves form an erect rosette, and the 10in (25cm) high thick stems carry two or three whorls of huge flowers from December to May in a wide range of colours, including orange, blue, white, mauve and pink. This species was introduced from China in the mid nineteenth century, and it was then very popular for the cold greenhouse – the catalogues from the end of the nineteenth century listing a wide range of varieties.

PRIMROSES AND POLYANTHUS

Many millions of primroses and polyanthus are now produced for the pot plant market. They may be found in every supermarket, flower shop and garden centre and are sold in flower from December through to March, culminating in the glorious displays for Mother's Day. The colour range covers the whole spectrum – red, yellow, blue and white and every conceivable shade in between. After flowering and when they no longer look their best they may be planted in a suitable place in the garden. They have been bred for many years under glass, and selected for good colour and form rather than hardiness, so inevitably they are less hardy than the strains recommended for the garden.

CULTIVATION: These plants always do better when grown cool, and they are happier with plenty of light in winter. On top of the television is not recommended.

PROPAGATION: The seed of the best strains is very expensive, so do be sure that the rather specific conditions required for successful germination are available before attempting to grow these plants from seed. The conditions for germination are identical to those for the non-hardy Asiatics described previously. When the seedlings are large enough to pot they be may either pricked out into seed trays 2in (5cm) apart or potted straight into 3–3½in (7–9cm) pots in a proprietary peat based compost and kept cool, moist and shaded for the summer. In the autumn they need to go into a frost-free greenhouse, and as soon as the flower buds start to form in the centre of the plant a liquid feed once a week is beneficial. When in flower they may be enjoyed in the house, but they will last longer and in better condition if they are kept in a cool, light and airy position.

Especially attractive forms may be split after flowering, potted up and grown on for the following winter. All the primroses and polyanthuses may be planted in the garden in the spring, and, although they are not as hardy as the outdoor types, they should give several years of enjoyment.

18
The Basics of Breeding

Contrary to popular belief the breeding of a new variety in the primula or auricula world will not yield any financial reward whatsoever, but it can be an absorbing hobby that will give great personal satisfaction.

There is a great deal of difference between collecting and growing seed and breeding new plants. The whole idea of breeding is that the parents are deliberately chosen in order to develop a new plant with certain characteristics.

In general it is only possible to hybridise plants within a section, the exception to this rule being the Candelabra and Sikkimensis sections. The species within any one section will often hybridise very readily, for example the species in the Auriculastrum section have hybridised in the wild wherever the distribution of two species overlap. The primula is still evolving, and many different species are little more than geographical variants, this being indicated by the ease with which they hybridise. It is this ability that has brought about the many hybrids that are present in our gardens today.

The aim of the breeder must always be to produce a new plant that is better than the parents, or at least significantly different. Consider all the variable characteristics relative to plants – leaf shape, colour, size, meal, flowers, flowering time, hardiness, vigour – the list is enormous. Generally the thing to look for is two parents with desirable characters, and to consider what would result if they were mixed. One parent may have a very attractive neat habit and insipid flowers, and the other parent might have messy leaves but very striking flowers – the offspring of mating these two plants might contain one plant with the desirable traits of both parents.

All the members of the Auriculastrum section hybridise with each other very readily, and despite the vast number of hybrids about there is still room for improvement. There are some lovely Pubescenses, that are marred by their slowness to offset and lack of vigour. Many breeders in the past have concentrated too much on colour and form to the detriment of health, and some good colourful plants for the garden would be a very worthy cause.

240

It is easier to use a pin-eyed plant as the mother, since there is less risk of the plant being selfed. The pollen is transferred, often by a very fine artist's paintbrush from the stamens of the chosen father onto the stigma of the mother plant, and it is then labelled. An easy way of labelling is to loosely tie a piece of coloured wool round the pedicel of the pollinated flower, and stick a label in the side of the pot with details, for example:

Blue wool, 3/4/89
'Harlow Car' x 'Blairside Yellow'

The name of the seed parent (Mother plant) is always first, and the pollen parent (father plant) second.

The greenhouse needs to be as insect proof as possible. If serious breeding is intended the doors and windows need to be covered with fine netting to keep all insects away.

It is advisable to remove all other flowers and buds from the seed parent, and when the seed is ripe it may be sown immediately or stored (See chapter 3).

The naming of new plants is a tricky subject. Theoretically it is not permissible to name a plant until one is invited to do so after it has been judged to be worthy of a name. There are special classes at the primula and auricula shows for new seedlings, and the best plants in these classes are then named by their owners. In reality many growers name their plants before they are shown.

19
Exhibiting

PRIMULAS

There are many shows where primulas can be exhibited, and growers enjoy both the excitement and the social gathering. The most important show in the primula growers diary must be the annual primula show of the Auricula and Primula Society, whether it be the Northern, Midlands or Southern section. The Northern Show is held by tradition on the first saturday in April, and not only are there classes for every conceivable type of primula, but also a few for auriculas, even though it is well before the main flowering time. The Alpine Garden Society and the Scottish Rock Garden Club also have classes in the spring shows for primulas.

A very important thing to remember about showing is that it is the losers that make the show – how boring it would be if the only plants on show were the three prizewinners in each class. There are two types of showman–the one who works for weeks, if not months beforehand, in order to be able to present his plants in the peak of condition, and the other, who looks round his greenhouse the day before, and selects any plants that are of a sufficient standard, and takes them along to the show. Showing is to be enjoyed, and it is amazing how the appearance of a plant can be improved by intelligent cleaning, tidying and arranging, known as 'dressing'.

The pot must be clean, and plastic pots can be carefully wiped with a damp cloth. Clay pots may need more work, with a nail brush etc.

All dead and dying leaves must be removed carefully, taking care not to mark or damage the flowers. Any flowers that are badly faded or marked need to be removed, taking care that the cut stalks are out of sight, below the level of the leaves. Weeds in the pot or dirty topdressing are unforgiveable, and the exhibitor will deserve all he gets, or doesn't, as the case may be. Experiment with a plant that is not going to the show in re-arranging the flowers to give a more pleasing effect – often two or three flowers moved slightly can improve a plant's appearance, transforming it into a winner.

Certain primulas, especially the allioniis, have sticky leaves, and once marked with sand or compost are virtually impossible to clean. Similarly the auriculas, members of the Farinosae section and other farinose plants can have the appearance of the leaves ruined by indiscriminate use of the watering can. This also applies to the flower stems of some varieties, and on close examination a delicate covering of farina will be seen, which can be marred by careless handling, or by the unthinking use of too much cotton wool. If a well mealed leaf is marked by just one spot, it can be left to dry and the mark can then be very gently brushed out with a soft brush, so that it no longer mars the whole appearance.

When exhibiting primulas there are few hard and fast rules. The plant must be in character and healthy, for instance a plant that is drawn and obviously forced will be down marked. Rarity and difficulty in cultivation of course counts, but a well grown speciment of a more common variety will still be judged on its own merits.

Do read the schedule carefully and if in doubt ask one of the committee for guidance, as even the most experienced show-man occasionally makes a mistake and puts his plant in the wrong class, where the judges will put an NAS card (not according to schedule). The judge's decision is final. There is always someone who thinks his plant better than the one given the red card (First). It may be, but like a football referee's decision, the judge's ruling must be accepted. The judge may be looking at the plants from a slightly different viewpoint, and however much the exhibitor may disagree, he does not decide, the judge does.

Opinions on top dressing the pots of the primulas vary. Often the use of peat or moss on the Petiolarids or other woodlanders enhances the plant, but take care, as any excesses will probably be downgraded. The European hybrids of the Auriculastrum group need to be top dressed with grit, preferably limestone in the case of the allioniis and marginatas. The size of the grit used is purely personal. The main criteria is that it looks natural.

GOLD LACE POLYANTHUS

As it is a Florists' flower the judging is along much stricter lines. This is not a full list of judging standards, but it is a good guide for the novice exhibitor:

a) One truss will be judged – any others must be removed or tied down.

b) The flowers must be thrum–eyed.

c) There must be a minimum of five expanded pips (flowers), as uniform as possible.

d) The pip should be ¾in(19mm) in diameter, and flat.

e) The colour must be unshaded, rich red or black.

f) Lacing narrow, unbroken, constant width, to pass around the edge and down the middle of each petal to the eye, which should be of the same colour as the lacing.

THE FLORISTS' AURICULAS

Do not top dress the compost, and it is preferable that the leaves cover the compost. For exhibition a single-stemmed plant with one rosette of leaves is the ideal, and the flowers must be thrum–eyed or the plant will be disqualified.

Many exhibitors these days are not dressing their auriculas. It is a very important part of showing, and many a good plant is judged as an also-ran when time spent arranging the petals, staking the plant etc., would transform it into a card winner.

ALPINE AURICULAS – will hold their flowers for seven to ten days. Symmetry is all important. An Auricula pip has six, seven or eight petals, and these need arranging so that one edge of each petal is overlapping the neighbouring petal, and the other edge is under the neighbouring petal. This is easily done with an opened-out paper clip, a plant label or a small piece of card. It is advisable to practise all the dressing methods on plants that are not going to be exhibited first.

EDGED AURICULAS – will stay in good condition for two to three weeks. The centre truss often has poor flowers, so it is not usually exhibited. If there are two trusses on a plant the one to be judged is staked, and the other is tied down so that it does not distract the eye from the important truss.

With the grey edges a great deal of care must be taken so that the meal is not marked. The greens can have their edges cleaned carefully, the proprietary cotton wool bud dipped in milk is recommended, with a very steady hand. If the green edge is marked with a little meal, this may be gently wiped off with surgical spirit, as the farina consists of tiny particles of a wax-like substance, which is soluble in alcohol.

SHOW SELF AURICULAS – only hold their prime form for two or three days, and so shading is essential.

AURICULAS: BORDER AND DOUBLES

The general comments on primulas apply here. There are no hard and fast rules, but it is possible that judging standards will be laid down in the near future for the doubles.

PRIMULA SIEBOLDII

This was described in chapter 14, but the following discussion of its importance as a Florists' flower in Japan is included here, because of its great suitability for pot culture and exhibition. Collecting and growing the cultivars of *Primula sieboldii* in Japan can only be equated with collecting Florists' auriculas in this country. In Japan it is known as *Primula sakurasoh*, and has been in continuous cultivation for 300 years. The societies devoted to the culture of these lovely plants are called 'Ren', and it is recorded that 'Shitay Ren' held the first flower show for new introductions of *Primula sakurasoh* in 1804. These Societies became very closed, and the rules regarding naming and showing became more and more rigid. Most of the followers belonged to the Samurai (Warrior) classes, and there were said to be up to 700 named varieties. In 1868 Japan opened it doors to the world, and *Primula sakurasoh* became less popular. It was never totally neglected though, and soon cultivation became the hobby of the aristocracy, with the emphasis on enormous flowers. In 1918 the 'Nihon Sakurasoh Kai' (Japan *Primula sakurasoh* Society) was formed, and held shows that were open to the public, and visitors could buy plants. The growing and showing of these lovely plants was promoted throughout Japan up to the start of World War II. After the war the enthusiasts reorganised, and a nationwide society 'Sakurasoh Kai' (*Primula sakurasoh* Society) was formed in 1952, and the plant again became very popular. Today there are small clubs all over Japan devoted to this hobby. The *Primula sakurasoh* are formally displayed in 6in (15cm) diameter bowls, planted four to five to a pot. There are many classes based on the shape and habit of the flower, ranging from perfect uncut primrose shape through to the lacey petalled varieties.

20
Pests and Diseases

Generally the primulas and auriculas are strong healthy plants if given the conditions they need. Even then it is sensible to keep a careful watch so that any pests or diseases can be checked before they reach epidemic proportions. Elementary hygiene plays an important role in the fight against pests and diseases. Dirty pots and seed trays should be thoroughly washed before they are re-used. Sand beds for plunging should be regularly disinfected with insecticides and fungicides. Dead and dying plant material must not be allowed to collect in corners. In the greenhouse a waste bin is a very useful piece of equipment, the odd dead leaves that are removed can be put in there, and if it is emptied regularly, this will help prevent the pile up of the bits that are so often seen beneath the benches.

APHIDS: Not usually a serious pest with primulas, but it has been noticed that plants (in particular the Nivalids) that have been overstressed by heat or drought may be completely crippled by greenfly. Remember that greenfly spread virus diseases, and this can be a problem amongst the Auriculastrum section. *Cure* – any conventional spray. Those containing dimethoate have a systemic action, which means they may be used as a drench rather than a spray.

BOTRYTIS, GREY MOULD ETC: Usually indicates that the plants need more fresh air, which is not always possible especially in the foggy days of autumn. If treating the Florists' auriculas or other plants that are to be exhibited it is possible that autumn treatment with fungicides can cause deformation of the flowers in the following spring. Good culture and hygiene is infinitely preferable to chemical treatment, though at times it becomes essential. *Cure* – the proprietary fungicides are effective, but do follow instructions, as some of the fungal diseases can and have built up a resistance to certain fungicides. Wherever possible it is advisable to alternate between different products to prevent this resistance build-up.

CATERPILLARS: Can cause havoc in a bad year. They seem to develop a craving for auriculas and other primulas in early spring and in August. *Cure* – systemic insecticides or aphicides are effective – picking them off by hand is downright tedious. Search amongst the chemicals in the local garden centre.

RED SPIDER MITE: Are only a problem in a really hot summer. This pest is not visible to the naked eye, and should not be confused with the little red money spiders. Yellowing and blotching of the leaves and a general appearance of ill-health indicate its presence, and close examination of the undersides of the leaves with a hand lens will reveal the spidery webs and tiny mites. A yellowing of the outer leaves in late summer and autumn is natural. *Cure* – spray with cold water regularly and use a dimethoate spray. If other methods fail the different smokes can be very effective, but be careful to close all the doors and windows, and follow the instructions implicitly.

ROOT APHIDS (MEALY BUGS): This pest is usually seen as a white woolly deposit on the end of the roots where they poke through the drainage holes, or around the neck of the plant. If the infected plant is knocked out of the pot, this white deposit may be seen coating the surface of the ball of compost. It is often a symptom of underwatering and it seems to be the neglected plant, in a corner, in desperate need of repotting, that is affected first. Evidence indicates that a proportion of peat in the compost, or a systemic aphicide will keep this pest at bay. It seems to be very prevalent at present, possibly as a result of two extremely mild winters. *Cure* – Aphicides containing dimethoate are very effective, especially when applied as a drench at regular intervals. Early spring and late summer seem to be the times when an outbreak is most likely to occur.

ROOT ROT: Is often indicative of poor cultivation on the part of the grower. Drainage needs to be improved, and possibly a reduction in watering helps. It can be caused by overfeeding in the case of the Auriculastrum! As a temporary measure repot into a grittier compost with less food, and cut away any diseased roots back to clean healthy root where possible. *Cure* – Improve growing techniques, and a systemic fungicide may help.

SCIARID FLY: These are the tiny black flies that quickly fly off the surface of the compost when disturbed. Their larvae are small, thin and a translucent off-white. They are most common in moist environments, and where peaty composts are used. *Cure –* They have a very short life cycle, so drench an infected area with an insecticide at fortnightly intervals until there is no sign left of this irritating pest.

VINE WEEVIL: This is the real nasty! White maggots with brown heads can be found in the pots rapidly munching their way through the complete root system of the plant. *Cure –* Not very easily treated, but certain insecticide dusts mixed in the compost do deter the adult beetles from laying their eggs. Late repotting (July or August) can help if the old compost is disposed of completely, for the eggs will also be thrown away.

VIRUS: Many of the older varieties of auriculas and primulas are said to be virused. Good growing regimes can go a long way towards minimalising the effect of Virus. Certain plants show badly distorted leaves, and if this continues for more than one year, it is safest to assume it is badly virused and burn the affected plants. Some of the edged auriculas suffer occasionally from 'Brussels Sprout Disease', whereby the leaves appear curly and distorted, like a sprout. If the plant does not grow out of this problem, the only solution is to burn the plants concerned. *Cure –* there is no cure. Micropropagation reduces virus in plants. Virus diseases are spread by inattention to hygiene in propagation, and dirty knives will spread the disease from one plant to the next. Aphids also spread virus, so strict control measures must be taken to eradicate greenfly.

Be very careful with the chemicals used to control pests and diseases. Read and follow all instructions to the letter. The large chemical companies are only just discovering how dangerous many of these pesticides are, and some, for instance 'Aldrin', is now completely banned. The chemicals that are available to the amateur are in many cases the same as those used by the professionals (farmers and other growers), and by law the professional has to wear breathing equipment and protective clothing. Never put chemicals in other containers, and always keep them under lock and key where neither your own nor other people's children can get to them. It is sensible to keep all children and pets out of the way when dealing with chemicals, and away from recently treated plants.

Appendices

I SUPPLIERS OF PLANTS AND SEEDS

The following nurseries are not all open to customers. Some are small, one-man concerns who do all their own propagating, and hence cannot cope with people arriving unannounced. It is usual to enclose stamps when writing to nurseries or amateurs for details.

Brenda Hyatt Auriculas, 1 Toddington Crescent, Bluebell Hill, Chatham, Kent ME5 9QT.
  Auriculas, show, alpine and others. Write for list.

Craven's Primulas, Hall Barn Nurseries, Windsor End, Beaconsfield, Buckinghamshire HP9 2SG.
  Auriculas, Barnhaven Strains including Cowichans, Gold Lace Polyanthus, Asiatics including sieboldii and a few Petiolarids.

Donington Plants, Donington House, Main Road, Wrangle, Boston, Lincolnshire PE22 9AT.
  Auriculas, including doubles. Holder of the National Collection of Double Auriculas. Barnhaven Strains. Nursery open, list available.

Edrom Nurseries, Coldingham, Eyemouth, Berwickshire TD14 5TZ.
  Asiatics including Petiolarids, Nursery open, but advisable to phone or write first as rarities are not in general display area. Mail order, list available.

Hartside Nursery Garden, Low Gill House, Alston, Cumbria CA9 3BL.
  Asiatics including Petiolarids, Auriculas, Vernales sections including double primroses, and Europeans. Nursery open, list available, mail order.

Hopleys Plants Ltd., Much Hadham, Hertfordshire SG10 OBU.
A good range of double primroses, Barnhaven Strains etc.
Nursery open, list available.

Jack Drake, Inshriach Alpine Plant Nursery, Aviemore,
Inverness-shire PH22 1QS.
Unusual primulas, including Soldanelloides, a few Petio-
larids, European primulas, and of course the Candelabras.
Nursery open, list available, mail order.

Martin Nest Nurseries, Grange Cottage, Hemswell, Gains-
borough, Lincolnshire DN21 5UP.
European Hybrids including allioniis and marginatas. Vernales section including double primroses, Gold Lace Polyanthus, auriculas, easy Asiatics. Nursery open, list available,
mail order.

Charlie Johnson, Waincliffe Garden Nursery, 24 Bradford Rd,
Northowram, Halifax, West Yorkshire HX3 7HH.
A few allioniis and other European primulas. Lovely display
garden. Nursery open by appointment.

Wharfedale Nurseries, Alec Stubbs, 4 Springfield Rd, Grassington,
Skipton, North Yorkshire BD23 5LD.
Small European hybrids and other primulas. Write for list.

Amateurs willing to sell plants:
Derek Telford, 109 Crosland Road, Oakes, Huddersfield HD3
3PW.
Florists' auriculas (alpine and show varieties) only. Write
first.

Ailsa Jackson, 'Paddocks' Moira Rd, Shellbrook, Ashby de la
Zouch, Leicestershire LE6 5TU.
Old double and single primroses, 'Wanda' hybrids, etc.
Write first.

II NATIONAL AND INTERNATIONAL SOCIETIES

Alpine Garden Society: Lye End Link, St. John's, Woking, Surrey GU21 1SW.

The American Primrose Society: B. Skidmore, 6730 West Mercerway, Mercer Island, WA 98040, USA.

National Auricula and Primula Society
  Northern Section: D.G. Hadfield (Hon Secretary), 146 Queens Rd, Cheadle Hulme, Cheadle, Cheshire SK8 5HY.
  Midland and West Section: P.G. Ward (Hon. Secretary), 6 Lawson Close, Saltford, Bristol BS18 3LB.
  Southern Section: L.E. Wigley (Hon. Secretary), 67 Warnham Court Rd, Carshalton Beeches, Surrey SM5 3ND.

Scottish Rock Garden Club: Miss K.M. Gibb (Hon. Subscription Secretary), 21 Merchiston Park, Edinburgh EH10 4PW.

III FURTHER READING

Asiatic Primulas: A Gardeners' Guide, Roy Green (The Alpine Garden Society, 1976)

Auriculas & Primroses, W.R. Hecker (Batsford, 1971)

Auriculas: Their Care and Cultivation, Brenda Hyatt, (Cassell, 1989)

Primulas of Europe and America, G.F. Smith, B. Burrow and D.B. Lowe (The Alpine Garden Society, 1984)

Primulas: Old and New, Jack Wemyss-Cooke (David & Charles, 1986)

The Plant Finder – 3rd edition, Chris Philip (Headmain 1989)

IV GLOSSARY

Annual   A plant which germinates, flowers and sets seed in one year or less.

Anther   The part of the stamen which bears the pollen.

Body Colour   Exclusive to show edge and fancy auricula varieties. The inner margin of the body colour should be smooth and circular, the outer margin feathering out into the edge.

Calyx   Made up of sepals and usually green, the outside part of the unopened flower bud.

Campanulate   Bell-shaped.

Candelabra   An unusual type of flower head where the flowers are arranged in whorls up the main stem.

Carrot   An auricula term meaning the thick, usually near vertical, underground part of the stem from which the roots grow.

Dentate   With pointed teeth.

Edge   With reference to auriculas – a mutation of part of the petal which has taken on the characteristics and colour of a leaf.

Efarinose   Completely without farina (meal).

Farina   The white to yellow powder that oftens covers various parts of a primula. Also referred to as meal.

Farinose   Covered in Farina.

Footstalk   Usually referring to auriculas, this is botanically known as the pedicel, and is the stalk of a single flower in a truss.

Germination   The process whereby the seed starts to split and the young shoot and roots emerge.

Globose   A rounded flower head.

Habitat   Natural home of plants in the wild.

Hose in Hose   A type of flower which has sported and where one flower fits inside another.

Jack in the Green   A collar of leaf-like structures surrounds the flower, immediately behind the petals.

Meal   Also called 'farina' – the powdery coating that can be present on the leaves, flowers and stems.

Mutation   'Sport' – a change in the cell characteristics of a plant, giving rise to a new variety (not by seed).

Offset   A young plant that may be detached from the parent plant easily, usually with roots. Generally used with reference to the Auriculastrum section.

Paste   A circular ring heavily coated in meal (usually white) around the centre of the flowers of show auriculas, often with a glistening enamel appearance.

Pedicel *see* Footstalk.

Pendant Drooping or hanging downwards.

Pin-eyed Here the stigma or pin is carried above the stamens.

Pip An individual flower in auricula terms; an expanded pip is a fully open flower, and should be flat or nearly flat.

Pollen The fine powdery grains on the stamens (the male part). The pollen needs to be transferred to the stigma (the female part) for fertilisation to occur.

Rhizome A stem which is usually horizontal and has roots growing out of it and is either on or under the soil.

Scape In primula terms the whole flower stem including the flowers.

Selfed The transfer of pollen onto the stigma of the same plant.

Sepal The individual parts of the calyx, which in primulas are fused together to form a cup shape.

Stamen The male reproductive organ which bears the pollen.

Stigma The female reproductive organ which is ready to receive pollen when it becomes sticky. The stigma is also known as the pin.

Stratification The alternate freezing and thawing of seeds in winter that helps germination.

Systemic Insecticides that are absorbed into the plant, making the plant poisonous to the predator (e.g. aphids).

Thrum-eyed Here the stamens are above the pin.

Truss The head of flowers.

Tube In auricula terminology this is the part of the flower which contains the stamens, ovary and stigma. It should reach to the flat part of the open flower, be yellow, and viewed from above, circular.

Umbel A many flowered head where the pedicels all start at the same position.

V LIST OF KNOWN PRIMULAS IN THEIR SECTIONS

Section 1: Cortusoides
Subsection Eu-cortusoides

Primula cinerascens(1)
Primula cortusoides(1)
Primula eugeniae(1)
Primula kaufmanniana(1)
Primula lactiflora(1)

Primula mollis(1)
Primula polyneura(1)
Primula saxatilis(1)
Primula sieboldii(1)
Primula violaris(1)

Subsection Geranioides

Primula alsophila(1)
Primula eucyclia(1)
Primula geraniifolia(1)
Primula heucherifolia(1)
Primula jesoana(1)
Primula kisoana(1)
Primula latisecta(1)

Primula loesneri(1)
Primula minkwitziae(1)
Primula normaniana(1)
Primula palmata(1)
Primula pauliana(1)
Primula septemloba(1)
Primula vaginata(1)

Section 2: Reinii
Primula hidakana(2)
Primula kamuiana(2)
Primula reinii(2)

Primula takadena(2)
Primula tosaensis(2)

Section 3: Pinnatae
Primula cicutariifolia(3)
Primula erodiides(3)
Primula filchnerae(3)

Primula merriliana(3)
Primula ranunculoides(3)

Section 4: Pycnaloba
Primula pycnaloba(4)

Section 5: Obconica
Primula ambita(5)
Primula asarifolia(5)
Primula barbicalyx(5)
Primula densa(5)
Primula dictyophylla(5)
Primula dumicola(5)
Primula filipes(5)
Primula kwantungensis(5)
Primula kweichouensis(5)

Primula listeri(5)
Primula obconica(5)
Primula oreodoxa(5)
Primula parva(5)
Primula petitmenginii(5)
Primula sinolisteri(5)
Primula tsiangii(5)
Primula vilmoriniana(5)

Section 6: Sinensis

Primula rupestris(6)   *Primula sinensis(6)*

Section 7: Malvacea

Primula bathangensis(7)   *Primula malvacea(7)*
Primula blattariformis(7)   *Primula saturata(7)*
Primula celsiaeformis(7)

Section 8: Carolinella

Primula cardioeides(8)   *Primula huana(8)*
Primula chapaensis(8)   *Primula obovata(8)*
Primula henryi(8)   *Primula partschiana(8)*

Section 9: Vernales

Primula amoena(9)   *Primula megasaefolia(9)*
Primula elatior(9)   *Primula renifolia(9)*
Primula juliae(9)   *Primula veris(9)*
                                 Primula vulgaris(9)

Section 10: Amethystina

Primula amethystina(10)   *Primula odontica(10)*
Primula dickieana(10)   *Primula silaensis(10)*
Primula faberi(10)   *Primula valentiniana(10)*
Primula kingii(10)   *Primula virginis(10)*

Section 11: Cuneifolia

Primula cuneifolia(11)   *Primula suffrutescens(11)*
Primula nipponica(11)

Section 12: Petiolares

Subsection Petiolaris-Sonchifolia
Group vera
Primula cunninghamii(12)   *Primula hoffmanniana(12)*
Primula deuteronana(12)   *Primula petiolaris(12)*
Primula drummondiana(12)   *Primula sessilis(12)*
Primula gracilipes(12)   *Primula sulphurea(12)*
Group scapigera
Primula aureata(12)   *Primula irregularis(12)*
Primula boothii(12)   *Primula moupinensis(12)*
Primula bracteosa(12)   *Primula scapigera(12)*
Group taliensis
Primula comata(12)   *Primula taliensis(12)*

Group odontocalyx
Primula euosma(12)　　　　　*Primula sinuata(12)*
Primula odontocalyx(12)
Group hookeri
Primula hookeri(12)　　　　　*Primula vernicosa(12)*
Group edgworthii
Primula edgworthii(12)
Group sonchifolia
Primula chamaedoron(12)　　　*Primula chionota(12)*
Primula chamaethauma(12)　　 *Primula sonchifolia(12)*
Primula chionogenes(12)　　　 *Primula whitei(12)*

Subsection Chartacea
Primula chartacea(12)　　　　 *Primula petelotii(12)*
Primula lacerata(12)　　　　　*Primula veitchiana(12)*

Subsection Tongolensis
Primula pulchra(12)　　　　　 *Primula tongolensis(12)*

Subsection Griffithii
Primula calderiana(12)　　　　*Primula laeta(12)*
Primula calthifolia(12)　　　　*Primula nepalensis(12)*
Primula griffithii(12)　　　　 *Primula strumosa(12)*
Primula hilaris(12)　　　　　　*Primula tanneri(12)*
Primula jucunda(12)　　　　　 *Primula tsariensis(12)*

Subsection Davidii
Primula breviscapa(12)　　　　*Primula fagosa(12)*
Primula coerulea(12)　　　　　*Primula hylobia(12)*
Primula crassa(12)　　　　　　*Primula klaveriana(12)*
Primula davidii(12)　　　　　 *Primula leptophylla(12)*
Primula epilosa(12)　　　　　　*Primula ovalifolia(12)*
Primula esquirolii(12)

Section 13: Malacoides
Primula aromatica(13)　　　　 *Primula forbesii(13)*
Primula cavaleriei(13)　　　　 *Primula interjacens(13)*
Primula duclouxii(13)　　　　　*Primula malacoides(13)*
Primula effusa(13)　　　　　　 *Primula pellucida(13)*

Section 14: Grandis
Primula grandis(14)

Section 15: Bullatae

Primula bracteata(15)
Primula bullata(15)
Primula dubernardiana(15)
Primula forrestii(15)

Primula henrici(15)
Primula redolens(15)
Primula rockii(15)

Section 16: Dryadifolia

Primula chlorodryas(16)
Primula dryadifolia(16)
Primula jonardunii(16)

Primula mystrophylla(16)
Primula triloba(16)
Primula tsongpenii(16)

Section 17: Minutissimae

Subsection Eu-Minutissimae

Primula annulata(17)
Primula candicans(17)
Primula flagellaris(17)
Primula geraldinae(17)
Primula glandulifera(17)
Primula heydei(17)
Primula minutissimae(17)
Primula muscoides(17)
Primula praetermissa(17)
Primula reptans(17)

Primula rhodochroa(17)
Primula rimicola(17)
Primula rubicunda(17)
Primula spathulifolia(17)
Primula stirtoniana(17)
Primula subularia(17)
Primula tenella(17)
Primula tenuiloba(17)
Primula waddellii(17)
Primula walshii(17)

Subsection Bella

Primula barbatula(17)
Primula bella(17)
Primula moschophora(17)

Primula occlusa(17)
Primula primulina(17)

Section 18: Souliei

Primula aliciae(18)
Primula humilis(18)
Primula incisa(18)
Primula longipinnatifida(18)

Primula rupicola(18)
Primula souliei(18)
Primula xanthopa(18)

Section 19: Farinosae

European species known

Subsection Eu-Farinosae

Primula algida(19)
Primula darialica(19)
Primula farinosa(19)

Primula frondosa(19)
Primula halleri(19)
Primula ossetica(19)

Primula scandinavica(19)　　　*Primula stricta(19)*
Primula scotica(19)

Subsection Sibirica
Primula nutans (formerly *sibirica*)*(19)*

Subsection Auriculatae
Primula glacialis syn auriculata(19)　　*Primula luteola(19)*

American species known
Primula borealis(19)　　　　　　*Primula intercedens(19)*
Primula comberi(19)　　　　　　*Primula laurentiana(19)*
Primula egaliksensis(19)　　　　*Primula magellanica (decipiens)(19)*
Primula hunnewellii(19)　　　　*Primula mistassinica(19)*
Primula incana(19)　　　　　　*Primula specuicola(19)*

Asiatic species known

Subsection Eu-Farinosae
Primula algida(19)　　　　　　*Primula flava(19)*
Primula assamica(19)　　　　　*Primula hazarica(19)*
Primula baldschuanica(19)　　　*Primula intermedia(19)*
Primula blandula(19)　　　　　*Primula jaffreyana(19)*
Primula borealis(19)　　　　　*Primula knuthiana(19)*
Primula caldaria(19)　　　　　*Primula matsumurae(19)*
Primula capitellata(19)　　　　*Primula modesta(19)*
Primula clutterbuckii(19)　　　*Primula schlagintweitiana(19)*
Primula concinna(19)　　　　　*Primula sharmae(19)*
Primula erratica(19)　　　　　*Primula sorachiana(19)*
Primula farinosa(19)　　　　　*Primula stenocalyx(19)*
Primula fauriae(19)　　　　　　*Primula tayloriana(19)*
Primula fernaldiana(19)　　　　*Primula yuparensis(19)*
Primula fistulosa(19)

Subsection Gemmifera
Primula conspersa(19)　　　　　*Primula laciniata(19)*
Primula gemmifera(19)

Subsection Pulchella
Primula pratii(19)　　　　　　*Primula pulchelloides(19)*
Primula pulchella(19)

Subsection Yunnanensis
Primula fragilis(19)　　　　　*Primula kialensis(19)*

Primula membranifolia(19)
Primula umbrella(19)

Primula yunnanensis(19)

Subsection Inayatii
Primula inayatii(19)

Subsection Glabra
Primula genestierana(19)
Primula glabra(19)

Primula kongboensis(19)
Primula pseudoglabra(19)

Subsection Sibirica
Primula fasciculata(19)
Primula involucrata(19)
Primula oxygraphidifolia(19)
Primula pumilio(19)
Primula sibirica(19)

Primula tanupoda(19)
Primula tibetica(19)
Primula urticifolia(19)
Primula yargongensis(19)

Subsection Auriculatae
Primula auriculata(19)
Primula clarkei(19)
Primula efarinosa(19)
Primula elliptica(19)
Primula fedschenkoi(19)
Primula flexuosa(19)

Primula macrocarpa(19)
Primula obsessa(19)
Primula rosea(19)
Primula sertulum(19)
Primula warshenewskiana(19)

Section 20: Denticulata
Primula atrodentata(20)
Primula denticulata(20)
Primula erosa(20)

Primula erythrocarpa(20)
Primula laxiuscula(20)
Primula pseudodenticulata(20)

Section 21: Capitatae
Primula capitata(21)

Primula glomerata syn crispa(21)

Section 22: Muscarioides
Primula aerinantha(22)
Primula apoclita(22)
Primula bellidifolia(22)
Primula cernua(22)
Primula concholoba(22)
Primula deflexa(22)
Primula euchaites(22)
Primula giraldiana(22)
Primula gracilenta(22)

Primula hyacinthina(22)
Primula inopinata(22)
Primula mairei(22)
Primula muscarioides(22)
Primula pinnatifida(22)
Primula vialii(22)
Primula violacea(22)
Primula watsonii(22)

Section 23: Soldanelloides

Primula buryana(23)
Primula cawdoriana(23)
Primula chasmophila(23)
Primula eburna(23)
Primula fea(23)
Primula flabellifera(23)
Primula flaccida(23)
Primula jigmediana(23)
Primula ludlowii(23)
Primula nutans syn(23)
Primula reidii(23)
Primula sandemaniana(23)

Primula sapphirina(23)
Primula sherriffiae(23)
Primula siamensis(23)
Primula siphonantha(23)
Primula soldanelloides(23)
Primula spicata(23)
Primula umbratilis(23)
Primula uniflora(23)
Primula wattii(23)
Primula wigramiana(23)
Primula wollastonii(23)

Section 24: Rotundifolia

Primula baileyana(24)
Primula barnardoana(24)
Primula caveana(24)
Primula consocia(24)
Primula gambeliana(24)

Primula littledalei(24)
Primula ramzanae(24)
Primula rotundifolia(24)
Primula tzetsouensis(24)

Section 25: Nivales
Subsection Eu-Nivales

Primula amabilis(25)
Primula bayernii(25)
Primula boreio-calliantha(25)
Primula brevicula(25)
Primula cerina(25)
Primula chionantha(25)
Primula crocifolia(25)
Primula diantha(25)
Primula duthieana(25)
Primula elongata(25)
Primula farreriana(25)
Primula helvenacea(25)
Primula kiuchiangensis(25)
Primula limbata(25)
Primula longipes(25)
Primula macrophylla(25)
Primula melanops(25)

Primula minor(25)
Primula nivalis(25)
Primula obliqua(25)
Primula obtusifolia(25)
Primula obtata(25)
Primula orbicularis(25)
Primula poluninii(25)
Primula purdomii(25)
Primula rigida(25)
Primula russeola(25)
Primula sinoplantaginea(25)
Primula sinopurpurea(25)
Primula stuartii(25)
Primula tschuktschorum(25)
Primula woodwardii(25)
Primula youngeriana(25)

Subsection Calliantha
Primula bryophila(25)   *Primula mishmiensis(25)*
Primula calliantha(25)

Subsection Maximowiczii
Primula advena(25)   *Primula szechuanica(25)*
Primula aemula(25)   *Primula tangutica(25)*
Primula handeliana(25)   *Primula yuana(25)*
Primula maximowiczii(25)

Subsection Agleniana
Primula agleniana(25)   *Primula falcifolia(25)*
Primula elizabethae(25)

Section 26: Parryi
Primula angustifolia(26)   *Primula maguirei(26)*
Primula broadheadae(26)   *Primula nevadensis(26)*
Primula capillaris(26)   *Primula parryi(26)*
Primula cusickiana(26)   *Primula rusbyi(26)*
Primula ellisae(26)

Section 27: Sikkimensis
Primula alpicola(27)   *Primula ioessa(27)*
Primula chumbiensis(27)   *Primula reticulata(27)*
Primula didyma(27)   *Primula secundiflora(27)*
Primula erythra(27)   *Primula sikkimensis(27)*
Primula firmipes(27)   *Primula waltonii(27)*
Primula florindae(27)

Section 28: Candelabra
Primula anisodora(28)   *Primula mallophylla(28)*
Primula aurantaica(28)   *Primula melanodonta(28)*
Primula beesiana(28)   *Primula microloma(28)*
Primula brachystoma(28)   *Primula miyabeana(28)*
Primula bulleyana(28)   *Primula moorsheadiana(28)*
Primula burmanica(28)   *Primula poissonii(28)*
Primula chrysochlora(28)   *Primula polonensis(28)*
Primula chungensis(28)   *Primula prenantha(28)*
Primula cockburniana(28)   *Primula prolifera(28)*
Primula cooperi(28)   *Primula pulverulenta(28)*
Primula helodoxa(28)   *Primula serratifolia(28)*
Primula ianthiana(28)   *Primula smithiana(28)*
Primula imperialis(28)   *Primula stenodonta(28)*
Primula japonica(28)   *Primula sumatrana(28)*
Primula khasiana(28)   *Primula wilsonii(28)*

Section 29: Auricula
Subsection Eu-Auricula
Primula auricula(29)   *Primula palinuri(29)*

Subsection Chamaecalus
Primula minima(29)

Subsection Erythrodosum
Primula appennina(29)   *Primula pedemontana(29)*
Primula daoensis(29)   *Primula villosa(29)*
Primula hirsuta (rubra)(29)

Subsection Brevibracteata
Primula carniolica(29)   *Primula marginata(29)*
Primula latifolia (viscosa)(29)

Subsection Arthritica
Primula clusiana(29)   *Primula spectabilis(29)*
Primula glaucescens(29)   *Primula wulfenianum(29)*

Subsection Rhopsidium
Primula allionii(29)   *Primula kitabelliana(29)*
Primula integrifolia(29)   *Primula tirolensis(29)*

Subsection Cyanopsis
Primula deorum(29)   *Primula glutinosa(29)*

Section 30: Floribundae
Primula aucheri(30)   *Primula gaubeana(30)*
Primula edelbergii(30)   *Primula verticillata(30)*
Primula floribunda(30)

Index of Species, Hybrids and Cultivars

Note: page numbers in italic refer to illustrations.

HYBRIDS, incl. primroses and polyanthus
(D) indicates double primroses.

Primula

SPECIES, cultivars and natural hybrids, ()indicates Section.

265

Index of species, hybrids and cultivars

Index of species, hybrids and cultivars

Index of species, hybrids and cultivars

Index of species, hybrids and cultivars

General Index